CHILD BEHAVIOR

D0029718

Child

Behavior REVISED EDITION

From the Gesell Institute of Human Development

FRANCES L. ILG, M.D.
DIRECTOR EMERITUS

LOUISE BATES AMES, Ph.D.
ASSOCIATE DIRECTOR

SIDNEY M. BAKER, M.D.
DIRECTOR EMERITUS

HarperPerennial
A Division of HarperCollins*Publishers*

A hardcover edition of this book was published in 1981 by Harper & Row, Publishers.

CHILD BEHAVIOR (Revised Edition). Copyright © 1981 by Louise Bates Ames, Frances L. Ilg, Sidney M. Baker and Gesell Institute of Human Development. All rights reserved. Printed in the United States of America. No part of this book may be used or reproduced in any manner whatsoever without written permission except in the case of brief quotations embodied in critical articles and reviews. For information address HarperCollins Publishers, Inc., 10 East 53rd Street, New York, NY 10022.

HarperCollins books may be purchased for educational, business, or sales promotional use. For information, please call or write: Special Markets Department, HarperCollins Publishers, Inc., 10 East 53rd Street, New York, NY 10022. Telephone: (212) 207-7528; Fax: (212) 207-7222.

HarperPerennial edition published 1992.

Designer: Sidney Feinberg

LIBRARY OF CONGRESS CATALOG CARD NUMBER 91-50503
ISBN 0-06-092276-1

94 95 96 CW 10 9 8 7 6 5

Contents

PART THREE

PART FOUR

Preface

It has been interesting, in the course of this revision, for the authors to compare the advice given in the first edition, published in 1955, with what we have to tell you today, some twenty-five years later.

Clearly our basic thesis remains the same. We continue to affirm that behavior is a function of structure. People behave as they do to a large extent because of the way their bodies are built. And behavior to a large extent develops in a patterned, predictable way. Not only do individual behaviors develop predictably, but the ages themselves have their own patterned, predictable characteristics.

Each human being is a unique individual, though inevitably influenced by the way the world treats him. Thus, to quite an extent the way any child behaves depends on the special kind of body he or she has inherited as well as on the stage it has reached.

At the time we first wrote this book, many psychologists were still blaming parents for any and all kinds of aberrant or even mildly undesirable behavior: bedwetting, school failure, autism, even using the "wrong" hand. Fortunately in the years since 1955, most child specialists and most behavior clinics have stopped blaming "emotional factors in the home" and general parental ineptitude for the majority of child behavior problems.

Child specialists are becoming increasingly biologic in their interpretations of behavior. Increasingly it is accepted that something about the individual child, at the age and in the situation in which he finds himself, is causing his distress, discomfort, or misbehavior. Faulty behavior may be merely characteristic of a certain age or a certain pesonality. Or it may be that the child finds himself, or herself, in a situation which is unsuitable and overdemanding—a situation which parent or teacher may be able to change.

In general, then, interpretation has switched from blaming parents or teachers to an acceptance of the principles emphasized in our first edition. But now we and others have taken a giant further step. We are not only increasingly concerned with the treatment of undesirable, uncomfortable, or unhealthy behavior, but we are actually in a position to advise parents how, in many instances, they can prevent it.

That is, earlier we gave suggestions as to what to do about troublesome behavior when it occurred. We can now, at least to some extent, help to keep it from occurring. Three special areas in which preventive help can be given relate to health, to school performance, and to that extremely important aspect of human behavior—the child's vision.

It is our belief that as knowledge about the human body and its functioning increases, and as emphasis shifts from blaming parents and other aspects of the environment to an understanding of biological function, much of the troublesome behavior that has bothered parents in the past can not only be understood and dealt with effectively but may actually be prevented in the first place.

A special entirely new section has been included. It is an extremely detailed and, we hope, practical discussion of the child's physical health. In this section we advise parents about the major factors which they should consider whenever their child is ill. We give specific suggestions as to how they, in cooperation with their own physician, should go about looking for these crucial factors.

Thus, this revision should help you not only in effectively dealing with child behavior difficulties when they do occur, but also in preventing a good many customary and traditional probler. both behavior and health problems—before they even crop up, or at least before they assume serious proportions.

PART ONE

PART ONE

1   How Behavior Grows

Child behavior does make sense. Happily, the more you as parents know about it, the more sense it will make.

There are three vastly important things we can tell you about which should help you to become an even better parent than love and good will alone would insure.

The first is that human behavior—and that means the behavior of your own child—develops in a not only patterned but also highly predictable manner. Though obviously the way any child will turn out in the long run depends strongly on the way he or she is treated, the basic ways in which behavior develops depend on much more than what you do or do not do.

Dr. Arnold Gesell made it very clear, rather long ago, that behavior has pattern and shape, as does physical structure. And just as your child's body grows in a reasonably patterned manner, so does his behavior.

A second basic thing to keep in mind is that behavior is to a great extent a function of structure. This means that children behave as they do very largely because of the way their bodies are built. Different kinds of bodies behave differently, even though they may grow up in the same environment.

The combination of a child's basic inborn individuality and the stage of development he has reached are fully as important in determining his behavior as is the way in which he is treated by you and others.

This book will tell you of the stages by which many of the more common child behaviors develop in the first ten years of life. It will tell you a little about the ages themselves—what 2-year-olds and 3-year-olds and 4-year-olds and the others are like, and what general changes you can expect from age to age.

It will also tell you a little about the different kinds of personalities and how they behave. The stages of behavior which more or less have to take place as a child develops are in many ways remarkably similar from child to child. To get to the top, the child has to climb all the steps. But though the steps are pretty much the same for everybody, the way each child climbs these steps (or goes through the basic stages) is a little different for every child. The way he goes through the stages and the way he expresses the common patterns of behavior vary according to his own basic individuality.

We can tell you about the common stages of development. You, yourself, however, are the one who will need to discover and appreciate your own child's individuality. Anything we can tell you about different kinds of individuality is only a beginning. Recognizing and appreciating your own child's basic personality is one of the most difficult but one of the most rewarding tasks of parenthood. But you have to do it yourself.

Thus, ages and stages we can tell you about. These come first and are the easiest because they are much alike for all children. We can also help you a little with individuality or personality, though it is still up to you to recognize and appreciate what your own particular child is like.

A third factor, equally as important as these first two, which you need to think about is your child's environment. Environment is of course a highly individual matter. What might be best for one child or at one age, might not be ideal for another child or at another age.

Happily, there is one vital aspect of environment which can be understood and manipulated. A new idea, or actually a new understanding and approach to an old commonsense idea, is that one of the most important things parents can do for their children is to feed them right.

Obviously a good diet is essential if we wish to keep our children in good health. The new emphasis which is so exciting and so very important is that a proper diet not only produces better physical health but can also result in improved behavior. We are gradually coming to realize that poor diets and/or specific sensitivities to foods and food additives, as well as to inhalants, can have a highly adverse effect on behavior. They can cause problems ranging from moodiness, lethargy, and irritability to bedwetting, sleep disturbances, poor schoolwork, and in some instances even delinquency. All of these things in addition to what might ordinarily be expected—poor health.

Children in real difficulty in almost any area of behavior can often be helped substantially when attention is paid to their diet. Even children who seem to be making out more or less all right can often be helped to even more effective living by proper nutrition and by being protected from foods and other substances which cause often-undetected allergies.

You have a challenging but exciting task on your hands when you set out to bring up a child. We hope we can make that task a little easier by giving you information about how children grow and about the way in which the foods they eat influence their behavior.

Better and Worse Stages

As the child's body matures, it tends to get larger and larger. Physical growth may seem to stand still now and then, but at least it doesn't go backward. Your child is not likely suddenly one day to get smaller.

Behavior growth is more complicated. We can be pretty sure that as they grow older, your children will get bigger; but unfortunately we cannot always guarantee that they will get better. In the long run they will become more self-sufficient. They will be able to use their bodies and their words and thoughts more effectively. We can be assured that 10-year-olds are less exacting of their parents' time and patience than are 18-monthers. And in many ways late-adolescents bring more joy and less trouble to their parents than they did as a babies or preschoolers.

But scientific studies of normal children have shown that this general trend toward "improvement" in behavior is not steady and uninterrupted. It does not go forward consistently and without setback. Each new age level tends to bring its own advantages and disadvantages.

In the early stages of our research we assumed that as the child grew older, his or her general behavior would or should become smoother and better balanced and would move from an early stage of disequilibrium on toward increasing equilibrium. If and when behavior took a turn for the worse, we looked to the child's environment for the source of any sudden appearance of disequilibrium.

But in studying early postural behavior, we discovered that as the baby lay on its stomach in the first year of life, stages in which arms and legs were flexed seemed to alternate with stages when they were extended. The baby showed repeated stages first of one kind of behavior and then the other. The same was true when we considered bilaterality versus unilaterality. First behavior was bilateral, then unilateral, then again bilateral, and so on.

Applying our observations of simple and basic postural behavior to the child's more "important" ways of behaving in everyday life, we soon came to appreciate that personal-social as well as postural behavior tended to develop in an upwardly spiraling fashion. And that stages of disequilibrium and equilibrium alternated at least through the first sixteen years of life.

This discovery clearly has practical as well as theoretical implications. It helps you understand not only *why* but *when* your child's behavior may be expected to take a turn seemingly for the worse. And it also helps you appreciate that any stage of so-called good behavior must break up before a more advanced stage of equilibrium can be attained. One cannot simply move up the "good" side of life. Equilibrium must break up and, at least temporarily, be replaced with disequilibrium if maturity is to be attained.

Thus, the baby who used to be so docile about being fed may at a year demand his own feeding implements, with which he splashes in his food and generally disrupts the business of feeding. The added maturity of the 2½-year-old, who at 2 years may have been so easy to manage through his daily routines, may cause him to demand, "Me do it myself." Added maturity may bring a drive toward independence in the 6-year-old which expresses itself in, "No, I won't. Try and make me!"—though at 5 he took pleasure in obeying his mother. Added maturity may turn a helpful 10-year-old into a rebellious Eleven who shouts angrily, "I don't *want* to help you with the dishes." It may change an enthusiastic, outgoing 14-year-old into a brooding, moody Fifteen.

Fortunately, all of these changes do not occur simply at random. Rather, they take place in a lawful and patterned way. Thus, in general (and there are of course exceptions), ages when the child seems to be in better balance, both within himself and with the people and forces in his world, alternate with ages when he appears to be unhappy and confused within himself and also at cross-purposes with much of the outside world.

So if your child's behavior suddenly takes a turn for the worse, the reason for this turn may not necessarily be that something has gone wrong in his environment. Or that he is just naturally difficult. It may be that a stage of equilibrium has been succeeded, as it often will be, by a stage of disequilibrium. Thus 2-year-old equilibrium quite normally breaks up and behavior becomes worse at 2½. The good 5-year-old becomes the explosive Six. Docile Ten becomes recalcitrant Eleven.

Figure 1 gives a basic timetable that shows the customary and more-or-less-expected ages of equilibrium and disequilibrium in the first ten years of life.

"Better" or "worse" behavior tends to alternate with the ages in a fairly lawful sequence of unfolding. There is a second, equally rhythmic alternation. Too concentrated or *focal* behavior, as we call it, at one time, is followed by too diffuse, widespread, or *peripheral* behavior at a succeeding time. A good example of focal behavior is seen in the average 5-year-old who tends to hug his

Disequilibrium   Equilibrium

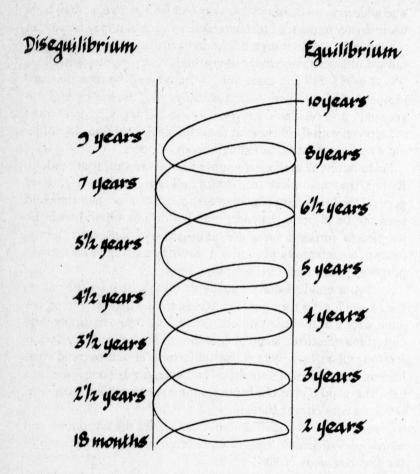

10 years

9 years

8 years

7 years

6½ years

5½ years

5 years

4½ years

4 years

3½ years

3 years

2½ years

2 years

18 months

mother's skirts, to shadow her wherever she goes. Six, in contrast, is in a peripheral stage. He may be all over the neighborhood, never at home, always ready for new places, people, experiences. It is the task of growth eventually to help the individual be neither one extreme nor the other, but to intermesh these extremes.

You may prefer your child's stages of equilibrium to those of disequilibrium. You may enjoy him most when he is conservative and close to home. Or you may prefer him when he is expansive and adventurous. But whichever stage you prefer, try to have patience with its opposite. Because the child seems to grow through these opposite extremes. One kind of behavior appears to be as necessary to growth as the other.

We can try to smooth over the child's "worse" stages, curb some of his expansiveness, or try to spread him out a little when he is in a too-close-to-home stage. But if we can accept all of these extremes, "for better or for worse," as necessary parts of growth, and not just blame them on somebody (teacher, other parent, neighbor, child himself), we will be looking at things realistically.

Suggestions

Each kind of behavior which will interest you (eating, sleeping, elimination, all the others) develops, as we have told you, through a series of patterned stages. In Part Two of this volume we are going to discuss these behaviors.

But it is not only the various kinds of behavior which develop in a predictable and describable manner. The very ages themselves can also be characterized and described. Behavior at any age is not simply a sum of the specific things that the child can do. It is almost as if each age had a personality of its own.

However, we would like to give you two warnings. The first is this: Do not take our "timetable" too seriously. Do not try to match your own child exactly to it. We are here describing more or less *average* behavior for each age level. That is, when we describe something as being typical 4-year-old behavior, we mean that of any hundred presumably normal 4-year-olds, approximately half of them may be behaving in the manner described when they are 4 years of age. One-quarter of them will already have gone past this kind of behavior, and one-quarter will not yet have reached it.

So your own child may, quite normally, be a little ahead of or a little behind the behavior discussed as being typical of his or her age. Your child will in all probability go through the stages we describe in the order given, but the rate of advancement will be his or her own. Do not worry, then, if he or she is a little faster or a little slower than the supposed average.

Another possible variable is that any given child's theoretical spiral of behavior could be displaced either to the right or the left of the one pictured in Figure 1. If it is displaced to the right, he or she will be most of the time moving toward the equilibrium or "good" side of life and even in his most disorganized swings will not move far toward the side of disequilibrium. If your child's spiral is displaced toward the left of the pictured figure, then you may expect rather customary disequilibrium, with fewer "good" spells than one can hope for in the so-called average child. That is, your child's behavior may be a little better or worse, most of the time, than that which we describe.

Your task, then, is not so much to compare your child with the "average" as to compare him with himself—as he has been in the past and as he might be in the future. Our age sketches are not absolute "norms" of behavior that every child "ought" to exhibit exactly at any given time. Rather they aim to help you to know the probable *direction* of the changes you may expect as your child grows older.

A second misunderstanding which we hope you will avoid is this: Some people believe that when we describe some unattractive behavior as being typical of a given age (the 4-year-old uses terrible language; the 6-year-old says he hates his mother), we mean that there is nothing they should do about it. They think we are advising them to say, "Oh that's just a stage," and to sit back and do nothing. Far from it! But knowing that an unattractive behavior is in all probability "just a stage" will, we hope, help you to be a little more relaxed about it; help you not to blame too many people for the behavior.

Knowing what to expect doesn't automatically relieve you of all responsibility for doing something about undesirable behavior. It may, however, help you cope with this behavior more successfully than you might have if you were shocked and surprised by its appearance. It should help you handle undesirable behavior more effectively as it occurs. Sometimes you will brush over it. At other times you will substitute other interests. At still other times you will do what you can to prevent its occurence. But there will also be times when you will come to grips with it.

2   Ages and Stages

Cycles of Behavior

As we describe succeeding age levels, you will note that the same
general kinds of things seem to be happening over and over again.
Careful analysis of behavior trends in the first 10 years of life—
supplemented by later studies of the years from 10 to 16—make
it apparent that a rather distinctive sequence of behavior stages
seems to occur repeatedly as the child matures.* Thus the first
cycle occurs between 2 and 5 years of age, repeats itself from 5 to
10, and occurs once again between the ages of 10 and 16.

Some of you may find it helpful to think of behavior in this
somewhat abstract and overall way. Others will find it quite
enough to consider one age at a time. For those who prefer the
long-range view—here are the cycles of behavior which you may
be able to discover if you observe closely the behavior of the child
from 2 to 16 years of age.

First of all, we have observed that 2, 5, and 10 years of age all
constitute focal points at which behavior seems to be in good
equilibrium, the child having relatively little difficulty within himself or with the world about him. Each of these relatively smooth
and untroubled ages is followed by a brief period when behavior
appears to be very much broken up, disturbed, and troubled, and
when the child shows himself to be in marked disequilibrium.
Thus the smoothness of 2-year-old behavior characteristically

---

*Data on the years from 10 to 16 will be found in F. Ilg and L. Ames, *The Years
from Ten to Sixteen*, rev. ed. (New York, Harper & Row, 1981).

12

breaks up at 2½; 5-year-old behavior breaks up at 5½ to 6; and 10 breaks up at 11, the 11-year-old child characteristically showing himself to be at definite odds with his environment and with himself.

Each of these ages is followed, once more, by a period of relative equilibrium at 3, 6½, and 12 years, respectively, when life's forces seem to be in good balance. The child is happy both within himself and in his environment.

These are followed by ages when there is a very pronounced inwardizing or drawing in of outer impressions and experiences, to be mulled over, thought about, and digested within. These ages are 3½, 7, and 13 years. At 3½ this inner process often has disturbing side effects of general emotional instability, a variety of fears, poor spatial orientation, hand tremor, whining and high tremulous voice, stuttering and stumbling. Seven and 13 are more stable ages and better ready to stand the strain of this inwardizing period of growth. The side effects at these latter ages are more apt to be expressed in marked sensitivity and touchiness, excessive withdrawal and moroseness, and a minor and pessimistic attitude toward life in general.

All three of these ages are followed by periods of extreme expansiveness: 4, 8, and 14 are all times at which the child's behavior is markedly outgoing in most major respects. He is even in danger of expanding too much. He wanders from home and gets lost at 4, demands to ride his bicycle in the street at 8 and may get hit, and gets all tangled up in his multiple and conflicting social plans at 14.

The next three ages (4½, 9, and 15) are the ones about which we perhaps know the least, but we do know enough to recognize certain similarities between the three periods. In each of them, behavior is less outgoing than at the age which directly preceded. In each it is in less good equilibrium. Child specialists have frequently used the term *neurotic* to describe each of these three ages, though they may each represent perfectly normal stages of growth.

And then once more, in each instance, we come to ages of stability and of relatively good equilibrium: 5, 10, and 16.

We have here started this summary of cycles of behavior at 2 years of age, but actually it could have been begun in infancy, when the same kinds of alternation of ingoing and outgoing periods, periods of equilibrium and disequilibrium, do occur. It is important to note that in early infancy salient changes are very rapid and show up clearly at weekly intervals. As growth progresses, these changes are clearer at two-week intervals. The 6-week-old child smiles spontaneously, but the 8-week-old child smiles as a social response. With increased age (from 12 weeks to a year) monthly increments are readily defined. From 1 to 2 years, the intervals of change lengthen to three months, and from 2 years to 7 years, to six months. From 7 to 10 years (and on to 16 years) these salient changes appear to take place less frequently—at about yearly intervals. It is probable that this spiral of growth slows down even further during the 20s and 30s, but it seems quite probable that predictable age changes are continuing to take place, though less clearly defined, during these and the succeeding years and probably throughout the human life span.

A brief and rather schematic tabular presentation of the age changes from 2 years on, as described above, follows:

2 years	5 years	10 years	
2½	5½–6	11	Breaking up
3	6½	12	Rounded, balanced
3½	7	13	Inwardized
4	8	14	Vigorous, expansive
4½	9	15	Inwardized-outwardized, troubled, "neurotic"
5	10	16	Smooth, consolidated

The first row reads: 2 years / 5 years / 10 years — Smooth, consolidated

For a pictorial version of this same spiral, which illustrates graphically the rhythmic swings that take place as the child matures between stages of equilibrium and stages of disequilibrium (and often, as it turns out, between ages of outwardized and inwardized behavior), see Figure 1 (page 8).

Warning about Age Levels

Most of you will realize, without any special warning from us, that any description of age levels such as that which we have just given you is a gross oversimplification. When we describe characteristic behavior for any given age, we do not mean that all children of that age will behave in just that way all of the time. In fact, some of them will rarely behave that way.

It is *the order* in which these stages follow each other which is most important—far more important than the exact age at which any certain child reaches any one of these stages. And each child gives his or her own individual twist to these age sequences. Also important is the fact that periods of relative equilibrium tend to be followed and preceded by periods when the behavior is less calm, less well adjusted.

Among the many possible exceptions to our suggestion that behavior in general at around 4 years of age tends to be out of bounds, could be the following:

First of all, your child may quite normally reach this 4-year-old out-of-bounds stage a little ahead of time or a little behind time or may be of such a gentle nature that even at his worst he does not go far out of bounds. Or he may be of such a vigorous nature that at *every* age he is more or less out of bounds.

Furthermore, even at a rather disorderly stage, there may be times when his environment fits especially well with his own personal needs and his behavior is quite calm.

And lastly, though 4 years of age may be in many an age when there is considerable disequilibrium between the child and his environment, some children seem to be relatively in harmony and at peace within themselves even at ages when their behavior is quite disturbing to those around them.

Thus it is more important for you as a parent to recognize the rhythms of growth, the alternations between expansive and inwardized ages or between harmonious and inharmonious periods, and to recognize that calm is very often followed by storm and vice versa, than to expect your own child to fit exactly into any given timetable or pattern. Each child is an individual, and you must always keep that in mind.

It is also extremely important to remember that every age has its positive as well as its negative aspects, and that there is always a "better" side even to the "worse" ages.

Thus your 4-year-old may often seem overbold, but he at least expresses a self-confidence and an independence which were lacking at 3½.

Similarly, your 6-year-old may often be rebellious, aggressive, demanding, selfish. But he also shows a tremendous enthusiasm and love of life. Some things may be terrible to him, but others can be equally wonderful. He may hate you one minute, but he loves you madly the next.

And Seven, though he may at times be morose and moody, complaining and unhappy, often expresses a great thoughtfulness and restraint which comes as a pleasant change after the boisterousness of Six.

Thus each new age may bring changes for the worse, but it is also quite certain to bring other changes for the better. Try to discover the good while at the same time you smooth over the bad. Here are some of the outstanding characteristics of the first ten years of life.

Four Weeks

What can the 4-week-old infant do in the way of behavior? What can we expect of him or her?

Very little if we compare the infant with the sophisticated 1-year-old baby. Certainly he cannot creep, walk, or talk. But compare him with himself a mere three or four weeks earlier, and he can do a very great deal. Never again, in fact—except in the period before birth—will so short a time mark so great an advance in the way of accomplishments.

To begin with, at a purely physiological level, he now breathes with regularity. His heart has steadied its pace. His body temperature has ceased to be erratic. His muscle tonus is already less fluctuant than it was, and he responds with noticeable motor tightening when you pick him up.

He also now sleeps more definitely and wakes more decisively. He opens his eyes wide and does not lapse so often into his earlier shallow, ambiguous drowsing. When awake he tends to have a preferred position—usually lying (when on his back) with his head turned to a preferred side and with the arm on that side extended, the other crooked. He thus may already be giving an indication of what is to be his later preferred handedness, since his preferred hand and arm will likely be the ones most often extended.

Occasionally he will regard his mother's face, but it will be only briefly. Though he may vocalize with small throaty noises, he is not quite ready to smile socially. However, he does react positively to comforts and satisfactions. He reacts negatively to pain and denial. And he can cry. He is already beginning, in his small ways, to impose his wants on the outside world and in turn to respond to that world.

Sixteen Weeks

The 16-week-old infant seems already quite mature, at least in terms of what has gone before. Not only have motor and verbal abilities increased tremendously, but he has, to some extent, become a social being! He likes the experience of lying on a big bed, and he begins to invade the house more than he did earlier. Feeding is no longer uppermost in his mind, and he can sometimes wait for it.

He is no longer as content to lie on his back as he was when he was younger. Rather, he likes to be held, or propped up for brief periods in a sitting position, so that he can face the world, eyes front.

In fact, there is something which at least hints at the social person he or she will later become in the way eyes glisten, shoulders tense, breathing quickens, and face breaks into a smile as the infant is lifted up to the sitting position.

Motor behavior is much better coordinated than it was even

four weeks earlier. Twelve weeks, in most fields of behavior, in many children marks a period of definite disequilibrium. Placed on his stomach on the floor or other flat surface, a baby of this age kicks and struggles fruitlessly and awkwardly. (Feeding, too, may raise definite problems around this time of life. And sleeping behavior—particularly getting to sleep—may not go too smoothly. There may also be a very great deal of crying around the 12-week period, especially in the evening.)

Much of this behavior is smoothed out at around 16 weeks of age. Feeding goes better. (You probably think you have finally hit upon the right formula if the infant is bottle-fed.) Hunger can be very intense at certain times, but he may refuse his 6 P.M. feeding for the very good reason that he is not hungry. He gets to sleep more easily and is more likely to sleep right through the night.

Postural behavior above all may be considered to express the good equilibrium which characterizes the 16-week age zone. Put him on the floor, and he no longer struggles helplessly as he did earlier. He may even, for brief moments, be able to maintain the poised position which we know as *swimming.* That is, both legs extend at full length, arms flex with fists at shoulders, and (something we ourselves would find difficult to accomplish) lower abdomen lifts well up off the floor.

Eyes now follow a moving object—often through an arc of as much as 180 degrees. Hands reach out for a desired object—even though he or she cannot as yet do much about grasping it.

And, best of all, from the parents' point of view, the infant is becoming socially responsive. He coos, chuckles, laughs aloud. He can even smile back when you smile at him. He is well on the way to becoming a responsive member of the family group.

Twenty-eight Weeks

If your 16-week-old infant seemed to you to be delightfully mature, that maturity was, nevertheless, nothing to what he or she will be able to achieve at 28 weeks of age.

Baby now not only prefers the sitting position, but can, under favorable conditions, maintain it for long periods of time.

But by now he is so mature that the mere business of sitting up by no means utilizes all his abilities. He is no longer content just to sit and look. Now he wants to touch as well, and he wants to be held standing and to bounce.

Whether lying on his back or stomach or sitting in his high chair, he must have something in his hands. He now can not only reach out toward desired objects, but can, if they are not placed too far away, pick them up in a crude grasp and finger them. He is most likely to bring them to his mouth. (Even feet are grasped and brought to the mouth as he lies on his back—no mean achievement.)

The baby of this age not only likes to grasp and to finger objects, but to shift them from one hand to the other. This behavior we call *transfer,* and he can spend many happy minutes thus engaged. Or he may delight in banging simple objects on the tray of his high chair.

He can, indeed, amuse himself alone for long periods. But this does not mean that he is not interested in people. The baby of this age is an extremely social individual. He likes to smile at onlookers and is usually enthusiastically friendly to both intimates and strangers. In fact, he presents an amiable union between self-sufficiency and sociability. He alternates with ease between self-directed and socially referred activity. He listens to words spoken by others and particularly likes his father's low voice, which frightened him at an earlier age. He listens also to his own private verbalizations.

He gets on well, whatever the situation. For 28 weeks, like 16, represents an age of extremely good equilibrium. Behavior patterns and emotions (which actually are in themselves behavior patterns) are in good focus.

However, as Dr. Gesell has commented, this period of equilibrium, like all such, tends to be short-lived. For the growth complex never fully stabilizes. New thrusts, new tensions of development, soon upset any state of balance, producing unstableness, which is in turn resolved by further temporary stages of equilibrium.

Thus 16 weeks was, as we suggested, in most a period of excellent equilibrium. New efforts—efforts to do things which he is not able to do—produce at 20 weeks a period of definite disequilibrium. The 20-week-old infant, for example, tries to get his knees under him as he lies on his stomach. He fails. He may try to sit alone. He fails. He reaches out for objects and may try unsuccessfully to grasp them. He cries when his mother leaves him. He is aware of strangers.

All of this produces frustration. Increased abilities coming in at 24 to 28 weeks help to resolve many of these frustrations.

Forty Weeks

Forty weeks marks still another temporary stage of equilibrium in the baby's path of growth. At 28 weeks he paused, momentarily, at a delightful point at which his drives and efforts were happily well balanced by his abilities. He was trying many new things— but temporarily he seemed, for the most part, to try only those things at which he could succeed. And to be satisfied with such successes as he could achieve.

All this, in many, changes at 32 weeks. New awareness at this age makes for new sensitivity. Thirty-two weeks, for example, marks one of the high points for withdrawing from or even crying at the sight of strangers. This is not a step backward, actually, for it is the result of an increased ability to tell the difference between the familiar and the unfamiliar.

Posturally, too, the 32-week-old baby may have some difficulty. Unable as yet to get to hands and knees and creep, he or she nevertheless tries to make progress toward unattainable goals by pivoting in a circular direction. This often leads to confusion and frustration.

For these and other reasons which you may observe in your own infant, 32 weeks tends to mark a brief period of considerable disequilibrium. Crying and laughter are very close together and sometimes indistinguishable.

All the more welcome, then, the age range from 36 to 40 weeks when many babies settle down to a brief period of fine equilibrium.

Socially they are not only well adjusted but often extremely responsive. Many can respond to "bye-bye." Some can pat-a-cake. Vocally most are extremely fluent. Friends and strangers alike are received with warm smiles.

Posturally, too, things are going along excellently. The child of this age can, if in a favorable position, sit alone indefinitely and can even manipulate objects while sitting unsupported. He can get over to prone from sitting. (In another month he will be able to get to sitting from prone.)

He can get up to hands and knees, which puts him in a position where he can very shortly move about by creeping. A whole new world becomes his when he can actually locomote. He can also pull himself to standing—another new dimension conquered.

Furthermore, his ability to grasp and manipulate objects has advanced, along with other abilities. Grasp is no longer predominantly pawlike. Not only can he poke accurately at tiny objects with extended forefinger, but he can grasp these same tiny objects precisely between thumb and forefinger.

He has become increasingly aware of his social world. Not only may he wave bye-bye and imitate pat-a-cake, but he can now respond to gestures, facial expressions, and sounds. He can heed "No, no"—a most useful social accomplishment and one which he will need to use extensively before he in turn becomes a parent. He not only vocalizes spontaneously, but he can imitate such simple syllables as "da-da."

All in all, your baby adds greatly to the social scene.

Fifty-two Weeks

Forty weeks of age marks such a peak of infant accomplishment in many fields that you might wonder what the baby will achieve next. Admittedly, he does not change as much between 40 and 52 weeks as he did in any preceding twelve-week period. The rate of growth is slowing down. We shall soon start measuring age changes in larger units of time.

However, there are changes. The greatest, perhaps, is that the baby can now creep about freely on hands and knees. The mobile 1-year-old is thus a quite different person from the 40-weeker who could cover only a small amount of space, if any.

He or she can not only get about freely on hands and knees, but can now "cruise" along beside some object of furniture and can probably take at least a few steps hands-supported.

Socially—after going through another period of disequilibrium at around 44 weeks in which he tends to be "strange" with strangers—the infant shows himself serene and self-confident and friendly. He loves to have an audience, recognizes social approval by repeating performances laughed at, enjoys the give and take of social games, and can imitate simple social actions. He particularly enjoys such games as peek-a-boo and loves to be chased as he creeps.

Increased motor abilities may temporarily, with some, interfere with daily routines. For instance, the baby may prefer to stand up while being fed. Or his love for manipulating the spoon himself may further interfere with eating. But give him scope for his newfound abilities—that is, let him stand up in his high chair supported by an extended harness and give him a spoon of his own to play with while you feed him—and feeding may go as smoothly as ever.

With a little skill on your part, you can give your 1-year-old opportunity to express growing abilities and at the same time get him or her through the day's routine without too much difficulty. Because 1 year, though not an age of startling new behavior advancements, tends to be a period of reasonably good, smooth functioning in all fields of behavior.

Fifteen Months

As compared with 1-year-old behavior, that which the baby exhibits at 15 months may be far from smooth. But this is partly because so many new abilities are coming in all at once. The child is suddenly trying to do so much, and doing it so vigorously, that it is small wonder if the total behavior pattern loses a little of its earlier harmony.

Fifteen months has been characterized as a dart and dash and fling age. The earlier two-way relationship of give and take has been replaced by one-way behavior (which will become even more one-way at 18 months). The 15-month-old child is no longer a mere creeping and cruising baby. He or she can now walk, strains at the leash with newfound locomotor abilities, and objects to both leash and playpen. A mere verbal "No, no" has little effect. There is too much to be done—too much to be seen. Not only agile on flat surfaces, the baby now can (and will, if allowed to) climb stairs endlessly, though this is more common at 18 months.

He gets into everything. He is ceaselessly active and knows very little inhibition. He definitely does best if kept out of the living room and restricted to places where he won't get into trouble.

If confined to his playpen, he is likely to pick up each toy with which you have provided him and cast it outside. In fact, throwing things is one of his favorite pastimes. He throws things and then shouts for you to bring them back to him. He also loves to put one object after another in and out of any given receptacle, but tends to dump more than to fill. He is more likely to stay willingly in his pen if there are interesting things going on within sight, such as traffic going by.

Language is coming in—though it has not yet progressed very far. However, the 15-monther can often ask for what he wants by vocalizing and sometimes by pointing, can indicate refusal by bodily protest, and can respond to a few key words and phrases.

Some can now allow a dish to stand on their tray without grasping at it. Some may have given up the bottle, and may even be able to hold a cup, though awkwardly, for drinking; or feed themselves, also awkwardly, with a spoon. They may possibly cooperate in dressing by extending an arm or leg when so requested.

Moods are shifting, and temper, while quickly aroused and vigorously expressed, tends to be short-lived. Diversion is easy, and the child is easily entertained. It is largely a matter of the adult's having enough energy to keep up with him.

Eighteen Months

The 18-monther walks down a one-way street, though this one-way street can be rapidly reversed. And this street more often than not seems to lead in a direction exactly opposite to that which the adult has in mind. Asked to "Come here, dear," he or she either stands still or runs in the opposite direction. (The 18-monther may even like to walk backwards.) Ask him to put something in the wastebasket, and he is more likely to empty out what is already in it. Hold out your hand for the cup which he has just drained, and he will drop it onto the floor. Give him a second sock to put on, and he will probably remove the one which is already on his foot. His enjoyment of the opposite may be the reason why it works so well, if he is running away from you, to say, "Bye-bye," and walk away from *him.* Then he may come running.

Not only does he not come when called—he seldom obeys any verbal command. "No" is his chief word.

It is not so much that the 18-monther is bad as that there are so many abilities he has not yet mastered. He has not yet reached the place where he is easily motivated by words. He has not yet reached the place where he can wait. "Now" is the one dimension of time important to him. Thus efforts to get him to wait a minute are for the most part doomed to failure, and he cannot stand any frustration. (Unfortunately, no matter how much you try to protect him in the way you set up the environment, he cannot seem to keep from frustrating himself.)

Interpersonal relations are almost completely dominated by ideas of taking—but not of giving. Actually, except for his parents, he may treat other people, especially other children, more as if they were objects than people. He will as likely step on a friend as walk around him. He has not even a beginning concept of sharing.

Eighteen months is not one of the "better" ages if we measure goodness in terms of minding, responding to commands, keeping within reasonable bounds. However, if we can appreciate the immaturity—of motor ability, language, and emotions—of the 18-monther, it can be fairly easy to keep his behavior within reasonable limits.

Thus, if you would like to have him move from wherever he is to wherever you are—lure him, pick him up and carry him, but for best results, do not call him. He is simply not mature enough to respond, in most instances, to such a verbal command.

If you wish him to stay away from certain areas in the household, for best results make it physically impossible for him to get to them. Physical barriers, you will find, work better than do verbal prohibitions.

When you do use words, keep them short and simple: "Coat—hat—out" is about as complicated a command as the average 18-monther can follow.

It is important in dealing with an 18-monther to keep in mind at all times that he is an extremely immature little creature. He understands more words than he can say, but even his understanding is extremely limited. He can walk and even run and sometimes climb, but his balance is very unsteady. And with his quick temper and need to have everything "Now," his emotions are as immature as any other part of him.

If you expect very little, keep your demands that he "mind" to a minimum, and give very close and rather constant physical supervision, you may find that you get on very well with and enjoy your 18-monther. However, in many households the phrase "bad boy" is used so commonly that the child may think it is either his own name or perhaps the name of the forbidden activity.

Be sure to give plenty of outlet for boundless physical energy—stair climbing is one of the best. And for the rest, it may be a kindness to him to use a harness, especially when he is in new territory.

And don't be above using guile. If he is playing with an object that you don't want him to have, try doing something interesting like playing the piano or crumpling some paper in another part of the room. You may be surprised at how quickly he will leave his activity to take part in yours.

Two Years

The child's behavior at 2 years of age is so much better organized than earlier from the adult's point of view that we sometimes fall into the trap of expecting a steady improvement from here on—and are thus unhappily surprised when the customary difficulties of 2½ make themselves apparent. (Though many people speak glibly of the Terrible Twos, this is a misinterpretation. For about six months around the age of 2 many children are cooperative and comfortable. In general, it is Two-and-a-half, not Two, who can fairly be described as terrible.)

At any rate, regardless of what may come after, here at 2 comes a brief breathing space for child as well as mother. For 2 is in most children, compared to the ages which immediately precede and follow it, an age of rather marked equilibrium.

Things are much smoother with respect to nearly every field of behavior. Added maturity and a calm willingness to do what Two can do and not try too hard to do the things he or she cannot manage largely account for this greater smoothness.

The 2-year-old is much more confident motorwise than he was at 18 months. He is less likely to fall. He runs and climbs more surely. Thus, he no longer needs to be so preoccupied with keeping his balance and getting around, and can turn his attention to other things. Also, the adult does not have to be so much on guard to protect him.

He is also surer of himself languagewise. Not only does he now understand a surprising amount of what is said, but he himself can, as a rule, use language with remarkable effectiveness. Being able to make his wants known and being understood by others relieves much of the furious exasperation which he felt earlier when he could only point or cry and hope that someone who knew his ways and wants would be on hand to interpret. At 21 months a wrong spoon or a wrong bib could be the cause of a long crying spell.

Emotionally, also, Two finds life easier. Demands are not quite as strong as they were. Ability to wait a minute or to suffer slight or temporary frustration if necessary has tremendously increased.

Furthermore, people mean more to him than they did earlier. He likes, sometimes at least, to please others; and he is often pleased by others. Thus he can, as the 18-monther cannot, occasionally do things just to please people, can occasionally put another person's wishes above his own. Though he cannot as yet share with other children, he will on occasion, if so directed, be willing to find substitute toys for these other children. This marks a whole new dimension in social relations over those of six months earlier.

Two also is, on many occasions, loving and affectionate and can be warmly responsive to others. This, along with his increased good nature, makes him, at home or nursery school, a much easier person to deal with than he was when younger. Much can be, and often is, said in praise of the 2-year-old. He is a loving companion and a real joy in many households.

Two-and-a-Half Years

This is an age about which parents may need warning because so much that the child now does naturally, almost inevitably, is directly contrary to what his or her parents would like. The 2½-year-old is not, temperamentally, an easy, adaptable member of any social group.

The change in behavior which takes place between 2 and 2½ can be rather overwhelming, perhaps to child as well as to the adults who surround him. Two-and-a-half is a peak age of disequilibrium. Parents often say that they can't do a thing with the child of this age.

Actually, once they understand a little about the structure of behavior at this time, they often find that, awkward as it may be, it does make sense. Working *around* the behavior characteristics of Two-and-a-half is often much more successful than trying to meet them head on.

We'll list some of these outstanding characteristics:

First of all, 2½-year-olds are rigid and inflexible. They want exactly what they want when they want it. They cannot adapt, give in, wait a little while. Everything has to be done just so. Everything has to be right in the place they consider proper. For any domestic routine, they set up a rigid sequence of events which must always follow each other always in exactly the same manner.

Second, they are extremely domineering and demanding. They must give the orders. They must make the decisions. If they decide, "Mummy do," Daddy cannot be accepted as a substitute. If they decide, "Me do it myself," then no one is allowed to help them, no matter how awkward or incapable they themselves may be.

Two-and-a-half is an age of violent emotions. There is little modulation to the emotional life of children of this age.

Furthermore, it is an age of opposite extremes. With no ability to choose between alternatives (it is almost impossible for Two-and-a-halfs to make a clearcut choice and stick to it), children of this age shuttle back and forth endlessly between any two extremes, seeming to be trying to include both in their decision. "I will—I won't," "I want it—I don't want it," "Go out—stay in." If someone doesn't cut into this back-and-forth shuttling, it has been known to go on for upwards of an hour or more. The decision of what clothes to wear may usurp a whole morning for a conflict-ridden 2½-year-old.

Thus any caretaker of a 2½-year-old will need to streamline all routines, make the decisions herself, try to avoid situations where the child takes over.

Another unfortunate characteristic of this age is perseveration—that is, the children want to go on and on with whatever they are doing. Not only right at the moment but from day to day. If you read four stories before bedtime yesterday, they want four stories—and the same ones, too—today. It is very difficult with many children of this age to introduce new clothes, new pieces of furniture, new things to eat. They want things to go on just the way they have always been or at least hold on to the old as new things are added.

Total all of these characteristics together and you have a child who is not easy to deal with. Vigorous, enthusiastic, energetic, the typical Two-and-a-half may be. But he or she is not an easy person to have around the house. However, mothers will find that great patience, a real understanding of the difficulties of the age, and a willingness to use endless techniques to get around rigidities and rituals and stubbornness will help get through the time till the difficult 2½-year-old turns 3.

Three Years

Things quiet down, briefly, at 3 for most children. Two-and-a-half seemed to love to resist. Three seems to love to conform. The typical 3-year-old uses the word "Yes" quite as easily as he or she formerly used the word "No."

Two-and-a-half seemed to be all "take." Three likes to give as well as take. He likes to share—both objects and experiences. "We" is a word used frequently. It expresses the child's cooperative, easygoing attitude toward life in general.

Three tends to be in good equilibrium with people and things around him, perhaps because he is in better equilibrium within himself. He no longer seems to need the protection of rituals, of always doing everything the same way. Greater maturity has led him to feel much more secure—secure within himself and secure in his relations with others.

Not only has the need for rituals dropped out, but almost every other aspect of 2½-year-old behavior which made trouble for him and those about him seems to have disappeared, or at least lessened, as well. The child is no longer rigid, inflexible, domineering, grasping. No longer does everything have to be done *his* way. Now he can not only do it *your* way, but can enjoy the doing.

People are important to him. He likes to make friends and will often willingly give up a toy or privilege in order to stay in the good graces of some other person—something of which he was incapable earlier.

Increased motor ability allows daily routines and other necessary activities to be gotten through with minimal difficulty. It also allows him to successfully carry out play activities which earlier baffled and enraged him.

But above all, an increased ability with and interest in language help him to be a delightful companion, an interesting group member. His own vocabulary and ability to use language have increased tremendously in most cases. His appreciation of the language of others has increased similarly. Now he can not only be controlled by language, but can be entertained and himself can entertain. He loves new words, and they can often act like magic in influencing him to behave as we would wish. Such words as *new, different, big, surprise, secret,* all suggest his increased awareness in the excitement of new horizons. Such words as *help, might, could, guess,* are active motivators to get him to perform necessary tasks.

Two-and-a-half often seemed to resist just as a matter of principle. It was safer. Three goes forward positively to meet each new adventure.

Three-and-a-Half Years

Temporarily at 3 many children reach what most parents and teachers consider to be a delightful stage of equilibrium. The children's wishes and their ability to carry out those wishes seem, for a while, to be in remarkably good balance. Three-year-olds, for the most part, seem to be well pleased with themselves and with those about them, and the feeling tends to be reciprocal. They seem also, at least so far as their outward behavior shows it, to feel secure within themselves.

At 3½ there comes, in many, a tremendous change. It is as though in order to proceed from the equilibrium of the 3-year-old stage to that which is usually attained by 5 years of age, the child's behavior needs to break up, loosen up, and go through a phase of new integration. All this comes to a head in many at 3½ years of age—a period of marked insecurity, disequilibrium, incoordination.

Thus, poor or new coordination may express itself in any or all fields of behavior. It may express itself only temporarily and very lightly in some children, for a considerably longer period and much more markedly in others. It is so characteristic of this particular age that though environmental factors certainly may exaggerate it, in many cases we can fairly consider that it is caused by growth factors alone.

You may look for incoordination in any or in all fields of behavior. Motor incoordination, for example, may express itself in stumbling, falling, fear of heights. A child who has previously shown excellent motor coordination may go through a period of extreme motor disequilibrium.

Hands alone as well as the total body may be involved. Thus, a child whose hand and arm movements have up till now been strong and firm may suddenly draw with a thin, wavery line; may build with a noticeable hand tremor.

Language may be involved. Stuttering very often comes in at this period in children who have never stuttered before.

Eyes and ears may be involved. Parents are often worried by the temporary (or more persistent) crossing of the eyes which comes in here. Or children may complain that they "can't see," or "can't hear."

Tensional outlets are often exaggerated in this 3½-year-old period. Thus children may blink their eyes, bite their nails, pick their nose, exhibit facial or other tics, masturbate, suck their thumb excessively.

And lastly, along with motor and verbal difficulties often come tremendous difficulties in relations with other people. Three-and-a-half-year-olds express their emotional insecurity in crying, whining, and frequent questioning, especially of Mother: "Do you love me?" Or perhaps in complaints: "You don't love me." They are also extremely demanding with adults: "Don't look," "Don't talk," "Don't laugh." Or they may demand that all attention be focused on themselves, and thus become extremely jealous of any attention paid by members of the family to each other.

With friends, too, children of this age show considerable insecurity and great demand for exclusive attention. The emotional extremes which they express (very shy one minute, overboisterous the next) also make them uncertain contributors to any social situation.

If the adult in charge knows in advance that all this uncertainty, insecurity, incoordination quite normally mark the 3½ age period, it can help considerably. First of all, it can keep you from blaming various aspects of the environment for any or all of the different incoordinations. It can stimulate you to improve the environment. And it can help give you patience to show the child the extra affection, the extra understanding which he or she so desperately needs at this age.

Moreover, the age of 3½ is not without its charm. One of the more amusing aspects of this age is the child's often vivid imagination, expressed most strikingly in his enjoyment of imaginary companions. Though some people have felt that only the lonely play with imaginary playmates, our own research and that of others makes it very evident that it is often the highly superior and nicely imaginative child who invents these creatures. They are very real to him, very important, and, we can assure you, quite harmless. Even though it may be a nuisance to have to lay a place at dinner, keep an extra seat in the family automobile or a place on the family couch for this "friend" who exists only in your child's imagination, it is probably well worthwhile.

Four Years

For every age it seems possible to discover a key word or words which describe the structure of behavior at that time. If we can find and remember those words, it often helps us tremendously to understand and appreciate the child of that age.

For Four the key words are *out of bounds.* If we can remember those words, and smile sympathetically when we say them, it can be of immeasurable aid in helping us to deal with any 4-year-olds who may come our way. For 4-year-olds are, almost more than children of any other age, out of bounds—and out of bounds in almost every direction.

Thus they are out of bounds motorwise. They hit, kick, throw stones. They break things. They run away.

They are out of bounds emotionally. Loud silly laughter alternates with fits of rage. "You make me so *mad*," he or she will tell you.

Verbally Four is almost more out of bounds than in any other way. The language of a typical 4-year-old can be almost guaranteed to shock anybody except perhaps a hardened nursery-school teacher. Profanity (Where did he ever hear such awful language?) is rampant. Bathroom words come into common use. He uses them not only incidentally or where they might be appropriate, but may dwell on them and rhyme with them—accompanying his rhyming with much silly laughter which shows that he fully appreciates their inappropriateness.

And in interpersonal relations he is quite as out of bounds as anywhere else. He loves to defy parental commands. In fact, he seems to thrive on being just as defiant as he can manage. Even severe punishment may have little chastening effect. A terrible toughness seems to have come over him—he swaggers, swears, boasts, defies.

Imagination, too, seems at this time to have no "reasonable" limits. This newfound flight through imagination, which often begins at 3½ years, may be a high point for the enjoyment of imaginary companions. These, most parents accept fairly well. Four's tall tales, particularly when they strike the adult as just plain lies, are less well accepted. Yet to the average 4-year-old the line between fact and fiction is a very thin, flexible one. He or she may not actually be telling falsehoods. It's just more interesting that way, and the children may come to believe their own imaginings, which become real to them.

How firm a stand you, as a parent or teacher, take toward all these out-of-bounds behaviors is up to you. Certainly there are limits. Even the very simple social situation of a nursery-school group requires a certain toning down of 4-year-old exuberance. Home life requires perhaps even more.

You will, inevitably, need to use a good deal of firmness in dealing with your 4-year-old. But you will feel less hopeless and less angry if you can keep in mind that behaving in an out-of-bounds manner is not only an almost inevitable but a probably quite necessary part of Four's development. The 3½-year-old was, certainly, too insecure for practical purposes. Four seems to most of us overly secure and too brashly confident in his own abilities. Nature seems to have this awkward way of going to opposite extremes as the child develops. Eventually the swings of the pendulum become less extreme and settle down to a narrower range as the individual's basic personality is less swayed by age changes.

The 4-year-old needs to be allowed to test himself out. He needs to be allowed to go up the street on his bike in both directions and with expanding limits. We hope there are neighbors whom he can visit and who will receive him and will notify his mother of his visit. He needs to be allowed to run ahead on a walk and to wait at the next street corner. He is surprisingly responsive if he has been allowed some initial expansion. The reins of control can be held loosely, but there are always those moments when they need to be pulled up short and sharp.

Four-and-a-Half Years

The 4½-year-old is beginning to pull in from those out-of-bounds 4-year-old ways. He or she is on the way to a more focal 5, when life is more matter-of-fact and not so deep.

The 4½-year-old is trying to sort out what is real from what is make-believe, and he does not get so lost in his pretending as at 3½ and 4 years, when he really *was* a cat, a carpenter or Captain Kangaroo. "Is it real?" is his constant question. Making a *real* drawing of an airplane, he includes a long electric cord so the people can plug it in. He can become quite confused as he tries to straighten out what he pretends, what happens on TV, and what is real.

This mixture of reality and imagination can be quite exasperating to parents. Thus when one mother, completely out of patience, threatened that the Sandman would come and get him, her 4½-year-old considered and replied, "O.K., well, I think I better take my cowboy boots and shirt—will you get down my suitcase?"

Four-and-a-half-year-olds are a little more self-motivating than they were earlier. They start a job and stay on the same track much better than they did at 4 years, and with less need of adult control. When they start to build a farm with blocks, it ends up as a farm—not, as at 4 years, becoming first a fort, then a truck, then a gas station.

Four-and-a-half-year-olds are great discussers. Reading a book about fires might lead to a long discussion about the pros and cons of fires. They often have a surprising wealth of material and experience to draw on and seem to be prompted by an intellectual, philosophizing sort of interest. They are concerned with details, and they like to be shown. Their desire for realism is sometimes entirely too stark for adults—they may seem almost too frank as they demand the details about death, for example.

Children of this age are improving their control and perfecting their skills in many ways. Their play is less wild than at 4; they are better able to accept frustrations. Their fine motor control as expressed in drawing is markedly improved, and they will often draw on and on. They show a beginning interest in letters and numbers and may count quite well, though skipping certain numbers.

Four-and-a-half-year-olds show a beginning interest, too, in seeing several sides of the picture. They are aware of front and back, of inside and outside. (One child wanted to know what her back looked like.) They may even draw a man on one side of a paper, then turn it over and draw the back of his head on the other side.

Four-and-a-half, with its increased control and its interest in improving and perfecting skills, is a "catching-up" time for some children, especially for boys who have been slow in motor or language development, or it may be an age of rapid intellectual growth.

Five Years

Five years of age marks, in many children, a time of extreme and delightful equilibrium. "She's an angel," say many mothers of Fives, in awe and wonderment.

"He's almost too good!" others worry.

Five is indeed a good age. Gone is the out-of-bounds exuberance of the 4-year-old. Gone is the uncertainty and unpredictability of 4½. The 5-year-old tends to be reliable, stable, well adjusted. Secure within himself, he is calm, friendly, and not too demanding in his relations with others.

Secure and capable he seems, because he is content to stay on or near home base. He does not seem to feel the need to thrust out into the unknown, to attempt that which is too difficult. Rather he is content to live here and now. He tries only that which he can accomplish, and therefore he accomplishes that which he tries.

His mother is the center of his world, and he likes to be near her. He likes to do things with and for her, likes to obey her commands. He likes to be instructed and to get permission. To be a good boy is not only his intention, but it is something which he usually can accomplish. Therefore he is satisfied with himself, and others are satisfied with him.

Many parents wish, when the customary 5½- to 6-year-old breakup of behavior comes, and when their "good" little Five turns into an often less-than-good little Six, that they could have their docile 5-year-old back again.

Looking backward in this way is, of course, fruitless. It is like wishing that your 18-monther, when he gets around the house too briskly and gets into too many things, were once again in the precreeping stage. Five is, surely, an enjoyable age for everybody while it lasts. But a growing child needs more than 5-year-old equipment to meet the world. He needs to branch out, as he does at 6. Unfortunately, in branching out, he often thrusts into areas which cause a good deal of difficulty for all concerned. That is the difficulty of 6.

Five-and-a-Half and Six Years

By now a certain rhythm of growth will perhaps have made itself apparent to you. You will have noticed that there is a tendency as children grow older for ages in which they seem to be in relatively good equilibrium—happy, easygoing, and secure—to alternate with ages in which this equilibrium breaks up. At the ages of disequilibrium children are thrusting out or in, trying new things, wanting too much, finding it difficult to adapt to others because their own demands are so strong.

Thus equable Five is followed by tumultuous Six. Actually, the breakup starts at around 5½ years of age. By 6½ things have usually smoothed down again. But for a period of six months or so around the age of 6 many parents find that their child is extremely difficult to deal with.

Behavior at this time is in many ways reminiscent of that which we have described as typifying the 2½-year-old. The child is, to begin with, violently emotional. And in his emotions, he functions at opposite extremes. He loves one minute—hates the next. Thus he may say, "I love you, Mummy," accompanying his statement with a big bear hug. And the next minute he bursts out, "I hate you!" This outburst may be elicited by nothing worse, on Mother's part, than moving some belonging of his out of its "proper" place.

What has happened is that Mother is no longer the center of his world, as she was when he was merely 5. Now *he* wants to be the center of his world, even though he hasn't yet developed a secure sense of self. He wants to come first, to be loved best, to have the most of everything. Mother has been moved to second place. And now he takes everything out on her. Whatever is wrong, Mother gets blamed.

And much goes wrong. Because Five-and-a-half and Six, like Two-and-a-half, is very demanding of others and very rigid in his or her demands. Boy or girl has to have things just so. Cannot adapt. It is the others who must do the adapting.

Also, the child of this age tends to be extremely negative in response to others. That he has been asked to do something is in his eyes sufficient reason for refusing to do it. He usually responds slowly or even negatively to commands, though if you can ignore his initial, "No, I won't," later he will often carry out the command spontaneously, as though it were his own idea. If he says "No," try, "See if you can do it before I count to ten." Or say, "I guess you're going to need three chances on that one." If you can give in a little and not demand instantaneous conformity and obedience, things will go more smoothly. However, admittedly, many 5½- and 6-year-olds are, much of the time, negative, rude, resistant, saucy, and argumentative in the face of direct commands.

However, this age definitely does have a good side. These children can be very delightful in their vigor, energy, and readiness for anything new. This is an expansive age, and 5½- and 6-year-olds are ready for almost anything. Their appetite for new experiences is prodigious.

But this may lead them to want all of everything. It is most difficult for them to choose between any two alternatives because they want them both. It is also most difficult for them to accept criticism, blame, punishment. They have to be right. They have to be praised. They have to win. They are as rigid and as unadaptable in their relations with others as they were earlier at 2½. Things have to be done their way. Others must give in to them.

If they are winning, everything is fine. Unfortunately, they are not above cheating in order to win. And if the others win, Five-and-a-half or Six is likely to go into a tantrum and accuse *them* of cheating. Thus, if all goes well, they can be warm, enthusiastic, eager, ready for anything. But if things go badly—tears and tantrums.

And, alas, 5½- and 6-year-olds are not above a little thievery on the side. *Mine* is very important to them; *thine* quite unimportant. It is hard for them to see why others should have more than they have, or even why anyone should have things that they would like to have. Thus they are very light-fingered. Best lock up pennies or nickels or other desirable objects till they develop a little more restraint.

Nor do 5½- and 6-year-olds always tell the truth. This is especially the case if you try to get them to admit to wrongdoing. They can be almost guaranteed to say that they didn't do whatever it was. If, for purposes of distributing blame, you find it absolutely necessary to discover whether a 6-year-old did or did not do a certain thing, it is usually easy to find out, if you don't accuse him directly. Just say, "Why, how could you reach that high shelf?" (From which he has just knocked off a valuable vase.) He will probably tell you, "Oh I just pushed that chair over and climbed up," not realizing what he is saying.

Whatever the situation, we can make it a little easier for the 5½- or 6-year-old, and for ourselves, by respecting the fact that he is having a difficult time within himself as well as in his relations with others. Use techniques where you can. Bypass as many unhappy incidents as you can. Get outsiders in to help carry through daily routines where you can—for children at this age behave worst with Mother.

Seven Years

Seven years of age is no exception to the rule that each new age period brings marked changes in behavior (as well as many new accomplishments). The 6-year-old child is typically brash and aggressive, ready for new adventures, falsely sure of himself. He meets new situations head on. Trouble occurs on the playground? He will stay and battle it out. Somebody tries to get something away from him? He will fight for his own.

Things are very, very different at 7. Though 7, like any other age, has its moments of exuberance, security and happiness, it is a more withdrawn age. Seven in many ways has calmed down and is easier to live with. But 7-year-olds are more likely to complain than to rejoice. More apt to retreat from the scene muttering than to stay and demand their own. They have, with justice, been described as morose, mopey, and moody.

Seven not only withdraws from combat, he just naturally seems to withdraw from other people. He likes to be alone. He wants a room of his own to which he can retreat and protect his own things. He likes to watch, to listen, to stay on the edge of any scene. He is a great television watcher and radio listener and possibly a reader. It is almost as if he is building up his sense of self by watching, observing, ruminating.

But his hands are also very busy touching, exploring, feeling everything he comes in contact with. Seven has an inordinate love of pencils and prefers the sharp, defined stroke of lead to the loose, sloppy stroke of crayon. His intellect is in the ascendancy. He is more discriminating and refined in what he sees and what he does.

Seven is not as belligerently uncooperative as is Six, but he often does not respond promptly, does not hear directions, and may forget what you have told him. He may start to obey and then get into a detour along the way. Best results are obtained by warning him in advance, reminding him when the time comes, and checking to see that he does not get off the track along the way.

He often demands too much of himself. He is aware of the task but not always able to complete it. He is apt to go on too long and then become suddenly exhausted. He needs to be helped to define stopping points. He has his good days and his bad days, his high learning days and his forgetting-everything days. An aware teacher will shift her intellectual fare on these different days. And a wise mother will keep her child at home if his bad day starts the minute he gets out of bed, as it so often does.

For a brief period life for some can be pitched in a definitely minor key. At these times Seven tends to feel that people are against him, that they don't like him, that they are picking on him. The other kids cheat; his teacher picks on him at school. Even his parents are unfair. Though only a few Sevens go so far as to figure that they are adopted, this fantasy does now and then occur, and it typifies the "nobody-loves-me" attitude of the 7-year-old. If his family is too "mean" to him, he may threaten to run away. Not from the expansive exuberance which sometimes drove Four out into the world, but simply to get away from the intolerable persecution which he thinks is his lot.

Even the facial expression of some 7-year-olds may reveal their dissatisfaction with life. Their lips may curl downward in a permanent pout.

Though Sevens tend to be less happy and satisfied with life than their parents would like, their good days will steadily increase in number as they get older, their fatigue will lessen, and they will be ready for most anything by 8 years of age.

The parent of a 7-year-old needs to steer a delicate course between being reasonably sympathetic with the many complaints the child will utter, and yet not taking these complaints too seriously (though headaches do need investigating). His teacher is probably not as unfair as he reports her to be, the other children probably not as nefarious, brothers and sisters not as wicked.

Eight Years

Seven withdraws from the world, but Eight goes out to meet it. Nothing is too difficult for the 8-year-old, in his or her own estimation. No task is too formidable to be undertaken. No distance is too great to cover. In fact, to the average 8-year-old, the new and difficult is an exciting challenge which he tends to meet with great zest. He often overestimates his own ability in meeting this challenge.

He will not always follow through in his activities. The burst of energy and enthusiasm with which he tackles each new task may be followed by failure, discouragement, and even tears if his failure is mentioned. But this will not stop him from starting something else new—tomorrow.

We often describe the 8-year-old as expansive and speedy. He seems to find it difficult to stay out of touch with any part of the environment. Therefore Eight is constantly busy and active, constantly enjoying new experiences, constantly trying out new things, making new friends.

In every way, the typical 8-year-old covers a good deal of ground. With characteristic speed, he covers it rapidly. But alas, with his newly increased powers of evaluation, he may recognize his all-too-frequent failures. Then, tears and self-disparagement! "I always do it wrong!" "I never get anything right!" With his tendency to dramatize everything, we sometimes suspect that he, in a way, relishes even his failures, or he at least makes use of them.

For all his seeming brashness and bravado, the child of this age is much more sensitive than one might expect. Eight needs protection both from trying to do too much and from too excessive self-criticism when failures occur.

Thus when his good beginning is followed, as it often will be, by a poor ending, help him from too great a feeling of failure. Plan with him toward a future time when he will carry through better or will not set an almost impossible task for himself.

Eight is a little better at carrying out requests than Seven. Eight usually delays somewhat in doing what you ask and may argue and find excuses, but he finally obeys with, "If you insist." He prefers to work for an immediate (cash) reward than simply for the sake of helping. Many Eights want just a hint or cue, not full directions which they consider babyish. Thus they prefer the one-word "Dinner" to "Wash your hands and get ready for dinner." Or, if full instructions are given, they may insist that these be worded "just right."

Seven was most concerned with self and how other people treated him. Eight has gone further than this in dealing with others. Now he is interested, not just in how people treat him, but in his *relationships* with others. He is ready for, and wants, a good two-way relationship. Furthermore, it is not just what people do which concerns him, but also what they think. He has more to give to other people than he did earlier, but he expects more of them as well. With his mother, especially, the 8-year-old wants and demands a close, understanding relationship.

The 8-year-old, in his expanding universe, gives us more than a hint of the kind of person he will be later on.

Nine Years

Exuberant! Expansive! Buoyant! Ready for anything! That was your typical 8-year-old. Nine, as many of you will have observed, is again on the quieter strain of 5 and 7. He lives more within himself, is surer in his contacts with the outside world, is more self-contained and self-sufficient than was the adventurous Eight, who just couldn't keep to himself.

Nine can be, in fact often insists on being, extremely independent. In his own eyes he is quite a man of the world, and he tends to resist too much bossing by his parents. However, many can now interrupt their own activity (so difficult just earlier) in response to a request or demand from the adult. Securing the child's attention in the first place may depend on his interest and willingness to carry out your request. He may wish to postpone the task till later, and then may become so busy that he forgets.

There is much less arguing back than occurred earlier. If the child does not like your directions, he may look sullen, cross, truculent; but if no issue is made, he will usually obey eventually. Many now prefer a fair appraisal of their work to praise or pay.

The average 9-year-old tends to be much more interested in friends than in family; and many, briefly, would like to withdraw as much as possible from the family circle. Certainly the opinions of their friends are much more important, to most of them, than are the opinions of their families.

Though the 9-year-old may be interested in adults from the point of view of what they can do with him—expeditions, excursions, shared interests—he is much less interested than he was earlier in the relationship itself. Therefore it is important not to impose yourself on the child of this age. He wants and needs to have his maturity, his independence, and his separateness respected.

If left pretty much to himself, if treated as the mature creature he considers himself to be, the 9-year-old usually gets along pretty well and does display a remarkable amount of self-reliance and capability. Nine can be an age of perfecting skills and of real, solid accomplishment. However, there is a disquieting side to the child of this age. He does tend to worry, takes things hard, can be extremely anxious and may, in fact, tend to go to pieces over something which would have brought only brief tears a year earlier.

Some people even go so far as to consider 9 a potentially rather neurotic age. Nine not only worries a good deal, but tends to complain. Complaints may be simply that tasks imposed, at home and at school, are "too hard." Or they may take the form of more serious physical complaints. Eyes smart. Hands hurt. Stomach aches.

These complaints nearly always do represent real physical feelings of discomfort. Nevertheless, it is interesting to note how often they occur in relation to some disliked task. His eyes hurt when he has to do his studying. Hands hurt when he practices. Stomach aches if he has to sweep the floor or rake the yard. He has to go to the bathroom as soon as it's time to wash the dishes. All of these complaints should of course be respected within reason but should nevertheless be recognized for what they are—Nine's way of meeting unpleasant situations. They are not, as a rule, really dangerous physical ailments.

Nine may be in some an age of considerable rebellion aginst authority. Some Nines, however, merely rebel by withdrawing—they can look right through you as you give them a command. Or they rebel by complaining, but actually do carry out your commands. And gradually the complaints and the rebellions and the worries diminish as the 9-year-old approaches the peaceful age of 10.

Ten Years

If your 9-year-old was something of a problem to you with his or her worries, anxieties, withdrawals, demands, he or she will in all probability more than make up for it when age 10 rolls around. For 10 is, to hear most parents tell it, one of the very nicest ages of all.

Perhaps this is partly true, from the parent's point of view, because of the fact that to the average 10-year-old his parents' word is so utterly law. Ask a question about almost any phase of behavior, and Ten will tell you, "Yes, I can do that. Mommy says it is all right for me to." Or, "No, Mommy says I'm not old enough for that."

Ten wants to be good and to do what is right. We'll let one of our own 10-year-olds speak for herself:

> Yes, I can usually tell right and wrong. It depends on what it is. Unless it was school work. If you were doing some work and it was the wrong question, I might not know. But if somebody was doing something to someone else that was wrong, I would know.
>
> My mother has told me some things; and Sunday School has told me some things; and other things I just know by myself. And the school has told me some things. At school they tell you how to act with other children and things like that. And my mother tells me manners for the table which are right and wrong.
>
> My conscience wouldn't bother me too much if I did wrong; but it would bother me enough to make me say I'm sorry.
>
> Yes [in answer to our question], I certainly try to tell the truth. And I always try to mind mummy except sometimes when I'm looking at television and mummy asks me to go to bed, sometimes I don't hear and sometimes it's too good to miss and I watch it just a little longer.
>
> About swearing, I always try not to. I don't think it's a good thing to do.
>
> I try to be good because I think God wouldn't like it if I was bad.

Ten not only obeys easily and naturally but seems to expect to obey and gains status in his own eyes by such obedience. "I try to be a good boy," he will tell you honestly.

Not only does Ten cheerfully obey Mommy (or Daddy), but he is for the most part extremely well pleased with both parents and with the rest of the family as well. Ask him what he loves best of anything in the world and he will tell you, "My mother and father, of course."

Ten is not only satisfied with parents and teacher, but with the world in general. He is pleased with life as he finds it, and he finds it easy to enjoy himself. He is nice and friendly to other people, and he expects them to be friendly to him.

Ten is matter-of-fact and straightforward, and also flexible. Doesn't take things too seriously. Ask a question about some behavior, and Ten will reply, casually, "Well, sometimes I do and sometimes I don't."

Ten, more than any age which follows until you get to 16 is an age of predictable, comfortable equilibrium. And never again, after 10, will you as a parent get quite the same wholehearted and unreserved acceptance of you, your actions, and your motives as you do from your 10-year-old girl or boy.

3   Individuality

So far we have described the way that behavior changes from age to age and have given you some idea of the general ways in which a 3-year-old differs from a 2-year-old, or a 6-year-old from a 5-year-old. That is, we've illustrated the fact that there are characteristic ways of behaving which tend to occur at each different age.

In the chapters which follow we shall describe the way in which the behaviors themselves—eating, sleeping, elimination, getting on with parents, and all sorts of other behaviors—change from age to age.

Thus, in most of this book we're emphasizing ways of behaving which all children have more or less in common. Before we go on, however, we'd like to discuss briefly the ways in which children differ.

That children do differ, and that each child has his or her own characteristic ways of behaving, is something that all parents know. Thus, in spite of the fact that all children tend to go through the same stages of behavior, you know that children go through these stages in their own individual way. You say, "Oh, Johnny's always been like that. You just have to let him take his time"; or, "He doesn't mix much with the other children, he just likes to play by himself"; or, "She's never been very good at her lessons, but she's a wonderful help at home."

Students of human behavior have been observing and studying these personality, or individuality, differences for a long time now. There are many different approaches to the study and classification of individuality. The one which we have found extremely helpful as a basic approach is the one that holds that we behave as we do (that is, our personality is what it is) because of the way our bodies are built.

This way of studying individuality is called *constitutional psychology*. We shall explain it briefly. If the technical terms we use seem confusing to you, or if at this point you'd rather proceed directly to finding out more about how children *in general* behave, and what solutions you may try for the everyday problems which confront you, you may prefer to skip this chapter or to come back to it later.

Physical Approach to the Understanding of Individuality

"Looks don't matter," some people tell us. And if by "looks" they mean superficial regularity of the facial features, they may be right. But if by "looks" they mean bodily structure—the way in which head, neck, trunk, arms, legs, and extremities are fashioned —we suspect that they are wrong. Because the way in which the body is structured appears to be the first and most important clue (for those who know how to interpret it) to what the human being is and will become.

One of the most important things that parents can do if they want to know more about their child's personality is to familiarize themselves, if not with the details, at least with the more basic aspects of the known differences in structure Because understanding these differences in structure will help them to understand differences in human behavior—that is, personality differences— as well.

This study of personality assessment based on measurement of bodily structure actually covers every aspect of human behavior. From the way a human being is built, many scientists believe that they can predict how he might act—his eating, sleeping, and social behavior, what kinds of situations he will seek or avoid, the possibility or impossibility of his being a success in activities requiring physical skill.

They can also get an idea as to whether or not he will be interested in competition, how and to what extent he will express his emotions, how much courage he will have for combat, and how brave he will be in the face of physical pain. The individual who shows stoicism and indifference in the face of pain is not merely exercising more "will power" than the one who flinches at physical pain. He may be responding differently largely because, being built differently, he actually is less physically sensitive to pain.

Understanding all these differences and respecting the fact that they are the result of basic and deep-seated differences in actual physical structure and not merely the result of the way individuals have been treated by their parents or the world around them can help parents in their efforts to understand their children. It can also help them to understand themselves.

All of this does not mean that human behavior is *entirely* determined by hereditary factors. What it does mean is that the body structure provides the raw material out of which personality is formed: that it is the instrument upon which the life forces, both internal and external, play. Tendencies to behave in certain ways are to a large extent predetermined, and these tendencies are then either reinforced or modified by the environment. So the same individual might develop along very different lines in contrasting environments—but certain behaviors would be less possible for him or her than others.

Three Physical Types

Though there do not actually exist different distinct "types" of body build, there can be identified three chief physical components.* Each person actually represents a combination of these three different components, but in most people one or the other tends to predominate. Thus we often loosely speak as if there were

---

*These different kinds of physiques are discussed in full in the following books by Dr. William H. Sheldon, *Varieties of Physique* (New York: Harper & Brothers, 1940) and *Varieties of Temperament* (New York: Harper & Brothers, 1942).

three different types of individual. These three components are endomorphy, mesomorphy, ectomorphy. And these three kinds of individuals may be described as follows:

The person in whom endomorphy predominates is referred to as an endomorph. These individuals have large stomachs and livers, that is, large digestive viscera. They float high in water and are usually fat. They are soft and spherical in shape. Their behavior is characterized by extreme relaxation and love of comfort. They are sociable, love food, love people, and are gluttons for affection.

Mesomorphs, in contrast, have big bones, a well-developed heart and circulatory system, and heavy muscles. They are hard, firm, upright, and relatively strong. Their blood vessels are large and the skin is relatively thick, with large pores. In their behavior, muscular activity and vigorous bodily assertion predominate. They love exercise and activity, love to dominate.

Ectomorphs, in extreme contrast, are the thin, fragile, linear people, flat of chest and with long, slender, poorly muscled or "pipe-stem" arms and legs. Their behavior shows restraint, inhibition, oversensitiveness, and a desire for concealment. They shrink from even ordinary social occasions.

The names of these three types may seem rather technical and specialized, but we believe that once you have mastered them, they will be extremely useful to you. Increasingly they are becoming a part of the common vocabulary.

Each of these three types of individual, because of his or her own special physical structure, has different drives, different responses, different interests, from each of the others. Sheldon sums up these differences by saying that the endomorph exercises and attends in order to eat; the mesomorph eats and attends in order to exercise; and the ectomorph eats and exercises in order to attend.

(It is very important to keep in mind that no one individual is *purely* one thing or another. In most individuals, one component or the other predominates and largely determines behavior, but we are each a combination of these three elements.)

The differences in the ways in which the endomorph, the meso-morph, and the ectomorph behave show up in eating, sleeping, emotional behavior—in fact, in every life situation.

Sleeping

Take sleeping behavior, for instance. You all know that in spite of tables and charts which tell you how much sleep a child of any age "ought" to get, children vary tremendously in the amount of sleep they do get and require, in the deepness of their sleep, in how quietly or restlessly they sleep, in how easily and quickly they get to sleep, and in how easily they waken. Some sleep so quietly that the bedclothes are hardly disturbed in the morning; others leave bedclothes completely rumpled.

According to Sheldon, endomorphs love to sleep, in marked contrast to mesomorphs who love to wake up and be active, and also in contrast to ectomorphs who hate to go to sleep but who, once asleep, hate to wake up and be severed from their dreams.

The sleep of endomorphs is deep, easy, and undisturbed. There is complete relaxation in sleep. They go to sleep easily and quickly. They can sleep comfortably in any position and usually snore. They love sleep—frequently becoming "sleep gluttons." It is diffi-cult to wake such people during the night.

Mesomorphs have low sleep requirements. It is important to remember this. They are voluntary early risers. Mesomorphs may sleep no more than six hours nightly and still retain boundless energy. They go to sleep readily and generally sleep well. But they sleep "vigorously," tossing and thrashing about. They seldom dream but often snore loudly.

Things are very different with ectomorphs. Insomnia occurs in adult life, and even in childhood habits of going to sleep are irregu-lar and erratic. It is hard to get children of this type to sleep unless they are close to physical exhaustion. They waken easily, but it is hard for them to get up. They sleep lightly, do not fully relax, seldom snore, often dream, are abnormally fatigued. They need more sleep than do the other two types of individual.

Thus you will see that it is not practical to make hard and fast rules about how much sleep your child needs—since sleep requirements vary so tremendously from one "morph" to another "morph" and from child to child.

Eating

There are certain children (and adults)—the slender, sensitive, fragile ectomorphs—who eat very little, seem never to gain weight. Their parents worry that they will be ill if they don't eat and constantly try to force on them "just one more" piece of bread or one more helping of potato. And yet, despite their lack of interest in food and the lack of "flesh on their bones," children of this type are often among the healthiest in any given group.

In the supervision of the child's feeding behavior, almost more than in any other sphere, it is important during the preschool years for mothers to recognize and respect the fact that different types of children have widely differing needs.

Many so-called feeding problems arise simply from the fact that the parent is trying to overfeed the child, especially the ectomorph who simply "hasn't room" for two tall glasses of milk, a second helping of meat and potatoes, and a dish of good, nourishing rice pudding.

We often find that the thin, "scrawny," or petite child who seems to care very little for food does better on four or five small meals a day than on three big ones. Children of this kind, when they do become hungry, become suddenly and sharply hungry. But their hunger does not last, and if you refuse them the snack they asked for "because it is almost mealtime and it would spoil your dinner," you may find that by mealtime that little spark of hunger is gone.

As to type of food needed, the ectomorph particularly needs protein, especially meat, and the easily digested carbohydrates. As to speed of eating, the ectomorphic child tends to eat very rapidly. Sheldon has commented that children of this type are often "misunderstood" and sometimes badly bullied by well-meaning relatives who try to normalize them and to make them not only eat as much as they "should," but sit patiently through a long, deliberate meal when, with their speed, they have finished—or could finish if allowed—in five minutes' time.

The fat, soft, roly-poly endomorph is, in contrast, almost never a feeding problem. This kind of child seems almost to live in order to eat. Endomorphs are characterized by "a love of food and a warm appreciation of eating for its own sake. This is not to be confused with a mere voracious appetite. There is deep joy in eating."

Endomorphic children are not fat simply *because* they eat. But they are almost invariably "good" eaters. They love to eat—it is a primary pleasure, and even when not eating, they love to talk about and to think about food. Approaching the stage of preadolescence, a child of this type may seem to do almost nothing but eat, and, if a girl, will find that she needs to resort to those dresses termed appropriately by the manufacturer "Chubbies." Such a child will often be interested in watching Mother prepare meals and, boy or girl, will often take great pleasure in being allowed to cook.

Digestion is usually excellent in the child of endomorphic build —all sorts of indigestible foods, such as pickles, mince pies, cucumbers, and the like, can be eaten with no embarrassment. "Roughage" is handled with no difficulty—and constipation, colic, and stomachaches are seldom experienced.

In fact, eating constitutes such a primary pleasure for individuals of this type that, from infancy on, their mothers have little trouble getting them to eat and drink all they "should."

Eating is such a pleasure, in fact, that to deprive an endomorph of supper (children seem hardly ever to be punished by being made to go without breakfast or lunch) is a really harsh punishment. The ectomorph, on the other hand, might hardly notice such punishment. Sheldon has noted that adult endomorphs probably never go on hunger strikes and that Gandhi was an extreme ectomorph.

The mesomorphs, to complete this story, are hearty eaters, enjoy "good plain food," and often eat too much. They like to "wolf" a large quantity of food at one sitting and, if permitted, may gorge themselves.

So, in general (though excess eating can produce a problem too), it is as a rule ectomorphs who tend to be classed as "feeding problems," and a clearer understanding of their real food needs can often take them out of the "problem" class.

Emotions

"That child just doesn't feel a thing, she's so unloving," complains Grandmother to Mother. (Skinny little Rosalie, a child of typically ectomorphic build, has just rejected Grandmother's efforts to give her a welcoming kiss as she came home from school.) "Really, I don't think she'd shed a tear if the whole family was killed all at once. She just looks so stony and secretive. I think she likes us all well enough in her way, but I don't believe I remember her ever showing any affection. Even as a tiny baby she wasn't cuddly the way the other children were.

"And it's so hard for her to thank anyone for anything. You can feel that she is pleased, but she certainly doesn't let herself go to any extent.

"Sometimes I think we ought to take her to a psychologist or something. She seems like such a normal child in so many ways. But she just seems to lack warmth and affection."

Such a lack could indeed, in a certain type of child, be a sign that something might be going wrong. But in a child of typically ectomorphic physique, as was Rosalie, such behavior may be considered not only quite normal, but to be expected. (This does not mean, however, that with shifting growth forces, effort, and experience some changes cannot and do not occur.)

According to Sheldon, the ectomorphic individual is normally characterized by secretiveness of feeling and emotional restraint. These people are tight-lipped and do their suffering in silence. They do not "let go" and reveal their emotions or feelings in the presence of others. "External expression of feeling is powerfully inhibited though there may actually be great intensity of feeling. Signs of emotional weakness are choked back as if subject to great shame."

Quite the opposite is the case with the fat, jolly endomorph. Rosalie's sister, Dorothy, was a typical endomorph, and her grandmother had no complaints to make of her. Warm, loving, friendly —she was, the family felt, satisfactorily responsive.

This too, we could have predicted from one look at Dorothy. It isn't necessarily that she loves her family more or appreciates them more than does Rosalie. It is just easier for her to express her feelings. Having the temperament which characteristically accompanies an endomorphic build, Dorothy finds it easy and natural to express her emotions freely. The endomorphic individual typically:

> gives way naturally and easily at all times to a free communication of feeling. Nothing is ever choked up or held back. There is no emotional inhibition. Feeling is smoothly and naturally communicated to whomsoever may be available as recipient. Whether the individual is pleased, grieved, disappointed or shocked, his feelings are to be read like an open book. . . . He conceals nothing. . . . Such a person "registers" delight or sobs and cries convincingly at the time when it will do the most good. He "wears his heart on his sleeve."

So, whether you have a Rosalie or a Dorothy, try to keep in mind that it is quite normal for different kinds of people to express their emotions differently and to a different degree.

The Overawarness of the Ectomorph

"Mamma, make him stop rattling the paper." Janice is practicing at the piano. In the next room her brother is reading the funny papers. The sounds he is making with these papers are barely audible, but Janice notices them and they interfere with her practicing.

"Janice," commands her mother firmly, "you just concentrate

on your practicing. You're a regular fussbudget. You just let your brother alone. He isn't bothering you."

Mother may be right from the point of view of harmony in the home. Everyone in the household, obviously, can't keep perfectly still just because one member is playing the piano.

However, she is wrong in her statement, "Your brother isn't bothering you." Because in making this remark she is reckoning without the fact that Janice is of an extremely ectomorphic body build (and temperament). An ectomorphic individual is perhaps supersensitive to any little disturbance of sight or sound, even those which he or she can just barely see or hear. As Sheldon says, "He is overaware, has a low threshold of attention, notices everything." (Though the ectomorph can, if completely absorbed in something which really interests him, such as an interesting book, be almost deaf to what goes on around.)

Thus in school, an ectomorphic boy or girl may be terribly distracted by a classmate who is drumming on his desk with his fingers, even several seats away. Ectomorphs will be particularly distracted if they are in a classroom where half the group is supposed to be studying, half reciting.

If doing homework, they may feel unable to concentrate if someone else in the family is making even a small noise in another part of the house. They may be unable to read unless there is perfect quiet in the room.

The tapping of a shutter, or any small, rhythmic sound (particularly if unidentified) may be so distracting that the ectomorph just can't seem to go on with any concentrated activity.

What do parents usually do when an oversensitive, overaware child complains of such noises or distractions? The child says that these noises bother him, make him nervous, that he can't concentrate.

Far too often his parents simply tell him to get on with what he is doing and not make so much fuss. Just put his mind on his work and forget about the distractions. That they won't bother him if he will just ignore them.

It is kinder and wiser to recognize that your child, if an ectomorph, will in all probability throughout life be of a supersensitive temperament, overly alert to and aware of the environment, easily bothered by little sights, little sounds. Help him to find, so far as possible, quiet surroundings for study and practice. When such surroundings are not available, sympathize with his need for them but help him gradually to adapt to less than perfect quiet. If he must, as most have to, put up with some minor distractions, at least don't make things worse by saying that he is foolish to be distracted.

The Noisy Mesomorph

"Joe! Come back into the house again and then go out and shut the door quietly. Don't slam it! There's no need to knock the house down every time you go in or out."

Or, "Joe! Don't shout so! Do you think we are all deaf? Honestly, everything you say can be heard at least three blocks away. Talk in a normal tone. There's no need to shout."

Well, in a way there's no need to shout. And in a way there's no need to slam the door when you could shut it quietly.

But if your boy or girl is of a basically mesomorphic physique (that is, with the vigorous, well-muscled, posturally alert body which we classify as mesomorphic), it will be natural for him or her to behave in these ways. For the mesomorph is just naturally noisy, vigorous, assertive, and dominating. The person of this build (whether child or adult) just naturally makes a lot of noise.

To speak softly, to shut a door gently, to work quietly, to move a chair by lifting it and then quietly putting it down somewhere else—all these are unnatural ways of behaving. A mesomorph would have to remind himself, on each occasion, to behave thus.

In public, as well as at home, this characteristic noisiness of the mesomorph makes itself felt. On the school bus, in the school cafeteria, at the movies—he shouts the loudest, laughs the most noisily.

The mesomorph's behavior is, therefore, in direct contrast to that of the ectomorph (the thin, bony, characteristically shy person). The ectomorph sits in the corner, speaks quietly, tries to avoid attracting attention.

Nobody taught the ectomorph to be so unobtrusive and quiet. He just naturally behaves this way. But just as the ectomorph almost automatically behaves in a way that will avoid attracting attention, the mesomorph acts in a way that will call attention to himself.

You can, within very narrow limits, help your ectomorphic child to feel enough self-confidence to speak up above a whisper. But it is unlikely that he will ever become conspicuously noisy. Conversely, you can encourage a mesomorph to tone down his voice and movements a little, especially if you choose certain specific situations and work on them. But he will remain a basically noisy, unrestrained individual.

Functional Approach to Individuality

A second, though not contradictory, approach to an understanding of individuality is to note how the individual behaves under certain circumstances and to determine the ways in which that behavior shows certain predictable qualities. Does the child concentrate well? Does he shift rapidly from one thing to the next? Is he more interested in people or things? These and other behaviors will be considered, a bit at random, in the following pages. These particular personality characteristics we are about to discuss have not as yet been related specifically to physical structure, though we have little doubt that such a relation does exist and that with further research we shall someday be ready to correlate these different factors.

You may find it interesting to think about your children and the children you know to see if any of the following functional items will help you to identify each child in his separate right. And to discover at least in part what distinguishes each child from other children.

Peripheral and Focal

Peter sits in a corner of the nursery-school playroom, his back to the group, building a house. Steadily, busily, ignoring the other children, he builds. Larger and fancier rises his structure. The morning goes by. Still he works on this one building, and still he ignores the other children.

Robert started out the morning sharing Peter's block play, but he soon tired of this quiet pursuit. So he rode a bike for a while, running into or over the people and things which crossed his path. Then he joined the group in the doll corner for a minute or two. He talked to the teacher. He fooled with the turtle. He made some biscuits out of clay. He had a conversation with one of the girls.

Their mothers were watching them from the sidelines. "If only Peter were friendly like Robert," complained Peter's mother to Robert's mother. "If only he would stir out of that corner and join into things. He ought to mix more with other children."

"If only Robert would stick to one thing better. He's so all over the place. He never stays still a minute and never accomplishes a thing. I wish he could learn to concentrate the way Peter does," replied Robert's mother.

And so, for as long as we have been observing children, we have seen these two sharply contrasting types. And nearly always their mothers are trying to change them. Trying to bring Peter out and to pull Robert in. Trying to broaden out Peter, who sits in the corner, and to make him more sociable. Trying to make Robert settle down, stick to one thing, concentrate and accomplish more.

Some children are of course mixtures of these two, but many more are of one temperament or the other. The names we use to describe these two kinds of children are *focal* (the one who focalizes or concentrates always on the one thing close at hand) and *peripheral* (the one who is all over the place, responding to many different things, quickly changing, flexible, versatile).

It is important for the parent of either kind of child to keep in mind two things: First, neither type of child will change basically through the years, though each may become "better" or "worse" at certain ages. Each will in all likelihood go on as he started, concentrating or spreading out. However, with increased age and environmental influences, growth tends to cut down the extremes of behavior. Though the peripheral child remains peripheral as he grows older, he can often learn to concentrate at crucial moments. And though the focal child remains focal, he can sometimes be pulled out into the periphery as needed.

Second, it should be remembered that there are many solid advantages to either one of these kinds of personality. If your child is extreme in either of these ways, it will be easier for you in the long run if you can adjust to and reconcile yourself to your child's personality, since you cannot in all probability make him or her over—even though time and experience tend to produce their mellowing effects.

As we earlier emphasized in our description of body types, we are each a combination of all three physical components—endomorphy, mesomorphy, and ectomorphy—in varying amounts. We are not just one or the other. The same is true of tendencies to peripheral and focal behavior. We each have some of both in varying amounts. We will also express these ways of behaving differently at different ages. Think of the focal attention and concentration of the 7-year-old and the spread and peripheral interests of the 8-year-old. The 9- and 10-year-olds try to combine these two forces so that less extreme behavior and modulation is possible. Age determines, as well as individuality.

Inability to Shift

"There are no problem children. There are only children with problems," say some people who work with delinquent youths. But delinquent children are not the only ones who have problems. Perfectly "good" children, as they grow up, have many problems too.

One of the major problems any child has to deal with, because it is a problem always present, is the problem of his own personality. And of all the problem personalities we have encountered, one of the most troublesome is the kind which cannot make shifts, which is poor at transitions. (That is, he cannot move easily from one thing to another or from one stage of behavior to the next.) The child who suffers this personality difficulty may be quite normal in all respects except that he is simply unable, without help, to move easily from one type of activity to another, from one situation to another, or from one stage of behavior to another. He gets stuck wherever he happens to be and cannot, without help, move on to the next thing.

Such a child usually ends up by being called "bad." "He is a bad eater, a bad sleeper, bad in his play, bad with people—in fact, I can say that he's just an all-round bad boy," one mother told us when she brought her attractive and intelligent but cross-looking little 3-year-old to the Gesell Institute.

A thorough psychological examination and a detailed interview with his mother brought out the fact that this boy was in reality a good eater. He had a hearty appetite and could feed himself nicely. But he tended to get stuck with one kind of food and did not like to shift (that is, to make the transition) to new foods. So he always made a fuss whenever a new food was added to his menu. He just wanted to go on and on eating the same thing for every meal.

He was also a good sleeper. He slept soundly for the "proper" number of hours each night. But he found it hard to get to sleep each night (that is, to make the shift from waking to sleep) and he also found it hard to come awake in the morning (that is, to make the shift back to wakefulness).

As to play—he actually played very nicely. He could entertain himself for long periods alone. But he found it difficult to shift within his play. That is, if he was playing with his wagon, he did not want to shift and play with blocks. And he found it hard to shift from play to any other type of activity. For instance, he found it hard to leave his play to come to dinner.

As to his relations with other people, he was "good" with one person at a time, but found it hard to shift from one person to another—for instance, from mother to baby-sitter. He had trouble both in separating from his mother at nursery school and in separating from nursery school to go home with his mother.

So it turned out that this boy was not really "bad" after all. He was merely bad at making transitions, and this was not, we believe, real badness but a definite characteristic of constitutional individuality. What he needed, then, was not scolding or punishment when he failed to make some necessary transition desired by his parents. What he needed was real and specific help from his parents whenever there was a transition to be made.

If a child does not see as well as he should, we help him in various ways. Sometimes he needs special visual stimulation. At other times he may need glasses. Similarly, if he cannot by himself make the necessary shifts from one thing to another, we should help him here too by providing the transitions which he needs and cannot arrange for himself. (When leaving nursery school, running to find his mother in her car rather than being met on the playground may well facilitate leave-taking. Or being given a new pair of pajamas may break into that going-to-bed ritual which has lasted all too long. These and many similar techniques will smooth the way for the poor shifter.)

Children Who Are Good in a New Situation and Then Deteriorate

Some children, however, have just the opposite response to change. "He's so much better since he went to this new school. The teacher says she just can't understand why that other school had so much trouble with him," explained Danny's fond mother to her husband.

He was bad in the old setup, but a change of environment has fixed him up and he's wonderful in the new. How many times we hear this theme repeated!

Two social workers were discussing one of their charges. "That little Davis boy—you know, he was getting along just terribly. But we put him in a new foster home and it's done wonders for him. The new foster mother says she can't understand why anyone couldn't get on with him. He's one of the best children we ever gave her."

The same story. He was bad in the old, but he is good in the new. Just a matter of taking a little pains and finding the right setup. We could go on indefinitely with similar examples, but let us instead return, after a six-month interval, to Danny and the little Davis boy.

Danny isn't doing so well in his new school. In fact, his new teacher is now making the same complaints that his old one did. Danny is rude, disobedient, uninterested, careless, and he makes trouble with the other children.

And the new foster mother has completely given up on the little Davis boy. She says he is disrupting the entire household, and she has asked the social worker to find him a new foster home.

What has happened? What went wrong? Danny seemed so happy and good in his new school. The Davis boy's foster-home placement seemed like such a favorable one.

A careful psychological evaluation of the personalities of either of these two boys might have allowed us to predict how things would turn out. It is likely that both of them belonged to that deceptive group of children who almost inevitably do well in a *new* situation.

Things going badly? Give them a new home, a new school, a new teacher, a visit to grandmother's, even a new bed (in case they have had trouble with sleeping) and, briefly, the change will work wonders. They behave beautifully. The new teacher, or foster parent, or relative takes credit for the improvement in behavior and blames the former caretaker for the former bad behavior.

And then the new wears off and the old patterns reappear. At this time you can make another dramatic change of environment and temporarily improve the behavior. Or you can decide to stay where you are and work on the problems from there.

(However, all of this does go to show that newness and change often do give the child a pickup even though it may be temporary. Let us hope that eventually the child himself will develop sticking power, some learning from experience, however slow it is. We as parents and caretakers may sometimes be guilty of accelerating a downhill pattern by anticipating too much, expecting too much too soon. We need rather to support the child and to protect him from himself.)

Left- vs. Right-Brained Individuals

Though this concept may still be a bit more at the theoretical than the practical level, there is a strong feeling around these days that in most individuals either left-brained or right-brained functions tend to predominate.

The story is that in perhaps the majority of right-handed people, the left cerebral hemisphere (left brain) is dominant. This hemisphere governs language functions, verbal communication, and the time sense. In left-handed individuals, presumably the right cerebral hemisphere (right brain) is dominant. This hemisphere governs visual-spatial configurations and manipulatory performance.

Thus, the so-called left-brained person is the one who is very good at talking, reading, writing, the supposedly "intellectual" functions. The right-brained individual may be less good at reading, writing, talking—the usual academic functions emphasized in most schools—but very good at manipulating objects, at seeing spatial relations.

The left-brained person may be thought of as a talker, the right-brained individual as a doer. Unfortunately our schools have given preference and reward to the left-brained boy or girl, ignoring the fact that right-brained people have their own different but equally important contributions to make.

Some educators recommend that teachers present information in such a way that students can, either simultaneously or alternately, use both hemispheres, and then can practice integrating information from them. Also, that when students are "not getting it," both teachers and parents should adopt practices that would appeal to each student's special aptitudes and abilities.

We have often spoken of the boy or girl who is better at doing than at talking. Without realizing it, we were referring to those right-brained individuals who are often made to feel like failures in school.

The Destructive Child

"We've got to have some help with Teddy," explained Teddy's mother. "He is without question the worst child in the neighborhood. Why, right while I'm phoning, he is climbing up the living-room curtains. We absolutely have no control over him."

An abbreviated list of 3-year-old Teddy's bad behaviors, which she later related to us during their visit to the Institute, included the following:

Teddy breaks everything he can get his hands on, even the handles of hammers. He especially likes to break windows.

He is "into everything," and he is so quick you can't stop him.

He ran away one Sunday at 6 A.M. without any clothes on and was brought back home an hour later by the police.

He is rough with children and adults. He hit his aunt over the head one day and knocked her out.

He constantly destroys neighbors' property.

He messes up stores if his mother lets go of him even long enough to pay for and accept purchases.

A careful psychological examination ruled out a first possible explanation of Teddy's behavior—that he might be "bad" because he was defective and unable to understand the normal demands of socialized living.

A second possibility was that his bad behavior was due to bad handling on the part of his parents. However, Teddy in our own hands behaved little better than with his mother. After two hours of his company we and the Institute were considerably the worse for wear.

The most likely conclusion, therefore, and the one which our tests indicated, was that this boy's personality was the thing at fault and the source of his difficulty. We found him to be a boy who had absolutely no ability to modulate or restrain his impulses. His drive to touch, to grab, to climb, to act, was very strong, and he himself had no ability to control or modify it.

Therefore, as we explained to his mother, the environment will need, for the time being, to be very firm and to provide the control that is necessary. It also needs to provide outlets for his desire to destroy and tear apart so that destruction can have its legitimate though temporary outlet.

However, when a child is overactive, or "hyperactive" as people now put it, there is a very good probability that this behavior may be caused by artificial colorings and flavorings in his or her diet. Dr. Ben Feingold in his groundbreaking book, *Why Your Child Is Hyperactive,* proposed this possibility. His work and his word have spread rapidly, leading to further writings on the subject, which include the useful books by Crook, Smith, and others (see page 349 for references).

Most certainly if your son or daughter seems overactive and destructive beyond what one may "normally" expect of an active preschooler, we urge you to read any or all of these books. And then, with the help of a competent physician or nutritionist, at least see if you can't improve your child's behavior through the avenue of an improved diet.

The Autistic Child

Another example—a special kind of personality which in its extreme form is described by child specialists as *autistic.* This kind of child is characterized chiefly by a marked lack of warmth in personal relations.

Dr. Leo Kanner was the first to describe the autistic child. More recently, several books helpful to parents and others dealing with autism have appeared. Bernard Rimland's *Infantile Autism* finally establishes a biological basis for this difficulty. Carl Delacato's *The*

Ultimate Stranger confirms this approach. And *Please Don't Say Hello* by Phyllis Gold is a book for children, which helps them to understand the special sensitivity of autistic girls and boys.

Briefly, autistic children do not relate in the ordinary way to people and situations, from the beginning of life on. People describe them as "in a shell" . . . "happiest when left alone" . . . "acts as if other people were not there."

These children often treat people as if the people were merely objects. They also seem to have little defined sense of self or of who they are. One autistic boy we know, when asked if he could write his name (usually one of the first words a child learns), replied in the typically hollow voice of the autistic child, "I don't know that word. That's just a middle-sized word and I only know big words and little words."

Their language, in the early years, often does not convey much meaning to other people, and their wish to communicate with others may be very mild.

They often repeat things just as you say them. Thus if you say, "Say good-bye to Mrs. Jones," they will repeat, "Say good-bye to Mrs. Jones."

Their surprising rote memory often encourages their parents, but their rigid demand that things be done always the same way (like the 2½-year-old) is often extremely trying. With such children relation to objects is nearly always stronger than relation to persons.

If you have a child of this type, it is important to recognize the fact that he was, in our opinion at least, born that way. Too many parents of autistic children have been counseled that the child acts as coldly and impersonally as he does because they, the parents, have rejected him. Too many are told that he is withdrawing from their own cold treatment of him. This is not, in our opinion, the case. We do not believe that you "make" your child autistic, no matter how coldly you might treat him. Your cold treatment— which he himself inspires in you—may exaggerate, but it does not cause, his coldness.

Your warmth, conversely, can help to "thaw him out," but it cannot change his basic personality.

If you have an autistic child, you will almost certainly wish to seek professional help, but it will undoubtedly encourage you to know that many autistic children do grow up to lead relatively normal and often highly productive lives.

Then What Can You Do?

Behavior is a function of structure. That is to say, the human organism seems to act as it does largely because of the way it is built. Whether we approach an understanding of individuality through measuring the way that the body is built or through an observation of the way that the individual behaves, we come to the conclusion that individuality is largely inborn.

A favorable environment (home or otherwise) can, it appears, permit each individual to develop his or her most positive assets for living. An unfavorable environment may inhibit and depress natural potentials. But no environment, good or bad, can so far as we know change a child from one kind of individual to another.

Some people don't like such ideas. They want to feel that it's all up to them. That their child's individuality is not predetermined, but that they can produce, by their own treatment of him, either a favorable or an unfavorable individuality.

They object to the idea that individuality is inborn, with such comments as, "You mean there's nothing I can do? I have to just sit back and accept the personality my child is born with? He won't benefit at all from a happy home and good loving care?"

Our answer is that there is plenty you can do about it. First of all, recognize your child's individuality for what it is and give up the notion that you either produce (except through inheritance) or that you can basically change it. Recognize it, understand it, accept it.

Accept the fact that no matter how "well adjusted" he is, your thin, wiry ectomorph will probably be at heart a shy, quiet individual who prefers to remain relatively inconspicuous. That your well-built, heavily-muscled mesomorph will be active, competitive, noisy, relatively insensitive. That your plump, pear-shaped endomorph will be jolly, friendly, sociable, easygoing, but will have little desire to compete and dominate.

Realize that your basically focal child will always be able to focalize and concentrate better than the more peripherally oriented person. That some children will always find it difficult to make transitions. That others will always have a tendency to put their best foot forward in a new situation and then gradually do worse as time goes on.

Understand your child's basic and inescapable endowments. Help him to understand himself. Then try to provide, so far as you can, the kind of situation in which each kind of child can feel comfortable and can do well. But don't try to change him and make him over.

Try to recognize and respect your child's basic, inborn individuality.

PART TWO

4 Eating Behavior

Twenty or thirty years ago, most parents' main question about their children's eating behavior was, "How can I get him [her] to eat? He hardly eats a bite." (This question was often asked even when children were quite obviously surviving and growing normally in size.

Today many mothers and fathers are more concerned about *what* they feed their children than about how much they feed them.

As time went on, perhaps due to good advice from specialists, perhaps due to their own common sense, the parents in this country have come to realize that if they do not push food and do not talk about amounts eaten or not eaten, if they serve small portions, and if they do not force their children to eat foods they especially dislike, mealtimes tend to go reasonably well.

Most children do, if it is available, eat enough food to keep them going. And if their not eating arouses no interest or consternation in their parents, they have much less incentive not to eat.

Thus, nowadays it seems that most American parents handle eating, as they do toilet-training, much more calmly than they used to. They make less fuss about it. As one mother put it years ago, "Even if I force myself not to say anything when my son doesn't eat, he can tell by the anxious look on my worried face that I care." Our advice, of course, is to keep that anxious look off your face and that worry out of your mind.

At any rate, many parents today appreciate that if their children find that they get no major payoff (in terms of receiving a great

73

deal of attention for not eating) chances are they will eat a necessary amount.

However, even in the best-regulated household, and even when parents remain calm and sensible about their children's eating, some problems do arise along the way. Here are some suggestions that may help.

Developmental Sequences

Infancy—The Heyday of Eating

Infancy is a time for its own special feeding problems, but on the whole appetites are good. In the first four months, they can be so excellent that the infant seems perpetually hungry.

It is really not enough to make general rules about feeding. We can and should get down to the specific demands of each individual infant. The so-called self-demand method of feeding, which allows the baby to nurse when hungry rather than by a set schedule, is called *self-regulation*, because it includes both a response on the part of the parents to the infant's demands and an adaptation on the part of the infant to the demands of the parents. It is an adjustment of take and give, of demand and acceptance. At some ages the demand is high, at others the acceptance is high, and at still others there is equilibrium between these two forces.

Not all children thrive on this method of feeding, though the majority do. It takes well-integrated infants who are capable of knowing when they are hungry and when they are satisfied to profit from this freer schedule. (Your pediatrician can help you here.) There are some infants, however, who do not know when they are hungry and who do not demand. There are others who tend to overdemand and thus do not come into balance. These two extremes thrive best on a more controlled and regular schedule.

Those infants who are on self-regulation usually organize more quickly than those who are on a strict schedule. They may demand as many as seven to eight feedings per day shortly after birth. This may reduce to five to six by 4 weeks of age, and may even settle down into the rather unusually advanced pattern of three feedings a day as early as 12 to 16 weeks of age. Such a reduction is possible only when the infant is capable of taking large quantities of food at one time.

With the coming of greater satiety by 16 weeks of age, there is often a noticeable reduction in appetite. Occasionally refusals of the early afternoon or early evening feeding are in evidence. With the poor feeders, vomiting may increase if excessive intake of food is urged.

By 16 weeks many infants are accepting some form of solid food. (Boys are often so hungry that they will accept and relish solid foods as early as 6 to 8 weeks.) Mashed banana is a uniformly preferred solid. However, the former tendency to force solid foods early is diminishing because there is so much refusal even as late as 32 weeks.

Cup feeding may be started as early as 16 to 20 weeks. The approximation of the infant's lips to the rim of the cup is at this age still very inadequate, and much spilling results. But in spite of this, the infant often enjoys the process of drinking water or fruit juices from a cup.

By 28 weeks infants show new awareness of the cup and spontaneously make demands to be fed from it. However, they are incapable of taking more than one or two swallows. They prefer water and juice to milk and may refuse milk from a cup.

In the second half of the first year, feeding is usually well regulated and is an activity of great enjoyment for the infant. In most things he or she is now an adjustable member of the household.

The first year of life can go very smoothly in the feeding realm if the parent is aware of the fluctuations of appetite and behavior which occur from meal to meal, from age to age, from individual to individual. The infant speaks out very clearly in his or her demands as well as refusals. If parents are aware of and sensitive to these shifts in infancy, then they will be more ready for the new demands and influences that are almost certain to show up in the succeeding years.

Appetite Retarded

In the second year of life appetites often falter. The generally smooth course of infant feeding seems to be broken by new interfering forces. For example, the gross motor drive at 1 year of age may make it difficult for the child to sit long enough to eat meals. Standing in a high chair or carriage supported by a harness may be the preferred posture for eating while this gross motor drive is strong, between 12 and 15 months.

Another interference stems from the child wanting to feed himor herself but being unable to do so. This occurs most frequently from 15 to 18 months. Help in filling the spoon may solve the problem. Giving the child food that can easily be finger-fed may be an even better solution. Those who still require puréed food may accept being fed, but like to have some activity of their own, at least a dish or spoon to play with.

Drinking from a cup may be at its lowest ebb in this second year, especially for the consumption of milk. Small cups that the child can handle and small portions can make this activity a continued interest. A colorful small paper cup, enticing the child's eye, easily handled, and unbreakable, is to be recommended. Whenever the 18-monther has completed a task such as drinking from a cup, he extends the cup to his mother as he says, "All gone." If she is not there to receive it, what else can he do but drop it?

New interferences hamper the appetite of the more aware 21-monther. His taste may be so discriminating that he will accept only certain foods prepared by his mother. He also becomes dependent upon a certain bib, a certain spoon, a certain dish, and these become a necessary part of a successful meal. If the parent is unaware of these demands, the child may cry until the parent finally guesses the right answer. The child doesn't yet have adequate words to express his desires.

Because of the 21-monther's heightened awareness, he is sensitive to all kinds of distracting stimuli. Even the kitchen may be too stimulating, and the meal may be more readily eaten in the seclusion of the child's room. Some 21-monthers even need to be served one food at a time because they are distracted by multiplicity. Mixing all the foods together and then not wishing to eat the new concoction is a characteristic trick of the child at this age.

Finicky—Fussy—Food Fads

The child's poor eating habits in the third year of life can be most distressing to the parent. The second year may have brought a reduction in appetite, but the third year brings all the exasperation of indecision and finicky choices. Preferences are high and may be related to taste, form, consistency, or even color. The child may want foods to be served very separately, without having one food touch another on the plate. Small helpings, even teaspoon size, are often best. This is the time for food jags, which had best be respected. What is wrong with stewed apricots night after night? But it is also important to introduce new foods under new and pleasant situations so that the child will have something to fall back on when the food jag suddenly wears itself out.

This ritual demand of the same thing time after time reaches its height at 2½ years of age and not only includes repetition of foods but also of dishes and arrangement of dishes, and even repetition of time when a certain food can be given. A soft-boiled egg may be accepted for supper but never for lunch.

It must be kept in mind with children of this age that appetites fluctuate markedly from very good to very bad. This type of fluctuation is characteristic of the age period and needs to be allowed to swing, within reason. As children become surer of their own likes and are able to feed themselves more adequately, the swings will lessen. Pouring their own milk from a little pitcher into a small cup may motivate their drinking more than if it is poured for them.

Though they desire to feed themselves, children of this age may continue to spill considerably. Some children don't mind this. Others judge it as failure and wish to be fed. A child may feed himself part of the meal—the part he likes—and want the parent to feed him the rest.

Calm

The 3-year-old is, in feeding as in all behavior, much easier to handle than the child just younger. Eating is definitely better. Appetite fluctuates less. The child has become a good chewer. He pours more deftly from a pitcher and handles a cup with ease and dexterity. He does best with a small cup and pitcher. He feeds himself more efficiently and even demands a fork to spear his meat. He is in fact often judged to be more capable than he really is. Surely if he acts so well, he is ready for the family table, parents think.

But with this added burden of the family table, the child may demand everyone's attention, want everything in sight, and wind up dawdling endlessly. By demanding too much, the parent has now put himself in a fix. Should he coax the child to eat; should he feed him; or should he leave him to finish by himself? Too often a vicious circle is set up which might not have been started in the first place if the child's meals had continued to be solitary, or at least apart from the total family group.

Speed and Incentive

Four is an age of speed, of new expansion, and of incentives. Four feels his age and wants to graduate to new demands and new activities. He wants to help set the table or even to help prepare the meal. His chief difficulties at this age are that he talks too much, has trouble sitting still, and quite frequently has to interrupt the meal by going to the bathroom.

Four might desire to eat to get big, to race with the baby, to finish within a certain time allotment, or to work toward a dessert goal. What Four does, he does with speed, including the drinking of his milk.

Appetite Rise

With many children there is a distinct appetite rise at 4½ to 5 years of age. Children of this age are more on their own, can handle more meals with the family, and are beginning to listen as well as to talk. Their choices and acceptance of foods are wider and may even be influenced by radio, television, or the man across the street. They are even branching out in their use of utensils and may use a knife for spreading, though not to cut meat.

Perpetual Motion

Six, in eating as in everything else, is all over the place, both predictable and unpredictable. His appetite may be tremendous, and he may wish to eat all day long. He may eat better between meals than at meals. Breakfast is usually his most difficult meal, especially if it precedes some demand such as going to school. He (or especially she) may complain of a stomachache or nausea, and may even vomit. In such cases a light breakfast which he can accept should be given, with the plan that he will have a ten o'clock snack at school. He makes up for his low intake in the morning by a rising intake during the day and often demands a sizable snack just before going to bed. Six may awaken in the middle of the night and ask for food.

Six-year-olds are, however, not good finishers, in food any more than in other things. Their eyes are bigger than their appetites and they will often ask for larger helpings than they can eat. Though they are interested in sweets, they may not be able to eat their dessert.

Six's perpetual activity makes him a menace both to himself and those around him. He simply can't sit still. He wiggles in his chair, teeters back on one chair leg, swings his feet vigorously, spills his milk, talks with his mouth full, eats with his fingers—until finally Father in exasperation sends him from the table.

Ravenous Appetite

Seven consolidates his appetite and may eat less than he did at 6. But Eight, with all his new inclusions and expansiveness, usually becomes an excellent eater. Foods he would not eat earlier, he now tackles. He is so hungry he even wolfs his food. He belches spontaneously. He feels so full he has to loosen his belt for comfort. He no longer is interested in listening to the family conversation as he was at 7. He wants no delay between main course and dessert, and he then wishes to leave the table and to go on about his 8-year-old business.

Even those who have earlier been very poor eaters are less of a worry to parents at 8. They don't necessarily have a very good appetite, but it is at least passable and they begin to show an interest in food.

In general, from 8 years on, appetites and quantities consumed increase steadily, even alarmingly. By 11 the child feels definitely full after eating and knows he or she has overeaten. But there is no further mention of feeling full at 12, and it sometimes seems as though Twelve has a bottomless pit for a stomach. Appetite begins to come into better control by 13, but it is not until 16 or later that a semblance of adult balance is reached. This is also true of table manners. The course is up and down. The down course is especially marked at 11, when behavior is reminiscent of the 6-year-old. Elevens even refer to their own *terrible manners*. Thirteen is the turning point toward better manners, and Fifteen shows a capacity to accept adult standards.

Appetite and Preferences

It is an odd commentary that the parent all too often spends the first 8 years of a child's life urging him to eat and the next eight years urging him not to eat. If the appetite were respected, it would be allowed to function as a part of growth. The typically fluctuating appetite has been noted. The good appetite of infancy is often followed by a very low intake in the second year of life. (Though milk intake in the second year may be very low, its substitutes in the form of butter and cheese may be very high.)

Appetites continue to be low from 2 to 3 years, but definite preferences for food are coming to the surface. Carrots and beets may be the favored vegetables for both color and sweetness. With the stronger advent of chewing at 2½, meat becomes a real favorite. Certain foods may be so desired that the child wants them repeated day after day. These food jags are very prevalent at 2½ years of age.

By 3, with a more stable appetite, the range of food choices is increasing. Green vegetables are now accepted, often for the first time. Raw vegetables are preferred. Desserts are more desired.

With a reduction in appetite at 4 years there is often a return to food jags, or the child goes on strike about certain foods which he or she had previously liked.

From 4½ to 5 years there often is an improved appetite which may steadily rise into the excellent appetite of 8. Throughout this age period of 4½ to 8 and older, though appetites are good, the demand is for plain cooking and there is a real antipathy to all casserole dishes, gravies, and fancy sauces.

Six's preferences and refusals are often very strong. One unfortunate experience with a certain food which has a stringy texture, or a rim of fat on his meat, might "put him off" that food for some time. He is often off dessert, especially rice pudding and custards. His newfound passion in life is peanut butter. Children can almost be placed in two different groups, those who love peanut butter and those who don't. This craze reaches new heights for those who do at 7 and 8 years of age and recurs in periods throughout the early teens.

Eight, with his definitely increased appetite, is ready to tackle new foods. He is often quite venturesome. And yet he is a sensitive being and may refuse to eat chicken if he has seen one killed. He also continues to be repelled by fat on his meat.

Acceptance of all foods is steadily increasing from 8 on. Food is definitely on the minds of 10- and 11-year-olds, even to the extent of dreaming about it. By 12 some like everything and in general there are many more likes than dislikes. Some favorites stand out at different ages, *e.g.* mashed potatoes with gravy at 12, and ice cream and steak at 14.

Since appetites are excellent and intakes are high in these early teen years, rapid weight gains may be expected. It is unfortunate when too much time and thought are given to restriction of food and dieting. True, there is such a thing as moderation. But this is no time for strict dieting. By 14 to 16 there usually comes a slimming down and a sense of the relationship of food eaten and weight gained.

Individual Differences

Some children live to eat. They are the round, often plump children. They are rarely feeding problems. But there are others who rarely think of eating. They are the small, petite, or even scrawny children. Hunger may come often to them, but it is usually sharp and short-lived. These children often do better on small, frequent meals, even five or six a day. Such children often become feeding problems. When food is forced upon them, they lose any little appetite they have and may be pushed into vomiting. They gain weight very slowly but are active and healthy, more healthy, often, than the larger, robust-looking children. If the parent can be guided by the child's slim appetite and keep portions small, few feeding problems are likely to develop. In due course these children, too, may eat with a ravenous appetite, especially in their teens.

Special Problems

Infantile Colic

An all-too-common accompaniment of feeding in the early months is infantile colic. Orange juice is one of the worst offenders and can fortunately be easily replaced in the diet by some other fruit high in vitamin C or by a vitamin C substitute which your doctor may recommend. If the infant is bottle-fed, a change in formula may be indicated. Prepared milk substitutes now available are more easily digested, but for some infants, food is not the primary offender. Since the colic seems usually to be limited to the first 12 to 16 weeks of life, there is undoubtedly a growth factor involved. But how to live through it is still a problem. Initially infants respond best to soothing protection from further stimulation. They quiet when rocked, held, or taken for a ride in the car. But as they grow older, they respond best to the stimulation of light and sounds and movement around them.

Vomiting

Regurgitation, or spitting up, may also be an early accompaniment of feeding. Just as the young reader in the first grade doesn't know which way the letters go, the gastrointestinal tract in some infants doesn't seem to be sure in which direction it is operating. "Should the food go down or come up?" By 28 weeks, growth has taken over, and the downward direction is usually established.

Some infants, however, continue to vomit into the second year and as late as 21 months. By this age they may know in advance that they are going to vomit and may reach a container in time. They will also be forewarned and will refuse food at the meal when they feel that their gastrointestinal tract is in indecision. Before this period of greater self-awareness, it is up to the parent to judge at what time the gastrointestinal tract is most unstable. Is vomiting most apt to occur at the noon or evening meal? Whenever it is most likely to happen is the time for a reduced feeding or a "split bottle," with an hour between the two halves. There should be no alarm over this behavior. This is a part of growing up for some children.

Holding Onto the Bottle

And then there is the problem of holding onto the bottle. Most bottle-fed infants give up their bottle at about the same time they would have given up the breast—in the last quarter of the first year. They may even go so far as to fling their bottle out of the crib. But there are some who cling tenaciously. Parents often continue bottle-feeding because they fear the child will not otherwise receive his or her quota of milk. Actually, this is not necessary. Ten to sixteen ounces is adequate, and this can be given on cereals, in puddings, and so forth, as well as sipped in small amounts from a cup.

Some drastic change in the nipple at 15 to 18 months will often help the child give up the bottle. Substituting a new nipple, especially in color or style, or enlarging the holes or cutting off the tip to induce drinking rather than sucking, may encourage the baby to give up his or her bottle.

However, some children are so attached to the bottle that it is wise to continue one night bottle until 2 years of age or even later. A bottle is often sleep inducive and insures the milk intake without anyone's having to think about it.

With those children who refuse milk completely when taken off the bottle, the provision of bright-colored cups or glasses with a small pitcher for them to pour from may produce an interest in drinking. The use of a straw may also help. Serving milk at a "tea party" may give it a new value to the child. And, of course, chocolate milk may be more pleasing to the palate.

Refusal of Solids

Some infants are slow to accept any form of puréed or mashed foods in the first place and then will only accept this consistency and will go no further. They choke on chopped foods. They chew poorly. They will accept only extremes—the puréed foods that slip down easily or the crispy foods like bacon or melba toast that must be chewed first. Such children are often found to have a very small throat opening and one which gags readily. They have trouble with in-between consistencies before 3 years of age and may delay until 5 years. Some experience away from home, such as a birthday party, may give them the courage and incentive to eat the same kinds of food as their contemporaries.

Refusal to Feed Self

The children who cling to puréed foods may be the very ones who will not feed themselves. Often these children have shown poor hand-to-mouth responses earlier. They may have refused to feed themselves a cookie at 8 to 10 months. They do not suck their thumbs. Some, on the other hand, have tried to feed themselves and have failed. They are the ones who dislike spilling. These children may delay any attempt at self-feeding until 5 to 6 years of age. Their fine motor behavior improves at 4½. But the motor movement of filling a spoon and bringing it to the mouth is more complicated than we sometimes realize. Feeding younger siblings may be easier and will give these children a feeling of success. Then they will more likely attempt to feed themselves.

"Spicy" Appetites

Why all children's diets should be bland is a very real question. There is a certain group of petite girls (and sometimes boys) with high emotional tone who may hit real eating snags at 2 years of age unless their parents recognize their peculiar preferences. Even as early as 1 year of age a little onion juice may make bland mashed potatoes acceptable to such children. They accept and seem to need salty foods, strong cheeses, olives, salami, lobster, mushrooms, avocado pears, and spicy sauces on their spaghetti. They crave this more stimulating diet, which can be given at least in moderation.

General Rules to Help Children Enjoy Food

1. Serve food attractively.
2. Give small helpings.
3. Serve food without comment.
4. Do not stress amount of food to be eaten. Many children who have small appetites to begin with absolutely revolt at any mention of how much food they are expected to eat.

5. Be aware that some food refusals many indicate an (unsuspected) allergic reaction to that particular food.

6. Try to maintain a calm, unworried attitude toward your child's eating. Nothing creates a feeding problem more quickly than an overanxious attitude on the part of parents.

7. Don't stress table manners with young children. Manners can come later when a positive attitude toward eating has been established.

8. Allow finger-feeding until the child has become fairly proficient at eating and is interested in food.

9. Do not have children eat at the family table until you find they are ready to do so.

5   Sleeping and Dreams

Getting the Child to Sleep

Getting children to sleep and keeping them asleep can be one of the most trying and exasperating tasks in a parent's day.

Of course theré are those children who fall asleep the minute their heads touch the pillow and who sleep soundly all night long. If your child is one of these, you are indeed fortunate. There are such children.

But there are many others who from infancy on have sleeping difficulties. Particularly do they find the transition from waking to sleep to be a difficult one. If you have such a baby or such a child, it is most important to keep in mind that his inability to fall asleep easily is a real inability, and not just perverseness or badness. Since it is a real inability, your best role is to help him to make this difficult transition, not to punish him for not making it.

The best ways for getting a child to sleep vary of course from child to child and from age to age. There are none which can be guaranteed to work. However, we shall tell you about some of the common methods which other parents have found useful.

Some parents of preschoolers do not set a bedtime hour. Rather they allow their children to play in the living room or family room till they become sleepy. This kind of permissiveness goes against the grain of some people and clearly gives parents less time for themselves. But some families prefer it to putting their children to bed before the children are ready and then spending much of the evening responding to, or trying to ignore, their demands for attention.

In Infancy

In infancy, release into sleep is not generally as difficult as in later years. To some extent the self-demand and self-regulation schedules which many pediatricians nowadays recommend approximate the conditions of a more primitive culture, and the child eats when hungry and sleeps when tired.

But if your baby is following a stricter schedule, he or she may need some help from you in getting to sleep. In that case, modern culture has, so far as we know, found nothing superior to rocking (in someone's arms or in a bassinet or carriage) for getting a baby to sleep. Rocking accompanied by singing will as a rule be especially successful.

From 8 to 12 weeks of age, the baby who cries and cannot seem to fall asleep may be helped to sleepiness by being given a light to look at or even by being brought out into the lighted kitchen or living room. He is hungry for lights, for movement, and for people as well as for food. With satiety he sleeps more readily.

At any age, giving the child a presleep breast- or bottle-feeding is a trusty method of inducing sleep. Music is successful with some. And often even a baby will go to sleep more quickly for someone other than Mother.

As the baby develops through his first year, he will often devise methods of his own to help him fall asleep. He may suck his thumb or rock in his crib. But as he goes on into the preschool years, being rocked or sung to, or even his own devices, may not suffice, and parents may need to vary their techniques and become considerably more ingenious. Letting the preschooler cry it out may have to be resorted to, but it is not usually recommended. Here are some methods which sometimes help to induce sleep in the 2- to 7-year-old.

The Two-Year-Old's Bedtime Demands

"It must be Heaven, it must be Heaven, to hear a baby cry!" was the refrain of a song popular in the late 1920s.

Well, maybe! But a lot of young parents certainly think otherwise.

And similarly, to the sentimentalist, the 2-year-old's bedtime request for "Just one more kiss, Mummy," might seem a sweet and lovely thing.

But to the average long-suffering parent of a 2-year-old it is a dismal sound. Because "just one more" is the call with which the young child, reluctant to leave his family and the joys of being awake, puts off his final lapsing into sleep.

"One more kiss," "A drink of water," "A hankie," "Go to the bathroom," are only a few of the demands the 2-year-old makes to get just a little more time and attention from Mother before she finally leaves for the night.

Parents soon come to realize that such requests—real needs or not—are in the nature of a racket. It is not simply the things he or she requested that the child actually wants, but Mother's continued presence. How you will deal with these demands is of course up to you. Some parents are more patient than others. Some children are more demanding than others.

With many children around the age of 2 years, you can shorten and simplify the bedtime scene by anticipating as many of the bedtime demands as possible. Be sure that you provide the child with a drink of water, a handkerchief, and a favorite toy. Be sure that he has been toileted. Give him his good-night kiss. Then leave, with a firm, "Good night," and if necessary, state that you are not coming back.

If you have an extremely docile or a very sleepy child, or if your past history of firmness has led the child to know that you really mean what you say, he may settle down at once to sleep, and there may be no further demands. Or he may call out once or twice, and, getting no response, give up and go to sleep.

He may! But what if he doesn't? What if the demands go on?

We know of no one solution to the problem which is guaranteed to work—but here are some things you might try.

First, remember that your child's demands for continued company and attention represent a real need. But, since it is a need that you cannot reasonably be expected to answer, you are going to have to help him get over it, for his sake as well as for yours.

Added age will be the surest remedy, but in the meantime, if his demands on Mother are too excessive, get Father to step in. A final kiss, a firm admonition from Father, "Now I'm not coming back again," will quiet many a 2-year-old who is too demanding of his mother.

Of course, there is another solution. If instead of a determined child and a gentle parent you have the combination of a gentle child and a determined parent, you may find that simply ignoring repeated calls (once you have gone back a "reasonable" number of times) works.

Two-and-a-Half's Bedtime Rituals

Two-and-a-half is an age of rituals. Children of this age don't like change. They don't like variety. They like everything to be in its place, and what they did yesterday they want to do again today.

Bedtime is no exception. The going-to-bed rituals of the typical 2½-year-old can be the despair of an entire household. Before you have realized what is going on, the child can build up a ritual about every single part of the going-to-bed activity.

Saying good night to the people downstairs will have to be done in just a certain way, and these good nights will have to be said in a certain order. A certain number of kisses. The exact same words to be said by everyone.

Then there can be a going-upstairs ritual. The getting-undressed, being-bathed, having-teeth-brushed rituals can be long and elaborate.

And then the prebedtime play! If on even one occasion you have rashly read three stories, played two phonograph records, allowed a little athletic activity, woe to you! Every night from now on (till this ritual age is over) your 2½-year-old may demand just these same activities in just the same order.

Then the child may want to arrange all of his or her belongings in a certain standard manner. One girl we know had to put her thirty-eight dolls to bed in a certain way before she herself would get into bed. Another child had to have a hat on each bedpost, each one turned just right.

And even after the child is once in bed, you may not have come to the end of the ritualistic demands. Many have to take certain special things to bed with them. One boy we know required a hammer, a green pepper, and a sharp pencil. This of course was rather unusual. Most are content with a favorite doll or soft animal. But often it has to be just the right one. Not any old doll or any old soft animal!

The possibilities are endless and formidable! But here as elsewhere, advance knowledge on your part, though it will not change the child, can help you to manage the situation.

First, knowing in advance how strong the rituals of the 2½-year-old can be, you will try at all times to keep bedtime activities as simple as possible. Try to avoid building up a too complicated ritual which the child will then insist on following.

Second, you can be more patient with Two-and-a-half's rituals when you know that they are perfectly natural for children of this age and that they act like bridges for him to cross when a shift of activity is demanded. It is easier for him to get to sleep if he is allowed the transition from waking to sleep which the ritual provides.

Bedtime—Three to Ten Years

Bedtime problems usually become less severe and less exasperating, or at least different, in the ages which follow 2½ years. At any of these ages a quiet period of music or reading can be one of the best ways to induce sleep. Roughhousing should in general be avoided at bedtime. It can overstimulate the child and leave him or her in no condition to go to sleep. (Although in some cases a physical workout, if held within limits, can result in the child falling asleep more quickly. It is the child who can't stop, who gets wound up further and further, who especially needs to be protected from roughhousing.)

By 3 years of age, bedtime problems are often much less troublesome than at 2½. Many 5-year-olds go to bed quite willingly, fall asleep with relative ease. (Their sleep problems may come later in the night.)

At 4, it may simplify things to allow children to read (some book they can look at by themselves, such as the *Golden Dictionary*) and then to turn out their own light. They may behave much better than if you turn out the light for them.

The 5- and 6-year-olds may like to have a little time for themselves to read and to color. By 6, many enjoy a brief chatting time with Mother or Father alone. At such a time they not only like to play favored games—especially number games—but this may provide a good opportunity for talking over and smoothing out any of the day's tangles.

By 7 and in the years which follow, the bedtime hour is improved for many by letting them have a small bedside radio. Then they may hurry through their undressing and into bed so as to be on time for a favorite program. The length of listening can usually be regulated by the number of programs you decide to let them enjoy.

These, and many other similar things which you will undoubtedly work out yourself, can help the child to end the day happily and to avoid those difficulties which sometimes accompany the business of getting to sleep.

However, by 8 and more strongly at 9, the problem of bedtime becomes again, in many, as it was in the preschool years, a real disciplinary problem. This in a way seems to have less to do with sleep as such than with a whole new attitude which the child may have toward parents and toward any parent-imposed task.

Even with children who have hitherto showed no resistance to sleeping, going to bed may suddenly become a sharp problem of discipline. The child tries by every means to put off bedtime as long as possible, and seems to feel that going to bed is something that his parents are trying to impose on him.

A later bedtime can help here—recognizing that children no longer need quite as much sleep as they did earlier and letting them feel that you respect their new grownupness.

But let the later bedtime depend on the smoothness of your child's bedtime performance. Let him feel that if he is ready for a later bedtime, then he is also ready to go to bed without stalling and without complaints. Also let him realize that you mean what you say when you announce bedtime. You may help him out by giving a little warning in advance, but try to make him feel that when you finally do say, "Bedtime," you really mean it.

Sleep Problems

Some children are by nature "good sleepers." Unfortunately, there are many others who are by nature light, fitful, restless sleepers. Who resist going to sleep. Who wake easily and often during the night. Who are disturbed by fears, by dreams, by physical pains.

Not only are there certain *individuals* in whom sleeping difficulties abound, but there are some *ages* at which even "good sleepers" may have difficulties. As in all things, a knowledge of some of the more common ones may help you deal with your own child's sleeping problems when they do arise.

Waking and Crying in the Night

More often than not, with a stable child whose routines have not been unduly upset by illness or visiting, night sleep is relatively undisturbed during the first months of life. This is particularly true if the mother dresses the baby warmly (as in a sleeper and perhaps later, when the child is more active, in a bathrobe as well), and sees to it that the room is reasonably warm so that no covers are needed. Then if he wakes, as many do, and plays around in his crib, he can fall back to sleep when he is ready without his mother needing to go in to cover him up.

If the mother does not go in to the baby when she knows him to be awake, most will play happily by themselves for a bit and then go back to sleep again. Many can, if necessary, lull themselves to sleep with their thumb, a blanket to be sucked, or a favorite toy.

A few can only relate themselves to some person, and can only be comforted by that person. With such children, the sooner you go to them, the more easily they can be quieted. A little food, a bottle, changing their diaper, or perhaps holding and rocking them a bit, may be all that is needed.

With most, waking several times in the night and crying for attention—or crying and refusing to be comforted—do not occur. If they do, great ingenuity on the part of parent or pediatrician will need to be exercised.

Middle-of-the-Night Activity at Three

Many 2-year-olds, once you have gotten them to sleep, do sleep right through the night without giving you, or themselves, much trouble. But at 3, with many children, an active night life begins. They go to bed nicely. To sleep nicely. And then, often after all the rest of the family is in bed and sound asleep, our hero gets up and starts his middle-of-the-night activities.

These activities often surprise and worry parents. It seems so strange to them for a small child to go wandering around the house in the middle of the night. Yet that is what some of them like to do!

Some get out of the crib easily by themselves, go to the bathroom, go downstairs and get some food out of the refrigerator, "read" a magazine after turning on the light in the living room, and may even be found asleep on the living-room couch next morning. Others go still farther afield and wander outdoors. Some merely play happily in their own rooms for an hour or two.

Such activity probably does very little harm *if* you see that outer doors are securely locked and that dangerous or valuable things inside the house are locked up. And if the child is not one who just naturally harms himself and things around him when left to his or her own devices.

Many children go directly to their parents' room. With others their parents' room is the one place they do not think of going. They want to set about their own activity, doing what they please. There is most probably the spirit of adventure in them. A few can contain their adventure within bounds, but the majority of these adventurous children need to be checked. Tying the child's door loosely with a bell attached will give the necessary warning that he is up as he attempts to open his door.

Such a child should be allowed his excursion to the refrigerator, the bathroom, or wherever he had planned to go. He may wish to look at a book for a while. He will settle down much more quickly after his needs have been satisfied.

We do not recommend spanking for this behavior. This wakefulness and need for night activity is a quite natural behavior for many children. This period of night waking often disappears when the child is around 4 years of age.

Getting into Parental Bed

Even when your child wakes in the night, you may not be *too* disturbed if he or she is one of those who can enjoy, and will be satisfied with, a *solitary* night life.

But, alas, not all children are so constituted. Not all are happy to be in their beds and to talk and play or even to wander about the house *entertaining themselves* for an hour or so. Some when they wake up in the night want their mothers. And what's more, they want to get into their mother's bed. This is in many no passing fancy or halfhearted notion. It is a real, strong demand, and they insist on it.

How you deal with this situation and whether you give in or not will depend on many things, but chiefly on three: on you, on your husband and on the kind of child you are dealing with.

In most cases, parents find that it does little harm and seems to do the child a lot of good to let him get into bed with them when he wakes and makes a strong demand. Usually you can put him back into his own bed as soon as he becomes drowsy again or when he falls asleep. If he wakes and objects, some parents find that it creates less confusion just to let the child spend the whole night with them. (Some parents, like Tina Thevenin, whose book *The Family Bed* describes this fantasy, recommend that the whole family sleep together. This sounds rather wild, but if it appeals to you, it is a possibility.

As a rule this demand to share the parents' bed does not persist for long, and you can speed its end by suggesting at bedtime after a few nights—or a few weeks, depending on your stamina—that he is not going to get out of bed *any more*. This suggestion can, if necessary, be strengthened by the explanation that if he does get up, and does wake Mother and Father, everyone will be too tired next morning to carry out whatever may be his favorite morning activity.

With most children, as we say, we have found it fairly safe to give in to what is usually only a temporary demand.

But with the child who is a strong perseverator, who holds onto patterns once established and will not give them up, it is wiser not to start anything that you don't want to continue. Such children can sometimes be discouraged from getting into their parents' bed by a clear-cut refusal and a show of real firmness.

This may mean having to let the child "cry it out" for a few nights, but you may consider that preferable to letting him or her get into a habit which will later be difficult to break.

Or, if you have gotten into the habit of letting your child sleep in your bed and he holds onto this privilege too long and simply refuses to start the night in his own bed, you may let him go to sleep in your bed but tell him that you will put him down in his own after he is asleep. Or you may plan so many nights a week with parents, and so many by himself.

The Big Bed at Four

Sometimes, if they have not already made the shift from a crib to a big bed of their own, the promise of a big bed (at 4) will get children back into the habit of sleeping alone. Four is an ideal age to shift to a big bed. At 4 the child is ready to try new experiences and to give up old patterns. Planning ahead with Four about a new bed may include the giving up of some undesirable sleep habits or other undesirable behaviors.

"When you're four and have your big bed, you won't get out of bed in the night *any more.*" "When you get your big bed, then you won't need to get into Mommy and Daddy's bed *any more.*" "When you're four and are sleeping in your big new bed, you won't suck your thumb [or wet the bed, or whatever thing you are currently concerned about] *any more.*"

The power of suggestion, the excitement of this dramatic new event, the importance of being 4, can for any children be the necessary stimuli to bring about the desired behavior. Plus the fact that by the time the child is 4 years old, many of the earlier preschool sleep difficulties are often about ready to iron themselves out anyway.

But let us warn you, don't overuse this technique. Give the child the idea well in advance of the shift, as you would plant a seed, and then watch it sprout when the proper time and situation come around. Also, be ready to judge whether this type of planning will work with your child. If he is still too immature, better not to use this method, or at least be ready to backtrack when it doesn't work, and tell him he'll be ready when he's older.

Bad Dreams and Nightmares

"I had a bad dream!" This is a common complaint among young children. But it varies in severity from a quietly voiced objection to loud screams of terror which waken a whole household and which can be quieted only with the greatest difficulty.

How common are such complaints? How early do they begin? What causes them? How can they best be dealt with?—parents ask us.

Even by 3 years of age, and sometimes earlier, children begin to report that they have been dreaming. Some 3-year-olds are wakened by their dreams, but as a rule these dreams are not particularly disturbing. The 3½-year-old may do quite a bit of dreaming, and may be disturbed by it, but as a rule he or she merely calls out and is easily quieted.

At 4 there may be less dreaming, but by 4½ to 5 years it frequently increases in amount and severity. And it is the 5-year-old who perhaps is most often really disturbed, and disturbs others, by bad dreams or night terrors. For dreams and nightmares definitely invade the sleep of many 5-year-olds.

Many children of 5 awaken screaming and have difficulty coming out of dreams and coming awake even when Mother is right by their side. Some, even when quieted and comforted, do not fully awaken and cannot report their dreams or tell what is bothering them.

As a rule, no matter how terrified children may be when they first call out, you will shortly be able to quiet them. Especially if you remain calm and confident and do not let yourself be disturbed lest there is "something wrong." Those who have trouble coming out of their nightmare may respond more quickly if they are taken into another room or have their face washed with cold water.

The 5-year-old may have considerable difficulty in going back to sleep after such an episode, and may need a great deal of soothing and Mother's continued presence until he or she is safely asleep again.

Five may be the worst age for this sort of episode. By 5½ or 6 many can wake up and run into Mother's room, where often they can tell their dream and, after a short, reassuring snuggle, go back to their own bed. Others may need a longer visit with Mother— but the terror is usually much less intense and more easily quieted when the child is 6 years old than 5. Still others may not wish to return to their beds, and prefer to remain in their parents' bed. An intuitive parent will know when the child's fear is real and when he needs to remain.

Bad dreams persist, though diminishing steadily to a low level at 8 years, often with a return rise at 9.

Six shows his extremes in his dream world as well as in his real world. First he may be frightened to death by the appearance of ghosts and skeletons in his dreams. Next he is soothed by angels. Animals bite and chase him, but friendly dogs lie under the table.

Pleasant dreams are steadily making their inroad—dreams about playmates, dreams of parties or of play at the seashore. Seven really enjoys himself in dreams, swimming with the greatest of ease or flying through the air. But an ominous note of drowning or of danger to his parent may invade his dream life.

By 8 all can be fairly quiet in the dream world and scary dreams can often be traced to their origin of stimulation through books, movies, radio or television programs. Whereas Seven cannot protect himself against these forces, Eight usually knows when to shut the book, hide his eyes at a movie, or switch the knob of his radio to stop the vicarious experience that he knows will invade his dreams. Parents need to be alert to these dream producers and to control them when necessary.

Nine can protect himself even further than Eight from scary dreams. He has his own ways of getting around this close relationship of his experiences and dreams. He knows that if he reads a scary book in the light of day, he will be protected from its influence which might occur if he read the same book in the darkness of bedtime.

By 10, nightmarish dreams may be decreasing, though at this age dreams are sometimes good and sometimes bad.

We have spoken as if nightmares and night terrors were a usual and expected part of growing up. This has undoubtedly been considered true in the past. However, evidence is mounting that artificial colors and flavors, as well as more usual foods to which an individual child may be allergic, may be the cause not only of night restlessness and wakefulness, but also of the more severe night terrors. As run-of-the-mill foods as milk, wheat, corn, or sugar may be at the root of much nighttime difficulty for some children.

Fears Related to Sleep

"But I'm afraid of the dark! Please don't turn the light off!"

"I think there's somebody hiding in the closet."

"I can't put my feet down. My bed's full of little bugs crawling all around!"

These are but a few of the bedtime fears experienced at one time or another by many perfectly normal children. The number and intensity of such fears, of course, varies considerably from child to child.

If your child does have such fears, no matter how silly they may seem to you, it is always important to treat them sympathetically and respectfully, and above all not to make fun of him or of them.

If it is the dark he fears, and in many this fear is especially strong at around 3½, leaving a low light on in the hall or in the next room may give him the confidence he needs. Or a faint light placed in the baseboard of his room may give the desired illumination without throwing frightening shadows. Attractive luminous pictures are now available which will glow softly in the dark for some hours, usually till long after the child has fallen asleep.

Another excellent way to help him get over his fear of the dark, especially when he is 4, is to let him keep a small flashlight under his pillow. Then he can turn it on whenever he feels the need. Often just having the flashlight there is enough. The child may not actually find it necessary to use it.

As the child grows older, it may not be so much the dark that he fears as the shadows. Shadows on the wall or ceiling may look like ghosts or burglars or other threatening figures. Such fears should never be ridiculed and preferably should not be belittled. Rather, if possible, by curtaining or otherwise, arrange that lights from outside, especially car headlights, will not throw scary shadows. Or shift the child's bed so that he is less disturbed by the shadows. Or if shadows absolutely cannot be avoided, take the trouble to show your child just how they are cast and convince him of their harmlessness.

The child who feared the dark at 3 and little bugs at 3½, may very likely have moved on to wild animals by 5½, to men under the bed by 6, to burglars and ghosts at 7.

Parents differ tremendously in the amount of sympathy and help they are willing to give to the child who is fearful at bedtime. Some, in spite of the specialists' advice, believe that all fears are nonsense, and will have none of them. The light is turned off, the door shut, and the frightened child ordered to behave and not be so silly.

Others, more imaginative themselves and the parents of imaginative children, go along with the child's fears and brush the "bugs" onto the floor, shoo the "wild animals" out of the room, exorcise the "ghosts" from the closet.

Both types of parents may notice that these bugs, wild animals, and ghosts exist only in the child's room. The parents' room may be miraculously free from all these frightening things. The child may go to sleep readily in the parents' bed and accept being transferred to his own bed after he has fallen asleep.

But, whichever path you follow, it will help the child if you recognize these two facts: (1) The child's fear is very real to him or her while it lasts; (2) with a little ingenious help and patience from you, most such fears can usually be dispelled after a short time.

Naps

The afternoon nap! Perhaps not a world-shaking topic to those of you whose children are past the age of naps. But a very important part of the day's schedule of both mother and child for those whose children are still preschoolers.

Here are a few general facts about nap behavior at the different ages through 5½ years.

4 weeks: The four to five nap periods which occur in each twenty-four hours represent a reduction from the seven or eight which characterized the earliest weeks. Individual differences as to their exact time and duration are marked.

16 weeks: Generally there are now three nap periods in each twenty-four hours. Naps occur in the early morning, late morning, afternoon, or evening. The early morning nap may merge with night sleep. The late morning nap may alternate with the afternoon nap. An evening nap is unusual.

28 weeks: Here there is a wide variety of nap patterns. There are usually two to three naps a day. The midmorning and afternoon naps are the most stable. Many children have a consistent pattern of a long morning and a short afternoon nap, or vice versa.

40 weeks: The most usual pattern now is a long midmorning and an unstable afternoon nap which comes and goes.

52 weeks: Now usually only one nap in midday, from eleven o'clock or eleven-thirty to twelve-thirty or two.

15 to 18 months: The nap usually follows the noon meal, and though the child may take favorite toys to bed, he or she often falls right to sleep. The nap lasts for around one-and-a-half to two hours, and the child usually wakes happy and wants to get right up.

21 months: Now there may be difficulty in release of consciousness, but most children play well by themselves till they do finally go to sleep. As they gradually become drowsy, Mother may need to go in and once more put them under the covers. They may now sleep longer (two to two-and-a-half hours), and many are fussy upon awakening.

2 years: Most are able to let the adult leave them, without making any demands, more easily at naptime than at nighttime. Some no longer sleep every single day, but even if they do not sleep, most will play contentedly in their rooms for an hour or more. If they do get to sleep, they often sleep for as long as two hours.

Many awaken slowly, and unless the nap is so prolonged that it interferes with night sleep, it may be better to let them wake up by themselves, rather than waking them.

2 ½ years: The nap is often a real problem at this age. Many are slow getting to sleep and are by no means willing to remain in their cribs till they do fall asleep. In fact, many just refuse to nap in their cribs at this age.

One solution is to let them nap in another room on somebody else's bed, though usually it is better to keep them in their own room. Tie the door, if necessary, and be sure that the windows are very safe. An active 2½-year-old is likely to climb on the window ledge.

When they have tired themselves out in play around the room, many are ready for sleep. Do not be too surprised if the child prefers to sleep in a bureau drawer, on the floor or in a blanket bed on the floor, or under the bed or on top of a (cold) radiator, or on a window seat. We do not fully understand some of these strange but definite demands of the child of this age—but we usually feel that it works out best to give in whenever we reasonably can do so.

The time of waking is apt to be stormy. The child may feel miserable and often cries harder the more his mother tries to quiet him. He responds best if his mother pays little attention to him, pulls up the shades, goes about her own activities. Then he will wish to approach her, and will calm down as he does so.

3 years: Now he may merely take a "play nap." If he sleeps, he usually goes to sleep more quickly and wakes more pleasantly than he did at 2½.

4 to 5 ½ years: Though some children in this age range still have naps and really sleep, the majority have merely play naps or no naps at all. (If the child still naps at 6 years, he or she may well not be ready for an all-day first-grade session and might better remain in kindergarten.)

There are a few common problems which arise with regard to napping which we would like to discuss briefly. One is the problem of the too long nap which interferes with night sleep. Some children, at around the age of 2½ or so, go to sleep so late and sleep so soundly and so long that, unless aroused, they do not wake up till five or even six o'clock. Then, obviously, they aren't going to be ready for bed at the customary six o'clock bedtime.

Here, of course, mothers have to make their own individual decisions as to when it best suits them to have the child asleep. If they welcome a long, uninterrupted afternoon and do not mind the delayed bedtime, there is no reason they should not arrange the schedule that way. But if Mother and Father both like to have their preschooler nicely out of the way by early evening, it will be necessary to wake him before he has had his afternoon sleep out in order for him to get back to bed again in time.

However, if, as often happens, you find that omitting the nap altogether produces extremely bad behavior in the late afternoon or during dinnertime, you may prefer to continue it, even though it does delay night sleep.

Waking the child from his nap may be easy or very difficult, according to his temperament. Some children wake easily and pleasantly. Others are extremely cross, irritable with their mothers, and often tearful when awakened. If your child is of this latter type, some indirect method of awakening him may work best.

Children vary tremendously in the age at which they give up their naps. Some are really through napping by 2 or 2½ years of age. Others cling to an afternoon nap till they are 5 or older. But whether he gives his nap up early, or clings to it late, the child's own rest requirements may well be the factor which determines how long and how late he naps. By requirements, we don't mean just what he *says*. "Don't want to take my nap" may express only a normal resistance to routine.

You judge more by his behavior than by his remarks. Does he sleep, or at least rest, during his nap period? Is his general behavior improved by this intermission? Or does insistence that he nap do little good and cause lots of trouble? These are the kinds of indications that will help you decide. In many cases the child will profit by a play nap after he has given up his regular nap.

Waking Behavior

Getting to bed, getting to sleep, staying asleep, and waking. Each phase of the sleep process brings its own problems, as most of you, except the most fortunate, know all too well.

Morning waking is no exception. In infancy, it is true, it does not create too much difficulty. The infant wakes, usually wet and hungry, and as often as not cries for attention. You give the attention and all is well. He or she expects a more or less immediate response. You expect to give such a response. So there is no trouble except that you perhaps aren't able to sleep quite as late as you might like.

Trouble starts, usually, at whatever age you decide the child should be able to lie quietly in the crib and entertain himself and not disturb you till you are ready.

Most preschoolers just aren't made that way. Most, in the years from say 2 to 5, wake very early indeed, often as early at 6:00 A.M. Most demand toileting at once and, as a rule, then refuse to get back into their own bed and play quietly. They often insist on playing in the parents' room, and even if they will agree to remain in their own room, their demands are numerous. As a rule, some one member of the family finds it necessary to give up the idea of further sleep once the 18-month to 2½-year-old child is awake.

With some, however, even around 18 months to 2½ years of age, if you provide toys and a little food, either where they can reach it from the crib (or elsewhere in the room if they can get out of the crib), they will entertain themselves for some time before becoming restless and crying for you.

(It is perhaps important for you to keep in mind that, contrary to what one might expect, keeping children up late at night does not usually result in making them sleep later in the morning.)

By 5 years of age or even earlier, some can take care of their own morning toileting and can play in their own room without bothering their parents. This is by no means the rule, however, and many parents find that their children need to be as old as 8 or 10 before they can manage entirely by themselves in the morning. And before they can grasp the important concept that their parents' morning sleep should not be disturbed.

In the teens, through one of the many seeming paradoxes of growth, children who earlier disrupted the entire family by their early waking and rising now seem to find it virtually impossible to get out of bed at all in the morning. Similarly, this same child who as a preschooler "ate like a bird," may in the teens be an absolute glutton for food. Remember that for many children both (morning) sleep and food requirements are very high when they reach their teens.

Individual Differences

Sleep requirements and sleep patterns thus change conspicuously from age to age, but it is always important to remember that they also vary tremendously from child to child. We have discussed this fact in detail earlier (p. 51).

Suffice it to say here that some children consistently sleep better, go to sleep more easily, and need less sleep than do others. Try to adjust the amount of sleep you require from your child to the amount he or she really needs—not simply to some arbitrary figure which you may have found somewhere in a sleep chart, or to the amount that other children in the neighborhood are getting.

Be as flexible as you can be. Remember that eating and sleeping are not only necessary for the human organism but can be real pleasures. Try not to spoil these natural pleasures for your children by making an unnecessary fuss over them.

6 Elimination

The age at which people try to toilet-train their children is becoming later and later. Years ago some pediatricians recommended, and some parents tried to begin, toilet-training even in infancy. And in some instances, Mother managed to combine child and potty at the instant that elimination was taking place.

Clearly in such instances it was the mother who was trained, not the child. Today most parents—in spite of some complaining and criticism from the older generation—do very little about potty-training till the child is 2 or even 2½ years of age.

The important thing to keep in mind is that success in toilet-training depends, with most children, not on the repeated experience of being placed on the toilet, nor on the child's "will power" or willingness to cooperate, but upon nerve connections which must mature. And these nerve connections develop more rapidly in some children than in others. All toilet-training or at least toileting "success" must wait for a certain amount of maturity in the child's central nervous system.

Really consistent success does not as a rule occur much before 2 or 2½ years of age. Mothers who have made little effort to train their children (these mothers are growing more numerous) often report that their children "trained themselves" at around 2½ years of age. (Boys in general attain dryness a little later than do girls.)

Bladder Control

The following timetable will help to familiarize you with some of the steps your child will go through as he develops the ability to keep himself dry.

4 weeks: Infant may cry during sleep when wetting and there may be a glimmer of wakefulness.

16 weeks: Number of daily micturitions has decreased and volume of any one has increased.

28 weeks: Soaking wet diapers. Intervals of dryness from one to two hours in length.

40 weeks: May be dry after a nap or after a carriage ride. Mother may have temporary "successes" placing child on pot.

1 year: Dryness after nap. Intolerance of wetness at certain times of day. Fusses until changed.

15 months: Postural difficulties (insistence on standing) have lessened. Likes to sit on toilet and responds at best times. At other times may resist. Retention span has lengthened to two or three hours. Placement on toilet may stimulate child to withhold urine. May release urine as soon as removed from toilet. Points with pride to puddles and may pat them.

18 months: Can respond with nod of head or "No" if asked if he wants toilet. May even ask, saying, "Uh," etc. May feel shame at puddles (if any) and may report accidents by pulling at his pants.

21 months: Reports accidents by pointing at puddles. Tells after wetting and sometimes before. Pleased with successes. But number of urinations increases, and lapses may multiply.

2 *years:*   Better control. No resistance to routines. Verbalizes toilet needs fairly consistently. May go into bathroom and pull down own pants. May express verbal pride in achievement. "Good boy." May be dry at night if taken up, though picking up may disturb his sleep.

2 ½ *years:*   Retention span lengthening. May be as much as five hours. Child may stop and then resume in the act of micturition. May have difficulty initiating release.

3 *years:*   Well routinized. Accepts assistance if needed. Most have few accidents. May be dry all night; may wake up by himself and ask to be taken to toilet. Girls may attempt standing up.

4 *years:*   Still routinized, but may insist on taking over own routine. Curiosity about strange bathrooms.

5 *years:*   Takes fair responsibility but may need reminding during day. Few daytime and only occasional nighttime accidents. Less reporting to Mother, though desires Mother's permission to go to the bathroom. May waken for night toileting and report to parent.

6 *years:*   Mostly takes responsibility, though may have to dash. Accidents are rare, and if they occur, child is disturbed by them. May need reminder before going out to play. Some giggling at sound of urine stream, and may mention this function in humorous or angry attack on others. Some require night toileting, but these can usually attend to themselves.

Individual Differences in Toilet-Training

Do not be disappointed if your boy or girl lags behind this schedule. Probably in no field of child behavior are individual differences greater than with regard to toilet-training. Probably in no field are parents more impatient.

Children do not always develop all of a piece. Not all their abilities develop at the same rate. Thus we have children who are "early" talkers but "late" walkers. Others are toilet-trained almost before you start thinking about it, but their social behavior may develop late. Still others are advanced (for their age) in every field of behavior except elimination.

If your child should be one who is developing slowly in this respect, and as so often happens a medical checkup has shown that there is nothing physically or medically wrong, we would chiefly advise patience and an unworried attitude on your part. We have seen many normal children who literally do not seem to know what goes on below their waists. This unawareness of their own "accidents," of which others are usually all too aware, may go on through 5 or even 6 years of age. Then suddenly everything may be all right almost overnight.

It is often a long wait, but in this as in other fields, patience is nearly always rewarded. It may help to remember that there is no "proper" age for staying dry. Practically all children go through the same stages which lead up to this desired ability, but each one makes his or her own timetable.

Bowel Movement Control

Training the child for bowel control is one of the less attractive but most necessary tasks of early parenthood. We would like, if we could, to lighten this task by recommending that you do not start in too soon, and that you take neither early "successes" nor early "failures" too seriously.

Even as early as 12 to 16 weeks of age the delay between feeding and the occurrence of a bowel movement may result in a temporary "success" if the mother is quick enough to get her baby onto a receptacle in time. Such a success means very little, except in terms of saving laundry.

Similarly, from 9 to 12 months some babies make vigorous sounds just prior to defecation, turn red in the face, and regard their mother as they defecate. This potential for success means little so far as consistent and sustained "good" performance is concerned because around 1 year of age many children no longer give these warning signs. Many go through a stage when they function best alone and standing up, at the crib rail or in their playpen.

At this time and for months thereafter they may function preferably while standing and may even resist being placed on the toilet seat. Or they may accept such placement but respond to it by withholding—releasing as soon as they are removed. Still others are apt to function during sleep, especially during naptime.

By 18 months many can associate some appropriate word with the function, thus increasing voluntary control. Many have few "accidents" after this age.

A temporary diarrhea comes in with many at around 18 to 21 months (followed by a period of constipation at around 2½ years).

By 2 years or shortly thereafter, some are able, if the mother removes their training pants for them and leaves them near the toilet facilities which they can use by themselves, to take care of their own needs. Some, however, do best if divested of all clothes, even their socks and shoes.

At around 2½ years, many develop a spirit of intense privacy about all toilet functions. "Mommy go way," they say, and even insist that the bathroom door be securely closed. Their demand for privacy, like other strong common growth stages, should of course be respected.

From then on, with most children, there are as a rule relatively few problems in this connection. However, it is important to keep in mind that expecting the child to have a bowel movement regularly every morning is somewhat unrealistic. From 3 years of age on there is a tendency in many to have it after lunch or after their nap, and this shift if it occurs should be respected.

"When Can I Expect My Child to Be Dry All Night?"

"How long do you think I'll have to wait before Danny will be able to stay dry all night?" Danny's mother asked us. "He's almost three now, and he's nearly always wet in the mornings. I've been hoping that if I just waited patiently, things would improve, but they don't seem to."

"Is Danny usually dry after his nap?" we asked her.

"Well, no, he isn't, most days. Why—does that have anything to do with it?"

"Unfortunately it does," we told her, and went on to explain the relation. Almost invariably we find that children are able to stay dry for the, obviously, shorter duration of naptime considerably before they are able to stay dry all night.

In the normal course of events, many babies wake dry from their naps as early as 1 year of age. By 18 months, many are reasonably well regulated in the daytime so far as toileting is concerned, though the responsibility for keeping the child dry is still the mother's. He does not yet indicate his toilet needs, but will wait a reasonable length of time for an opportunity to use the toilet.

By 2 years the child may be dry in the morning on waking if he or she is taken up during the night. (But this is often disturbing to the child of this age and we do not as a rule advocate it.) By 3 years of age, many are dry all night without being taken up. (Remember that boys are usually slower than girls in this respect.)

But this is only on the average. So we know that for many children it will be long past 2 or even long past 3 years before they can stay dry all night. In fact, many quite normal children are 5 or 6 years old before night dryness is established. And, as we have indicated, before you can even begin to hope that your child will be able to stay dry all night, he will in all probability need to have reached the stage of staying dry through his nap.

The child's awareness or concern over wet pants usually means that there will soon be no more wet pants. Dryness after nap means that you can at least start hoping for dry nights. But until these two preliminary steps occur, it is largely useless to look for the final control.

"Shall I Pick Him Up at Night?"

"Do you believe that picking a child up at night does any good? And if so, should he always be wakened thoroughly, or is it all right to toilet him without waking him up?"

These two questions usually go hand in hand, and they are asked, at some time or other, by nearly every young parent—except, of course, the extremely lucky ones whose children are "dry" almost from the moment of their arrival.

There is no one answer to the first of these two questions. As with so many problems of child rearing—it all depends.

If your child, regardless of age, has come to the place where he is customarily dry after his nap, dry during the day (even though with some assistance from you), and if by being taken up once or even twice during the night can manage to be dry in the morning, then your efforts are certainly being rewarded. You will probably feel that it is worth your while to take him up in the night.

If, however, you take him up, say at ten o'clock and again at midnight, finding him dry on each occasion, but nevertheless he is sopping wet when you go in to him at six or seven in the morning, you have not really saved much by your efforts. It might be just as well to see to it that he is arranged in sufficient rubber pants and pads to protect the sheets, and let him sleep through the night.

And if he is already wet an hour after he goes to sleep, or even when you first pick him up at ten o'clock, you have so far to go that you might just as well give up and wait till he can at least stay dry for the first two or three hours of the night. Or pick him up an hour or so after he goes to sleep to insure his comfort and save on the laundry, but don't expect him to be dry in the morning.

Not chronological age but how the child is actually functioning is the thing that should chiefly determine whether you pick him up or not.

As to waking him thoroughly when you pick him up, opinions

differ considerably about this. We ourselves advise, in most instances, that you do not wake him. Carry him to the bathroom if he is small and easy to pick up. Let him function in a bottle if he is a boy. Remember that picking him up is merely palliative. You pick him up in order to keep him dry and warm and to reduce the laundry. Picking him up does not *teach* him to stay dry. Therefore waking him does little good and may do serious damage in that once wakened, he may not be able to get back to sleep. A sleepless child may be more trouble to himself and others than a wet child.

However, the problem of picking up and waking is different at different ages. Even up through 2 or 3 years of age, many children are better off if not picked up during the night. In some, even being picked up more than once does not insure a dry night. In many, picking up disturbs sleep to such an extent that the child cannot get back to sleep.

The situation is different by 4 or 5 years of age. Then very often (assuming that the child is not entirely and consistently dry at night, as many are) picking the child up once two or three hours after he goes to sleep may insure dryness and is obviously well worthwhile. Some children are dry some nights without being picked up and tend to wet only after an especially exciting day. You may find that you need to pick them up only on such nights.

If your child is 6 or 7 years old and still wetting at night, then you judge by whether or not he has ever had any dry nights even with the help of being picked up. If there is no past history of dryness and he still wets within an hour after bedtime and is never dry in the morning, then you have a long way to go. You may still want to pick him up before he is apt to wet, usually one to two hours after he has gone to sleep and again when you go to bed, to make him feel more comfortable. But don't expect him necessarily to be dry in the morning.

However, if his span has even increased to two or, better, three hours after bedtime, the prospects are more encouraging, and just one pickup during the night may insure dryness. Remember that many perfectly normal children are as much as 8 years old before they reach this stage.

Snags in Toilet-Training

There are many snags in toilet-training, as there are in training the child in any other kind of behavior. We shall tell you about a few of the more common ones.

If you work hard at it, you can often "catch" a baby of 16 to 40 weeks, or in the last half of this first year, and can combine him and a suitable receptacle often enough and quickly enough that he stays dry most of the day, and you may have the illusion that he is toilet-trained. When he is just a little older, increased frequency and greater irregularity of urination along with changing motor patterns may result in "failures" and dispel your illusion. Then if you have been priding yourself on your early success, you will be disappointed and may feel that he is not doing as well as he did when he was younger. Yet actually the early "success" was your success, not his. Later on he will arrive at real success of his own, so don't be discouraged.

Especially discouraging is the reaction of some children, often seen at around 15 months of age. Placement on the toilet seat for many children around this age results in sphincter contraction or withholding of urine. They simply refuse to function so long as they sit there, releasing only after they have been removed and their diapers put on. This seems like deliberate badness to parents and is often punished. It will still be a nuisance, but you will be calmer about it if you recognize it for what it is—a stage of development which appears to be an immaturity. Actually it is an advance in that the child learns to inhibit, or to control, his sphincter by contraction. This more often occurs in the seated position and especially on the toilet, where he is expected to function. He often functions as soon as he is taken off the toilet and his diaper is put on. Part of the ease of release is because he is taken out of the demanding situation. Another part is that he functions best when he is extended in posture, either standing up or lying down. If this demand to function standing persists, it is wise to place a newspaper in a corner of the bathroom and allow the child to release his bowel movement on it. We need to recognize the wide distance between the cultural level and demands of our bathrooms and the level at which the little runabout is functioning.

Bedwetting

Bedwetting is an especially discouraging behavior, and "What can we do about the problem of bedwetting" is a question that parents ask and ask again. More often than not the answer is, "Wait awhile." In other words, more often than not the child in question, regardless of chronological age, is not yet mature enough in regard to this particular function to remain dry all night. If this is the case, you have no "problem" insofar as that nothing has really gone wrong, and there is no special thing that you can do to improve matters.

Some children are not ready to read at the conventional age. Some children do not begin to lose their baby teeth, like the majority, at around 5 or 6 years of age. And some are not yet ready to stay dry at the age when, norms show us, the average child has reached that desired goal—or even for years thereafter. Boys are more apt to be slow in developing control than are girls.

Check on your family history. Often you will find, or remember, a history of belated bladder control somewhere in the family. And the child's own elimination history will give you good clues. Was he (or she) much later than the average child in showing awareness of his own functioning or in staying dry after his nap? Is his span for dryness still short in the daytime? Is he already wet at eleven o'clock or even an hour after he falls asleep? Has he ever had periods, short or long, of being dry at night?

If, after making all these checks and after checking with your pediatrician, you then conclude that his inability to stay dry is just a matter of late development, pad him thoroughly at night, add rubber pants, and—if you can—forget the whole matter for a while. There is a certain group of children who do not even show glimmers of control before 6 or 7 years of age, and finally do stay dry at 8 either by being picked up or without help. Besides the more obvious evidence of occasional dry nights or of staying dry until picked up at eleven or midnight, the child's own feeling response to wetting can be very telling. If he isn't disturbed and hardly gives it a thought, then the necessary structure for control is not yet there.

If the child distracts his mother's attention and talks about the birds he sees outside or about other things as she comes to greet him in the morning, then she may know that this wetting is not congenial to him. For shame comes with new awareness. A mother should know that the child is most vulnerable at this stage and needs most help. The wetting child doesn't want the other members of the family to know that he has wet his bed. This can therefore be a secret between him and his mother. Then mother and child can work out ways and means by which he can learn control. The other children of the family must not be allowed to shame him.

If he achieved bladder control at 2 years and then, as can sometimes happen, lost this control at 4 (when tensional overflow is more often in the pelvic region of his body), he needs to be told that this happens to a lot of children.

Also the increased wetting that occurs during the turmoil period of 5½ to 6 years and also on the cold nights of autumn or just after a too exciting day or a frightening television program—all of these need to be understood and circumvented if possible by the parents. A half-day in first grade which cuts down fatigue or a happy chatting time with his mother after he is in bed may be all that is needed to break into a 6-year-old's tendency to wet his bed. An overnight visit to Grandmother's where he is happy and is given a lot of individual loving care may result in a dry bed and give him a real emotional uplift.

Years ago many psychiatrists felt that emotional factors alone were at the basis of bedwetting. Emotional factors could in certain instances play a part, but probably not with most children. That is, the old psychoanalytical notion was that children wet the bed because they were unhappy. We think it more likely that they are unhappy because they wet the bed.

If a boy or girl still wets the bed by 6 or 7 years of age, then we recommend that, after the usual methods have been tried and found wanting, parents try a conditioning device. There are a number of these devices now on the market.* The important thing to realize is that in bed-wetters there is a lack of relaying the simple message to the brain that the bladder is about to be emptied by the release of the bladder sphincter. Something needs to be devised to warn the child of this thing that is happening to him which he knows nothing of until he awakens later in a cold, wet bed.

Now easily available conditioning devices are constructed in such a way that the salt in the urine produces a short-circuit and thus sets up an electric current which rings a warning bell or buzzer.

At first the child may be slow to respond and before he awakens may have a sizeable puddle on the specially prepared pad on which he lies. But as his response to the bell or buzzer becomes quicker, the size of the puddle nightly grows smaller and smaller until it may finally be no bigger than a dime. It is then that he comes to the final stage of "beating the bell" (or buzzer). The child receives the warning from his bladder before the sphincter releases. This conditioning usually is accomplished within a period of a few weeks.

If the method doesn't work at first, put the device away until a later time when the child is more ready. Sometimes he responds well at first but then has a relapse later. Then an extra session of conditioning may be needed. As for using one of these devices before 7 years of age, this is obviously up to the discretion of the parents. Many prefer to wait to see if the child can't make it on his own.

Some parents have already tried setting an alarm clock to wake their child at some specific time during the night, but claim this doesn't work. Its failure, and the success of the conditioning de-

---

*Among the best of these devices is U-Trol, sold by J.G. Shuman Associates, Box 306, Scotch Plains, N. J. 07076.

vice, is probably due to the fact that the buzzer in the device rings only when the child has started to wet, at which time sleep tends to be light. The alarm clock rings at some arbitrary time, often when the child is very soundly asleep. (Bed-wetters tend to be sound sleepers.)

A newer and less mechanical possibility of a cure for bedwetting has been suggested by allergists who currently report cases in which bed-wetters have been cured by identifying food substances to which they are allergic and then removing such substances (in one instance milk) from the child's diet. We do not at present know in how many cases elimination of some specific food from the diet has brought about night dryness, but it's a possibility which some parents might like to consider.

Not Dry in Daytime by Three or Four Years of Age

Rarer than bedwetting but sometimes even more discouraging is the inability to stay dry in the daytime at an age when most children are fully "trained."

If a medical examination shows that there is nothing physically wrong, and if your pediatrician has no better suggestion, we would recommend the following. First, try to forget that your child is "old enough to be doing better." Just start in all over again as if dealing with a much younger child.

Find the time of day when he is most apt to be dry and see if you can get him to the toilet successfully at that time. Perhaps he will be dry right after his nap and you can catch him then. Then perhaps he will have a short dry spell following that, and you can catch him again.

At other times of day, keep the child in diapers and rubber pants, using training pants only at the times when you are hoping to have success.

As a rule, if you treat even the older child this way, you will find that he or she will run a course, even though slowly, quite similar to that of the younger child. If you start slowly and don't expect too much, the rapidity of progress may surprise you.

Can't Stay Dry at Play

Another related, though usually quite temporary, problem is that of the child (usually 3 to 4 years of age, and usually a boy) who cannot stay dry while out at play. When out with his mother, shopping or visiting, he never has an "accident." But almost every day when out playing, he comes in wet. And the mother usually finds that warning, scolding, spanking, or even keeping him in the house for a few days does no good at all.

The reason that spanking and punishment do not help is because such a child's difficulty is not badness—it is a real inability.

The complex task of stopping enjoyable play, leaving friends, and getting into the house in time is just too much. And so you will need to work with him, not against him. You need to help, not to punish. Your child needs practical help. And so you will need to plan with him about getting into the house.

You and he may, for instance, plan with him that you are going to call him in at intervals. You may be able to figure out what his time span is and call him accordingly. If you can't figure this out, and if his timing is very irregular, you can just call him in every hour, or half hour, or as often as you think necessary. A police whistle which he has helped to purchase may work better than just the human voice. And some surprise for him after he has gone to the bathroom will make coming in more enjoyable.

Soon his span may increase so that preventive toileting before he goes out to play may do the trick. Later he may reach the point where he can remember to come in without help—though he may wait till the last minute.

Wetting in School

Wetting in school, which occurs in a few first-graders, is often a sign that the child is immature for his or her age. It is often a warning that the child is not quite ready for first grade.

For any first-grader, ideally, toilets should be adjacent to the classroom, and children should be free to come and go as necessary. Until such architectural arrangements can be made universal, however, teacher and parent will have to help the immature child as best they can.

First of all, question the child's readiness for daily all-day attendance, and for being in first grade at all, for that matter. If he must so continue, then be sure that he takes the time to go to the bathroom just before and just after the class session. The teacher must recognize that she needs to take over a mother's responsibility—that the child is unable to take care of himself.

Scolding and shaming are of course to be entirely avoided. Most of these children are doing the very best they can.

Odd or Bizarre Toileting Behaviors

The following are not really "snags" in toilet training, but should simply be mentioned so that they will not worry you when and if they occur.

The 2-year-old's inordinate interest in bowel movements as you take him out for a walk shows his own level of development. His eyes seem to spot every dog's defecation in sight. Then he goes to these, points to them, exclaims over them, and all too often embarrasses his mother beyond words. We have often wondered if it isn't the very child who has been made too aware of his own functioning at home who is so conscious of the functioning of others, especially animals.

Many little girls around the age of 3 attempt to urinate standing up. This is a perfectly normal experiment and not in our opinion a sign that they have "penis envy" or have been overexposed to little boys. It may rather suggest their powers of observation.

Many boys and girls around 4 express an excessive interest in other people's bathrooms. Take them visiting and they are almost certain to say that they have to go to the toilet. A good hostess could perfectly well say to her 4-year-old visitor—who loves in any case to go exploring in another's house—"Would you like to see the rest of the house—the bedrooms, bathrooms, and everything?"

Throughout the preschool years some children exhibit rather bizarre toilet behaviors. Thus they may void in unusual or unsuitable places, or may save products or even store them away in bureau drawers. Such behaviors often occur in children who have slightly atypical personality patterns; but if these particular behaviors are the only atypical signs, as a rule parents should not be too concerned, though they will probably want to prevent the behavior if possible. If this kind of response is part of a whole group of unusual and atypical responses, parents will most likely wish to consult a child specialist.

Another thing which occurs especially around 4 is an excessive expression of need for privacy for their own toilet functions, but a tremendous interest in watching other people in the bathroom.

And lastly, also around 4 (and again at 6), many indulge in a good deal of name-calling related to toilet functions. "You old wee-wee pants," or, "You old bowel movement" are favorite epithets. You may wish to prohibit this, but you should not be too upset when it occurs, as it is extremely common.

Bowel Movement Difficulties

Most children have less difficulty with regard to bowel movements than with regard to urination. Many children are easily trained in this respect and a great many have no difficulties and no accidents after 18 months of age.

There are, however, a few snags which you may run into in this department. First of all, many children, especially boys, at around 15 months to 2½ years of age may insist on standing up to have their bowel movements, even though they may have earlier been perfectly good about sitting on the toilet seat. It is usually best to permit them to function standing while this demand lasts.

Stool smearing occurs transiently in many children at around the age of 15 to 21 months. It occurs probably most often at the end of the nap if you do not go to the child quickly enough. He simply has a bowel movement in his diaper and then plays with the product.

Aside from being messy, this is not usually a serious problem. Preventive measures chiefly involve getting to him sooner or seeing that his diapers or training pants fit more securely. If this behavior occurs frequently, excessively, and consistently, you may need to put on such securely fitting nightclothes that he can't get them off. Prevention is the secret here.

A more worrisome problem arises when a child (usually a boy) as old as 3 or 4 years of age absolutely rejects any efforts to train him so far as his bowel movements are concerned. He refuses to sit on the potty chair or toilet and has his bowel movement in his diapers.

When this is the case, a mother will need to start over at the very beginning. Give up the idea of having him use the toilet at first. Simply try to localize the behavior as to the time and place.

Try to determine at about what time of day he usually functions. (Unless it has narrowed down to some approximately regular time, you may just have to wait till it does.)

Then, at this time, let him play in the bathroom, nude or at least with his pants and underpants off. Have a newspaper on the floor, preferably in a corner behind the door, and indicate to him that when he is ready to function, he may do so on the paper.

Success is usually obtained within a remarkably short time. Once it has been established, you can gradually introduce a potty chair onto the scene and then can eventually shift from that to the regular toilet at such a time as he tells you he is ready for it.

Related to this refusal to function on the toilet, or sometimes not so related, is the problem of constipation, which may become quite severe in the preschool years.

There are several things you can do about this problem. First, as in other fields, be sure that you really have a problem. Remember that some children do not have a bowel movement every twenty-four hours. Also, there are ages when the child quite normally is a little more constipated than usual. This is particularly true at around 2½ years of age.

In other instances it turns out that the parents simply are not giving the child the privacy during elimination which he or she demands and needs. Added privacy often quickly solves the problem.

Equally simple is the giving of canned prune juice or a good nonabrasive laxative. Reasonable experimentation with laxatives and with a relaxing diet should certainly be tried before you conclude that your child's constipation is an "emotional" problem.

But if you have tried all reasonable methods which you and your pediatrician can devise and your child's constipation continues to be excessive and chronic, then you will probably want to consult a psychologist or psychiatrist and get some specialized help. You will most likely find that the child's excessive constipation is just his organism's way of telling you that something is wrong, for him, in his daily family life.

Another problem which may also require professional help is that which arises when a preschooler attempts to "control" his mother's actions by having bowel movements in his pants to get her attention. She may be entertaining company; she may be attending to Father or the new baby—whatever it is, she is not paying as much attention to him as he thinks he deserves. So he has a bowel movement and she has to stop whatever she is doing and clean him up.

Here, obviously, the problem is as much one of mother-child relations as one of elimination. And unless the mother can herself figure out ways of making the child's life more harmonious and satisfactory, she may well wish to get a little professional help with the problem.

Two last problems in this realm.

At around 5 to 6 years of age many children again go through a period of increased withholding, as at 2½. It often takes them so long to function that they simply do not bother. This difficulty can usually be controlled through careful checking by Mother and the use of prune juice or mineral oil.

Just the opposite difficulty comes in at around 6 years of age with some, when there is tendency to overrelease. The child functions almost without warning to himself—on the way home from school in the afternoon; or at school, also in the afternoon; or in Sunday school; or out at play. Children may be terribly embarrassed when this happens—and most parents are either embarrassed, worried, or angry. They think that the child is "old enough to know better." Actually, this represents a real developmental problem and should be treated as such.

What the child needs here is a little more supervision and help. He should never be scolded or frightened. See that he functions before he goes back to school in the afternoon. If he is a 6-year-old, try to arrange for him to attend only a morning session at school. Or if necessary, call for him at school and drive him home, since this behavior most often occurs on the way home from school. Or after school, be sure that he functions before he goes out to play. A little planning on the parent's part can usually overcome this temporary difficulty.

7 Tensional Outlets

Perhaps nowhere has the American attitude toward child behavior changed more in the last fifty years than in our feeling about what we now call *tensional outlets.*

No more than forty years ago, one of the main questions which parents asked the child specialist was, "How can I get my child to stop sucking his [her] thumb?"

By the early 1950s we specialists, as well as many parents, were more accepting. Parents were beginning to ask not, "How can I stop my child from sucking his thumb?" but rather, "Should I stop him?" We and others were referring to thumb sucking, blanket fondling, hair pulling, rocking, and other such behaviors not as "bad habits" but rather as "tensional outlets."

Our position was that just as many grownups feel tense at times and have their own ways of relieving their tension (smoking, drinking), so do children, also, sometimes feel tense and have a need to relieve their own tensions.

This approach quite naturally led to a friendlier and more accepting attitude on the part of parents. Then finally came a third stage in parental feeling about thumb sucking and related behaviors. A book by Kathryn Ernst titled *Danny and His Thumb* is addressed directly to young thumb-suckers in an effort to make them feel better about their behavior. The book points out that lots of children suck their thumbs and that gradually, by the time they get to kindergarten or first grade, they are just so busy with their hands that they don't have time to suck their thumbs *any more.*

Many parents in times past have thought of thumb sucking,

blanket fondling, rocking, head banging as bad habits, and have considered them to be a sign that the child was insecure or maladjusted. Many have felt that a child who was "all right" wouldn't do these things—that is, would "give up his bad habits"—or better still, wouldn't have gotten into them in the first place. A well-adjusted child just wouldn't do such things.

Many parents even go so far as to feel that if their child does indulge in such behaviors, it is because they have failed to make him or her feel secure.

Our own attitude toward all these kinds of behavior has always been quite different. We think of all these tension-relieving behaviors which we have just mentioned as tensional outlets. That is, we believe that many children, like many adults, feel at times certain normal tensions. The adult has many ways of relieving these tensions—smoking is one of the most common. The child, too, has ways of relieving tensions—and among these are the so-called bad habits which we are discussing.

We believe that your attitude as a parent toward these behaviors can significantly affect the situation. If you can think of them as devices for helping a child live with his tensions rather than as vices which must be cured, your own greater calmness and relaxation and acceptance of them will definitely benefit your child.

Nine times out of ten a child will grow out of these behaviors of his own accord. You not only will not find it necessary to break him of these habits, but often the less you say about them, the less you call them to his attention, the sooner he will get over them.

In fact, the nagging (well-meant correction) of a tense parent may often increase rather than decrease the child's thumb sucking or nail biting or whatever it is that you object to.

And so, as we say, perhaps the most help we can give parents is to try to help you take a calm, relaxed attitude toward these behaviors. Our best way of doing this may be simply to give you a timetable which shows the ages when we have found that the most common tensional outlets appear and the ages when they usually drop out.

You will note as you read this timetable that some behaviors such as temper tantrums drop out and then later reappear. Others, once they have finally dropped out, do not as a rule recur.

1 year: *Thumb sucking* strong, with or without an accessory object; occurs in daytime, just before sleep, and during the night.

Transient and somewhat accidental *stool smearing*.

Presleep *rocking* in crib, *bed shaking, head banging,* or *head rolling.*

Handling genitals and possibly some *masturbation. Crying.*

18 months: *Thumb sucking* reaches a peak. May go on for several hours a day as well as just before sleep, or even all night.

Rocking, bed shaking, head banging or *head rolling* may occur.

Occasional episodes of *stool smearing.*

Furniture moving. Takes objects out of bureau drawers.

Sit down *temper tantrums.*

Tears books or wallpaper.

21 months: Tears bed apart.

Removes clothes and runs around unclothed.

2 years: *Thumb sucking* less during the day. Has a positive association with hunger, frustration, fatigue.

May be some *stool smearing.*

Rocking, bed shaking, bouncing, head banging, or *head rolling.*

Many presleep demands.

Fewer tensional outlets at this age.

Left alone in a room, removes everything from drawers and cupboards.

2 ½ years: *Thumb sucking* less during the day. At night strongly associated with accessory object. Some sucking in daytime, often with accessory object.

Rocking, head banging in some.

Some *masturbation.*
Stuttering may come in with high-language children.
Tears wallpaper, digs into the plaster.
Completely disrupts playroom, both large and small objects.
Sudden aggressive attacks—may "sock" a stranger.
Temper tantrums.

3 years: *Thumb sucking,* often associated with accessory object, at night or occasionally in the daytime. Can tolerate having thumb removed from mouth during sleep.
Fewer tensional outlets.
May wander around house during the night.

3 ½ years: An increase in tensional outlets here.
Thumb sucking at night with accessory object. Can suck in daytime without object.
Spitting.
Considerable *stuttering.*
Nose picking, fingernail biting.
Hands may tremble and child may stumble and fall.
Much *whining.*

4 years: *Thumb sucking* may occur only as goes to sleep.
Out-of-bounds behavior: Motor—runs away, kicks, spits, bites fingernails, picks nose, grimaces. Verbal—calls names, boasts and brags, silly use of language.
Nightmares and fears.
Needs to urinate in moments of emotional excitement.
Pain in stomach and may *vomit* at times of stress.

5 years: Not much tensional overflow. Often not more than one type in any one child.
Hand to face: *nose picking, nail biting.*
Thumb sucking, before sleep or with fatigue, often without accessory object.
Eye blinking, head shaking, throat clearing, especially toward end of day—peak at dinnertime.
Sniffling and twitching nose.

5½ years: Number and severity of tensional outlets increasing. One child may show several types of overflow.
Hand to face: *nose picking, nail biting* increasing.
Some *throat clearing,* sometimes ticlike.
Mouthing of tongue and lips, tongue projection.
Less presleep *thumb sucking.*
School entrance may cause increase in *stuttering, nail biting,* and *thumb sucking.*

6 years: General restlessness.
Clumsy. "Falls over a piece of string."
Kicks at table legs as swings legs.
Sits on edge of chair, nearly falls off chair, pushes chair back.
Temper tantrums may return.
Makes faces with some relation to others, somewhat for fun.
Throat noises.
Heavy breathing, gasping with excitement.
Nail biting, tongue extension, spitting.
Stuttering.
Thumb sucking only in those with prolonged history, and may show an increased intensity.

7 years: Very few tensional outlets reported. Old ones dropping out. Those who still *suck thumb, bite nails,* or *stutter* are usually attempting to control.
Some *blinking* or reference to eyes hurting. Scowling.
Spontaneous undulating movements similar to St. Vitus's dance.
Headaches.
Things go "round and round" in head.

8 years: Very diffuse. Any of the earlier patterns may reappear; *eye blinking, nail biting, eye rubbing*—but all are less persistent.
A few persistent *thumb-suckers,* especially boys, still

suck during reading or listening or during illness or
fatigue.
Picking at fingers.
Crying with fatigue.
Making faces when given unwelcome command.
Stomachache.
Need to urinate before unpleasant task.

9 years: Stamping feet, rubbing hands through hair.
Fiddling, pulling off button.
Drops and breaks things, picks at self.
Growling and muttering.
Feels dizzy.

Tense Ages

Just a word should be said about the fact that not only may any
given child have a favorite and characteristic method (or methods)
of releasing tension, characteristic of him or her and liable to occur
at any age, but also that at some ages any child is apt to be notably
more tense than at others.

Thus 2½, 3½, and 5½ to 6 are, as the preceding table suggests,
even more than others, ages of tension. This means two things:
first, that at these ages you should particularly go out of your way
to prevent, or break into, situations which are likely to arouse
tensions in your child; second, that you may normally expect an
increase in tensional outlets at these ages and should try not to
worry too much about this increase.

Temper Tantrums

Daniel, aged 2½, was having a full-fledged temper tantrum. He
flung himself onto the floor and kicked and screamed. He
drummed his feet and howled with rage.

His mother, in the best current tradition, observed him calmly.
Most mothers find that if they can walk out on a child or remain
calm and unemotional while the child is having a tantrum, it is

over much sooner and is somewhat less likely to be repeated. If having a tantrum gets them nowhere, many children give up this way of expressing themselves after only a few trials.

But Daniel's grandmother was also present. (The apartment was so small that no member of the family could be very far absent.) And she did something more than watch him calmly. For she had, like other grandmothers, brought up a family of her own and she knew that handling a temper tantrum skillfully was only a first step. A second and even more important step was, if possible, finding out what had caused the tantrum and what set of circumstances was thus to be avoided in the future to prevent further tantrums.

"I know just how he feels," sympathized Grandma. "And I suspect that he needs a lot more space to move around in. This summer when you all come to visit us, we'll fence in the yard, and then he'll have all the room he needs. I think he won't get frustrated so often."

This is one of the most important things that the adult can do when dealing with a child who is bothered with (and bothers others with) tantrums. Try to find out what things, or what kinds of situations, cause these tantrums. Even more important than treating them calmly is trying to prevent their occurrence.

Temper tantrums most often occur when the child is tired or frustrated. Some frustration is inevitable and perhaps necessary as a child grows up—but frustration is most apt to end in tantrums when he or she is tired.

If you will take the trouble to keep a record of the situations when your child has tantrums, you will often find that they occur at a time of day when he is particularly fatigued. At such times you will find that his tolerance for frustration is low. The same refusals and denials which he might be able to stand early in the day or after a nap often bring on a tantrum when they occur just before lunch or suppertime, for instance. A snack before suppertime may help to break into his fatigue.

But not only fatigue brings on a tantrum. Sometimes some very simple incident will bring it on. That is why it is important for you to try to discover *why* your child explodes and *how* you can prevent a recurrence.

Thumb Sucking

Your baby, if he or she is going to be a thumb-sucker, may possibly be one of those who gets such an early start that already at birth the thumb bears guilty traces of having been sucked. More likely, however, thumb sucking will start, if it is going to at all, at around 3 to 4 months of age.

At this time the behavior most frequently occurs right after feeding. The baby has been sucking (at breast or bottle), and just keeps right on after the source of food has been removed. Later on, as you may have noted, this urge to suck spreads to the period before feeding, and then finally to other times of day as well.

By 6 months, with some, putting an object to the mouth may take the place of thumb sucking. But at around 7 months, when hand to mouth is such a favorite gesture—and posture—thumb sucking will be very strong in many. In fact, it may reach such a peak that sucking may take place during a good part of the day and for at least much of the night. If you remove the thumb forcibly from the child's mouth, it is likely to come out with a loud pop and to go back in at once unless forcibly restrained.

It is usually when sucking has reached such a peak that parents worry the most and are most anxious to do something about it. Unfortunately, this is probably the very worst time to interfere. Your efforts during such a period will have the least effect. It usually proves much more effective if you can wait till the behavior is on the wane before making any definite attempt to stop it.

(Here let's say a good word for this behavior which is looked upon askance by so many parents: The baby who sucks his thumb may cry less and may get through teething much more easily than the baby who doesn't. He is also likely to go to sleep more easily and to get along better in many other ways.)

After this 7-months period there may be a repeated rise and fall in the amount of sucking. First you think it's dropping out, and then you fear that it's getting worse. Then at around 18 months, with many, such a peak is reached that mothers become not only discouraged but worried, too.

It may encourage these mothers to know that there is a good chance (though by no means a certainty) that sucking may decrease, during the daytime at least, by the time the child is 2 years old.

Not only does it (often) reduce in amount around this time, but it often has a more positive association with hunger, sleep, frustration, or fatigue. If this does happen, it gives you something to go by. You can note the situations when it is most apt to occur and can try to prevent these situations or to reduce their difficulty for the child.

By 2½ to 3 years of age, sucking in many is much less frequent during the day and at night may be associated with a certain (accessory) object held in the free hand. If the child needs to suck in the daytime, he may have to go and get this object before he can enjoy his sucking.

By 3½ many can do their daytime sucking without the object, even though they use it at night. At this age, daytime sucking is often stimulated by such excitements as being read to, watching television, or looking up at an airplane.

And in the majority of children, if it has not already disappeared earlier somewhere along the way, by 4 or 5 thumb sucking will be associated only with sleep, and may then drop out of its own accord or with just a little help from Mother or Father.

Thus, perhaps the most practical suggestion we can give parents when they ask what to do about their child's thumb sucking is the following: We can suggest that they familiarize themselves with the more or less usual course which thumb sucking takes (in our children, in our time) and then check to see how far their own child has gone along this course.

If, as we have noted above, the thumb sucking is merely on its way in or has about reached its peak, efforts to stop it in all likelihood not only will be ineffective but may actually be harmful, since thumb sucking, if it occurs, seems to need to run its course.

If it is nearing its end, you can either wait till it has taken its normal course or you may take such direct measures as seem fitting to you to hurry a little this natural ending of the behavior. The gift of a kitten might be the necessary stimulus to stop thumb sucking in a 3-year-old. But in a 5-year-old the thumb itself needs to be attacked. Various means can be used with the child's cooperation. One method might be a nightly Band-Aid with a projecting tab that he can chew on. This may shift him out of his sucking habit.

Sucking with Accessory Object

"He not only sucks his thumb, but he rubs his nose with his forefinger at the same time!"

"He pulls the fuzz of his blanket with his left hand while he sucks his right thumb!"

"She twists her hair—or pulls her ear—all the time that she sucks her thumb!"

"He can only suck his thumb if he has his 'pretty' [or his 'cuddler,' or whatever name the individual child may have for his soft blanket, or sweater, or soft piece of cloth] clutched in his other hand!"

These very customary statements are usually made to us prefaced or followed by the question, "Did you ever hear of such a thing?"

And we note that most parents report these things with a combination of pride and discouragement. Pride that their child could have worked up something so complex and "unusual." Discouragement because they have a feeling that it is a pretty bad habit and that it may even be a sign that something is "wrong" with him or her.

Though it may occur at almost any age, we have found this sucking with an accessory object or gesture to be most common at around 2½ or 3 years of age, when it occurs mostly at bedtime.

(Yet some at this age cannot suck even in the daytime without their treasured blanket, or whatever they may have chosen.)

As a rule, if their desired objects are denied them, they usually cry or scream and become very much upset. This is not, in most, a good age to withhold the object or even to suggest withholding it.

Even by 3½, when many have gone back to being able to suck in the daytime without their special object, they still are not able to give it up at night.

But by 4 or 5 years of age, with many you can successfully attack the thumb sucking itself through this accessory object. With some you can merely say that the blanket (or whatever it is) is in the wash. Some will accept the story that it is lost. (If they do, the probability is that their thumb sucking has nearly run its course.)

With others you can frankly plan a giving up. A fuzz puller may agree to buy chintz and help cover a fuzzy blanket so that the fuzz will not be a temptation. Another child may agree to *try* going to sleep without his blanket. Or he may allow Mother to sit by his bed and hold his hand in place of his sucking his thumb and holding his blanket. ("It isn't working, Mother," one little girl said after several nights of this. "I guess I'm not ready to give it up yet.")

Whatever specific plan you yourself may find successful—getting the child to give up an accessory object or habit is one of the best ways to help him over thumb sucking—*if* you do not start in too soon.

Does Thumb Sucking Do Harm?

Does thumb sucking actually distort the shape of the child's mouth?

This problem is perhaps one which concerns the parents of thumb-suckers more than any other. Even if parents do not like to see their child sucking his or her thumb, many of them would have no major objection to the behavior if they were sure that it was not deforming the mouth. Conversely, even parents who do not object to the behavior as such feel that they ought to stop it because it may be interfering with the thumb-suckers later looks.

The answers given by different specialists to this question are extremely varied. The nature of the answer seems to depend largely on who is doing the answering.

Some, though by no means all, dentists do seem to feel that thumb sucking definitely mars the shape of the mouth and is thus specifically harmful. Most psychologists and psychiatrists, and many pediatricians, consider that it is basically not a harmful habit and that it does not in most cases alter the shape of the mouth. Particularly do they feel that it is harmless in this respect if it ceases before the second teeth come in, as it usually does.

These two points of view are pretty much opposed, obviously, and thus cause parents no end of worry. If the so-called authorities disagree, what are parents to do? How are they to know whether thumb sucking actually is, or is not, harmful to the child?

Dentists who really believe that sucking is harmful state flatly that it "directly displaces teeth" and should be stopped as quickly as possible. To stop it, some of them suggest a really horrid-looking device known as a *hay-rake,* a metal device which can be cemented to the teeth and which, with its vicious looking (and probably feeling) prongs, quickly deters the child from putting his thumb into his mouth. Merely looking at a picture of such a device would prevent most tender-minded parents from dreaming of using one.

Fortunately, many qualified dentists agree with the psychologist and psychiatrist (and with us) that in most cases thumb sucking does not permanently impair the shape of the mouth. As long ago as 1951, J. H. Silliman, writing in the *Journal of Pediatrics,* reported a fourteen-year follow-up study based on serial dental casts taken at least once a year on a group of children from birth through 14 years of age.

This author—and findings like his are increasingly reported—states clearly that in his opinion thumb sucking may affect the oral structure of children with "poor bites," but has little or no effect on those with "good bites." That is, if the child's mouth was well shaped to start with, thumb sucking did not distort it. Only in those cases where there was a poorly shaped structure to start with did the sucking possibly distort it further.

Specific Things to Do (and Not Do) about Thumb Sucking

Does all this mean that we must just sit by and do nothing about thumb sucking, you may well ask.

Not entirely! Some people can, of course. They are calm and patient enough, or objective enough, to wait and watch till thumb sucking has run its natural course.

Most parents, however, assuming that they basically dislike having a thumb-sucker around the house, want to *do* something about it.

Here are some of the things you can do.

At around 2 years of age, with many children, thumb sucking occurs less during the day than formerly, and when it does occur, it tends to be brought on by hunger, fatigue, frustration, or boredom.

Thus it is not too difficult for a mother to check up, to see in what situations and at what times it occurs. And having done that, she can often prevent the sucking *before* it starts. Arrange for an earlier nap to prevent fatigue. Provide a little snack to prevent hunger. Give a little more attention and help if your child is lonesome or frustrated.

Substituting another object for the thumb—that is, giving the child a toy to hold so that he or she cannot suck the thumb—works less effectively than many parents hope and expect. Especially if the desire to suck is still at its height.

Sometimes, oddly enough, going to nursery school will cut down thumb sucking. The new interest of nursery school has been known to stop this behavior as well as to cut down wakeful nights and to improve poor appetites, as it often does.

Just keeping a record of when and to what extent the thumb sucking occurs has been known to help many mothers, even though it does not actually keep the thumb out of the mouth.

Keeping a record helps you to view the behavior more objectively and allows you to see the progress and improvement which are usually brought about by time.

As a rule, the more you try to stop the child's sucking in the early stages, that is, during the first 3 years or so, the stronger it may become and the harder it may be to stop later. If you tackle it before it has run its course, you are likely to get into trouble. But by the time the child is 4 or 5, if you haven't made too much fuss earlier, the behavior will usually drop out by itself or with just a little help from you. (It may get worse briefly from around 5½ to 6, when tensional outlets normally do increase.) You can plan possible remedies with the child. Often something fairly simple, such as putting adhesive tape around the thumb with an extra tab to chew on, may do the trick. Wearing mittens to bed helps some to give up their sucking.

Biting

"What do you do to stop a child from biting? Bite him back? That's what some people advise us." Many a parent has asked this question, phrased in just this way.

Our answer is that biting back is one of the least desirable and often one of the least effective ways to prevent biting.

Biting is in many children an extremely temporary way of behaving, expressed only when they are in a social situation which is too difficult for them. Frustrated and unable to express themselves more effectively, they resort to biting. Two simple remedies are: (a) First simplify the play situation. Don't have the child play with so many or such difficult (for him) companions. And don't have him play for so long. (b) Give more adult supervision. Step in, not just to punish biting after it has taken place, but to prevent the need for it. Help the child to express himself in more satisfactory ways.

Just these two steps can often prevent any need for biting. And time itself takes care of things in most children. Behavior proceeds (or develops) from head to foot, scientists have learned. The child who bites in September may hit in December and kick in June. So in most cases, if you can keep him out of too difficult situations for a brief while, the urge to bite will disappear.

But suppose it doesn't? We have found in a nursery-school situation that if you have a biter on your hands, it often helps to have one teacher delegated to follow him around for a morning or two. Then every time such a child opens his mouth to bite, the teacher just cups her hand under his chin and gives a quick upward push. This, repeated every time he starts to bite for a few days, as a rule quickly discourages future biting.

Often we have found that biting can be "cured" by some such simple trick, by added age, or by just a little simplifying of the play situation. Or by a little extra supervision. Or by isolating the child from the group or from his playmates each time he bites.

If these things don't work, the biting, like any other aggressive behavior, may be considered a sign at least that something deeper is amiss. In such a case you may want to call in outside help. Play therapy for the child, or even help for the parent in smoothing out the whole home situation may be needed. We definitely do not recommend such drastic measures as biting the child back or washing his or her mouth out with soap.

Biting may be one special manifestation of a certain type of personality. It may eventually become significant in an individual's whole sweep of development. But—and this is our advice not only where biting is the problem—never seek the complicated explanation or remedy when a simple one will do. Biting is not necessarily a sign that something is deeply and ominously "wrong" with a preschooler.

Nail Biting

Nail biting is a slightly discouraging topic—in that it, unlike most of the other early tensional outlets (head banging, rocking, thumb sucking), it does not normally run its course and disappear by the end of the preschool years or shortly thereafter. Research into the tensional outlets of adolescents has shown us that nail biting is the most common and most persistent of the specific ways in which teenagers release their tension. Many continue this behavior till they are 15 or 16 or even, as many of you realize, right into adulthood.

Some children bite their nails only under extreme tension (nervousness about exams, excitement at the movies). Others just bite their nails.

Nail biting often seems to be a quite different kind of response from thumb sucking (though a few children are thumb suckers first and nail biters later). Nail biting is a pressure type of response and certainly is effective in releasing a good deal of nervous energy. With some children we do get the feeling that they need to do this.

Three of the possible courses of action which parents may follow in the case of nail biting are:

First, consider that the biting may be an indication that some specific thing is bothering the child. (We know, for instance, of a little girl who stopped it when she was moved to a different school.) Try to find out if this is the case.

Second, it may have started as a necessity, but then moved on into the "habit" realm. In this case, mere cosmetic arguments may suffice to break it up. (Point out to the child—if a girl—how nice her nails will look when long and polished. Or even, in the teens, let her wear artificial nails.)

Third, it may be something, like smoking (though actually less harmful), which the individual seems to need to do (or feels that he needs to do) and which may just go on without stopping until the individual is ready to exert the necessary controls himself.

Rocking

"My little boy gets up on his hands and knees in his crib and rocks back and forth. He rocks so hard that you can hear him all over the house, and he actually moves his crib from one side of the room to another. Did you ever hear of such a thing?"

Yes, we have.

"My little girl rocks herself to sleep every night of her life, and sometimes we even hear her rocking in her sleep. Do you think this is a sign that something is wrong with her?"

Not necessarily.

We repeat: We have often heard of it. And we don't think it is necessarily a sign that anything is wrong with the rocker.

Rocking, like many other outlets for tension, starts out as a perfectly natural and normal stage of development. At around 40 weeks of age many babies, able to get up onto their hands and knees but not yet quite ready to creep, rock their body backward and forward without actually moving from their original location. Hands and knees remain firmly on the floor (or mattress), but trunk moves forward and backward.

More often than not, this behavior drops out after the infant learns to creep. But sometimes it doesn't. In those cases this actually quite normal behavior may continue to express itself, particularly at bedtime or during sleep, long after the second birthday.

In such cases it often reaches its peak at 2½ to 3½ years of age, and then gradually drops out. Only in a minority of children does it persist after 4.

As with most such tensional outlets, it is usually best, if you can, to let this behavior alone till it runs its course. However, some of the things you can try, which may cut it down a bit, are:

Pad the child's crib heavily, be sure that the crib is screwed tightly together so that it does not creak unduly, and put a soft rug under the crib. This reduces the noise and movement, which are often among the things that make the behavior most satisfactory to the child.

Sometimes when the child is around 4, you can plan that he or she will move into a bigger bed. Some children are at this time susceptible to a buildup to the effect that *they won't rock any more* after they have the big bed.

Sometimes a more prolonged going-to-bed hour which involves some activity or activities especially pleasing to the child will reduce tension and can send him off to sleep without rocking. Or you may find that your child can respond to some prearranged signal—such as your knocking on the wall—by stopping the rocking.

Your own ingenuity may, or may not, find some means of cutting down rocking which will work in your particular case. But whether you find such a means or not, at least try to appreciate the normality of this behavior and do not be unduly concerned.

Till recently we have felt that aside from rather modest efforts to cut down the satisfaction a child receives from rocking (by reducing the movement of the crib) there was not too much that parents could or should do about the behavior. Recently some pediatric allergists are discovering that if they can help the child to feel more comfortable within his or her own body by removing from the diet foods to which the child is susceptible, the need to rock or bounce can be lessened or completely removed. Most certainly even though rocking in itself may not be harmful, being uncomfortable is. So it's well worthwhile if you have any rockers in your family, to check on their diet.

Tongue Sucking

A behavior less common than thumb sucking but equally worrisome to parents is tongue sucking. Tongue sucking, obviously, is harder to get at than thumb sucking. Many of the simple things which we can at least try to do to break into thumb sucking are of no avail here.

In general, with tongue sucking, it is more important to handle general behavior than to attack the sucking problem directly. That is, you do not make an issue of the sucking or try specifically to get the child to stop.

Rather, you attempt to improve the total life situation so that, perhaps, the tensions which get relief in the sucking will no longer be felt, or no longer felt so strongly. Nursery school or any similar activity which gives the child happy, pleasant experiences can be a great help. Or more time alone with Mother, or a satisfactory baby-sitter.

Some parents have found that gum chewing (even though not a very attractive behavior in itself) cuts into tongue sucking.

Head Banging

Somewhat similar to rocking but rather more frightening to parents, since it often causes actual bumps or welts on a child's forehead, is head banging. The child usually picks out the hardest surface available and then bangs his or her head against it. This is sometimes done in anger, sometimes not.

We have found that many, though of course not all, head-bangers have the following personality characteristics:

1. They frequently are highly aware of sounds and sensitive to them.
2. Often they have musical ability and interest, like to listen to music, and may sing on pitch early.
3. Many are ritualistic and patterned in their behavior.
4. They may be slow to approach a new activity or person, then slow to give it up.
5. They often are poor sleepers, waking up in the night and crying or singing to themselves.
6. Many have extreme temper tantrums. Desires are strong and ability to inhibit is poor.
7. They may be very cautious physically but have considerable energy.
8. Many are neat and show a marked dislike of dirty hands or of anything spilled.

Knowing these characteristics of course will not prevent the head banging. But it can at least help you to realize that the behavior must be fairly common if it is possible to describe head-bangers as a group.

The best methods of dealing with this behavior are picking the child up and comforting him, but without talking about the head banging. Or distracting him with music or some other device. Or, best of all, if you can, try to prevent recurrence of the kinds of situations which led up to the banging. Scolding or punishing is as a rule completely ineffective.

It is very unusual for a head-banger to do himself real damage (other than making black and blue marks) by his banging.

Head Rolling

Another similar behavior is head rolling. This may go on till a child is 5 or 6 years of age or later. Spanking and scolding, urging and bribing, usually are of no avail in stopping this. Some mothers try appealing to the child's vanity (since the behavior tends to snarl the child's hair and make it look untidy, or it can produce a bald spot). This too is usually unsuccessful.

What usually does work is providing some form of substitute outlet. Since the behavior usually occurs when the child is fatigued —it is at those times that you will need to provide him or her with something to think about or something interesting to do.

Playing music or reading to the child are two things which will be worth trying. (This behavior often occurs in the daytime as well as just prior to sleep.) Either may help. However, on the other hand, the child may roll or sway while listening. If he does, try having him color or play with clay. Or, instead of playing slow rhythmic music to which he may rock, try speeding up the music and getting him to dance to it.

You yourself may be able to think of other things which the child can do when he is tired and this urge to roll the head comes on. Whatever you do, it will be necessary to break into the behavior with some interesting, positive stimulus. It is seldom useful at the younger ages to attack the problem directly. If head rolling continues until the child is as old as 8 years, he may be motivated toward some goal he wants to achieve, *e.g.* he can go for a visit to Grandmother's as soon as his hair grows in.

Hair Pulling

An extreme and often actually disfiguring tensional outlet is the pulling out of hair. Some children pull out only enough to make small bald spots. Others pull out enough to make themselves completely bald.

As with all other similar behaviors, the parent can best attack this one in two ways, neither of them direct.

First of all, try to determine when and under what circumstances this behavior is most likely to occur. Then so far as possible, prevent the tension-arousing circumstances which cause the behavior or provide other more soothing and relaxing activities.

If the behavior is general and not localized to any special times or places, it will be necessary to try to find ways of simplifying and improving the child's life so that he will have less need of tensional outlets. Specifically what you do will of course be different for each child.

At the same time, it is possible to try to reduce the bad effects of hair pulling as well as the satisfaction which the child gets from it by providing a tight angora cap (provided that he or she will accept this; some who will not accept it in the daytime will accept wearing it at night). Such a cap allows the satisfaction of pulling at something, *i.e.* the fuzz on the cap, but protects the hair. It is less satisfying than pulling at the hair itself (though less frustrating than physical restraint of the arms). Often by the time one cap is worn out, the pulling will have come to an end.

Whining

Whining can be a tensional outlet. It may occur in any child at any age, though it reaches its peak in many at around 3½ years of age, at which time some children seem to their mothers to be whining all day long.

Many mothers threaten their whiners with, "If you don't stop that whining, I'll spank you [or send you to bed]!" And yet the best way to treat whining is actually to prevent it rather than to punish it.

No matter how much time you may be giving to your child, if he whines, he is giving you a clue that he needs more attention. Try to fill his days with activities that are more satisfactory than clinging and whining. He may need to be helped to play more creatively or for longer periods of time. Finger painting, clay play, block building, being read to—any of these might cut down on whining.

Your child may need someone to play with. Hiring an inventive sitter would cut down on the time that you yourself have to spend with him. Most children whine less for sitters than for their own mothers.

Or you may need to plan your child's day a little differently. He may require more rest or more frequent snacks, or more interesting things to fill his life. A chance to attend nursery school can, for example, often cut into whining.

You might try so-called behavior modification techniques which hold that a child will repeat and continue behavior which is rewarded, give up behavior which is ignored. A little difficult, true, to ignore somebody hanging onto you and whining; but so far as it is humanly possible, try to make such behavior unrewarding.

Or you might consider the possibility that ill-health is at the basis of this whining. At least check on the possibility.

Patience is what whiners need from those around them. Impatience is, unfortunately, what they most often attract.

Dirt Eating

Some preschoolers worry their parents considerably by their habit of eating dirt, paint, wallpaper, soap—whatever comes to hand. Though such a diet can lead to lead poisoning (if it is paint with a lead base which is consumed), it is amazing how much foreign matter of this type can be taken in by the child without any really bad effects.

However, this behavior is not to be encouraged, and most parents would like to know how to stop it. First of all, they should consider the possibility that this behavior indicates a lack of calcium in the child's diet and should check with their pediatrician to be certain that this is not the case.

Aside from this, the best approach is to give the child more supervision, and to try to provide him or her with more satisfactory and interesting activities.

It is very difficult to teach a young child (especially one of only 15 to 18 months) not to eat dirt, paint, wallpaper. If the hand-to-mouth reaction is still very strong, and if the child does not discriminate what hand puts to mouth, about the best you can do is to keep him away from these materials as much as you can, watch him as much of the time as possible, and try to keep him occupied as much as you can with permissible activities. If you try all three of these tactics, what little foreign matter does get into his mouth will hopefully do him no harm.

Tics

Definitely one of the most worrisome of all the tensional outlets are those automatic, repetitive, purposeless movements known as tics. Such movements may occur quite normally at certain ages in certain children, and they usually disappear more quickly if ignored than if attention is focused upon them.

Thus ticlike nose sniffing at 5, ticlike throat clearing around 5½ to 6, ticlike grimacing and head shaking at 6, eye-blinking at 6 to 7, general bodily writhing at 7, various facial tics and grimacing at 8 to 9—all may occur quite "normally" and briefly and may be a sign of no more than the normal tensions of the age.

Even when such behaviors are quite irritating or worrisome to parents, as a rule it is best neither to call attention to them nor to attack them directly. Usually they will be of short duration.

However, when they persist or become extremely exaggerated, it is generally wise to consult a child specialist. As a rule, *persistent* severe ticlike movements are considered to be a response to an environmental situation which is deeply disturbing to the child. They are usually considered to be signs of serious emotional strain.

In treating tics, with the aid of a specialist, first of all it is important to be sure to remove any and all possibly physical sources of irritation. Next, an attempt should be made to try to discover which parts of the child's life are causing unhappiness or concern.

Home and school conditions both will need to be carefully reviewed to find out how life can be made more satisfactory and less frustrating for the child.

Sometimes very simple changes in home or school can give the necessary relief, but in severe cases prolonged psychiatric treatment may be required. One reason why it can be useful to seek the guidance of a child specialist is that the mere fact that this particular child does respond to an adverse situation in this particular way is an indication that here is an unusually sensitive organism. One which is perhaps not too well coordinated. One which may, even after the immediate symptom is cleared up, be expected to respond to future difficult situations in a similarly extreme manner.

Stuttering

Broken fluency (repetitions and prolongations of sounds, syllables, and words) is a characteristic of normal speech development, and most young children manifest this behavior at some time or other. It comes and goes in waves during the preschool and early school years, and is more pronounced in some children than in others. We have found that such repetitive speech is most marked at the ages of 2½, 3½, and 6 years. Normally a child goes rather quickly through these periods, and then his or her speech again becomes relatively smooth.

On the average, the child from 2 to 6 years of age, who is still in the process of speech development, repeats forty to fifty times in every one thousand words. He may *re-re-* repeat a *s—s—* sound or syllable like this, a word *like like* this, or a phrase *like this like this.* He may have inappropriate pauses and prolongations.

Speech is a complicated process, and it is not surprising that the speech of the young child is unstable and subject to nonfluency. The young child is busy mastering sound production, new vocabulary words, syntax, and all the other complexities of spoken language. Even normal adult speech is characterized by occasional breaks and repetitions.

Although stuttering can follow an emotional shock or crisis, the onset of developmental nonfluency is usually quite gradual and commonplace, and it is, in the majority of cases, first noticed in the routine situations of everyday life.

Parents are often overanxious and alarmed by this behavior and are apt to label normal nonfluency as "stuttering." However, this behavior differs from that of the chronic or adult stutterer. The young child is seldom conscious of his "difficulty" unless someone in the environment brings it to his attention. He babbles along repeating in rather an effortless fashion. The older stutterer, on the other hand, is very aware of his speech hesitations and has many more complicated symptoms.

Parents who are alarmed by this behavior often wonder if "something is the matter with his tongue," or if he is "retarded" or "neurotic." However, repetitive speech occurs so commonly in children who are normal in every respect, with excellent home situations, good coordination, etc., that we do not necessarily think of it as a sign that anything is "wrong" with the child.

However, this normal nonfluency can be aggravated by adverse handling. The child who is forever interrupted when trying to talk, the child who is penalized for repetitions, who must compete for a chance to talk, or who is harshly forced to confess to a misdeed, is certainly apt to show intensified nonfluency and a more pronounced tensional outlet through speech.

Speech therapy is not recommended for the ordinary repetitive speech of the preschool child. But there is much that the parents can do to help their child progress more easily to fluent speech. The best approach is preventive and indirect. Here are some of the important *do's* and *don'ts* to serve as guideposts for parents:

Things to do:

1. Do give him the attention he deserves when he is speaking to you.
2. Do listen with patience and understanding as he tells you about something that has happened that is important to him.

3. Do let him finish what he is saying without interrupting him, no matter how much difficulty he appears to be having.

4. Eliminate as much as possible the causes of tension and frustration in his daily routine. Remove disturbing influences that seem to aggravate his nonfluency. For example, see that he has a chance to express himself at the table without too much competition from the older children.

5. Try to maintain as calm and restful an atmosphere as possible in the household. This can be done by slowing down your own pace and by handling routines in an easy and unhurried manner.

6. Try to speak more slowly, calmly, and simply to him. If you are relaxed and unhurried, he is apt to feel more relaxed when speaking to you. Sometimes it is difficult for him to "keep up" with adult speech. If you speak in shorter, simpler sentences and at a slower tempo, it will be easier for him to achieve fluency.

7. See that he does not have too much stimulation and is not overtired.

8. Do all that you can to keep him in good physical condition.

9. Try to keep the demands made on him in regard to his training within his capacity to understand and carry them out.

Things to avoid:

1. Don't refer to his nonfluency as "stuttering." Once it is called stuttering (or by any other name) in front of him, he may begin to react to the label and become self-conscious of his speech, and his difficulty may increase.

2. Never discuss in his presence the "trouble" he is having with his speech.

3. Try to avoid becoming anxious about his speech. It will be easier for you to relax in your own attitude if you remember that most children do go through perfectly normal developmental nonfluency and most come through it with normally

smooth speech. Anxiety can be transmitted to the child by the attitudes of those around him.

4. When he speaks to you, do not show in any way (by facial expression, impatience, etc.) that you notice his difficulty in speaking.

5. Do not ask the child to "Speak more slowly," "Stop and start over," "Take a breath," or "Think before you speak"—even if such suggestions seem to bring temporary relief. Such demands usually serve only to increase the child's difficulty.

6. Do not reward him for fluent periods or punish him for difficult periods of repetitive speech.

7. Never force him into upsetting verbal situations (such as reciting for company, apologizing, confessions, etc.).

Many of the above suggestions are aimed at preventing the child from becoming aware of his repetitive speech. This is our ideal, but it doesn't always work out that way. Perhaps a playmate or another adult might bring it to his attention. Should this happen, the wise parent will respond by reassuring his child. You might tell him that "everybody gets tangled up in speaking once in a while if they are excited or talking very fast."

If the child's stuttering persists and you do not feel that he is having longer periods of fluency, and especially if you feel that you do not fully understand his stuttering or feel capable of handling it, you should consult a speech specialist or speech clinic.

Masturbation

There are perhaps three main points of view about masturbation in babies and children. The position to the most extreme right is that this behavior is not only wicked but harmful, and that the child who masturbates should be punished and forcibly prevented from further indulgence in this activity. (However, it has been shown that masturbation causes no physical harm, and few people now hold the view that it is a sign of depravity in the young child.)

A second attitude is more middle of the road. It considers masturbation to be a common (though by no means universal) and relatively harmless activity—something in the same class with thumb sucking but a little less desirable. People in this group, in fact, deal with masturbation more or less as they do with thumb sucking. They do not attack the behavior directly, but rather attempt to improve the child's life in general ways so that he or she will be well adjusted and happier, or more interestingly occupied, and will feel less need of tensional release. They particularly try to note at what times and under what circumstances the behavior occurs. They then try as far as they can either to prevent the circumstances or to provide other outlets at times when the behavior is most likely to occur.

In addition, some parents are helped if they realize that masturbation, like thumb sucking, follows a definite course in many children. Thus they do not make too many (even indirect) attempts to prevent it when it is at its height.

Often parents find that their own attitude toward the problem relaxes if they can ask themselves not, "How can I stop him?" but rather, "Why does he [she] do it?" Sometimes the "why" becomes quite apparent, and you can then prevent the circumstance or situation which brings it on. In other cases, you can't find out the exact "why," but at least your attitude may be softened by the search.

A third and more recent point of view is that masturbation not only does no harm, but that excessive efforts on the part of parents to stop or prevent it actually may in themselves be harmful. We should like to quote Dr. Fritz Redlich on this subject. In his book *The Inside Story,* he gives the following possible arguments for ignoring this activity when it does occur:

> First, there is no danger that our child will suffer physical harm from a limited amount of masturbation. The old wives' tales about its causing blindness, insanity, bad complexion, and what not have been scientifically disproved. Secondly, there is some danger that an emotionally charged parental forbidding of the child's touching himself may result

in such repression of the child's sexual urge that when grown up he may not be able to function normally in this respect. Thirdly, there is comparable danger that the child may develop terrible self-loathing and lack of confidence when he finds he cannot (when half-asleep) completely keep himself from doing what he has been so forcefully told is unnatural and vile. Fourthly, we may be sure that even though we never say a word about it our child will pick up the idea that this is an activity about which people he admires are not exactly enthusiastic. Fifthly, if we have never frightened our child about masturbation he may feel free to tell us when and if little school friends make physical advances (which little school friends sometimes do), thus enabling us to protect him by insisting on supervision when the children visit each other's houses, or even by cutting out the visits for a while.

The last argument—perhaps most controversial of all—is that through allowing our child to keep a few deep dark secrets from us we may be reinforcing his grasp on reality and diminishing his unconscious tendency to believe in symbols and magic and other forms of unreality. That is, it may lessen his feeling that we are omniscient, if we seemingly are not aware of everything that he does. (Particularly since we are not sure of the wisdom of what we would say if we did say anything, and also since the child is likely to outgrow the behavior of his own accord.)

Of these three attitudes we cannot say which one you will choose, but we hope that it will not be the first.

III Health

Colds! Earaches! Sore throats! Stomachaches! These may not seem to fall exactly under the heading of tensional outlets. Yet it is true that many children when overtired and overtense do respond with physical illness.

Many children seem to have one special kind of illness with which they respond to any overdifficult situation. They *always* get a cold, or are sick to their stomachs, or become constipated.

In addition to these special individual ways of responding, there are also certain ages when children are likely to have certain sicknesses. Of course no disease is unique to any one age. And even when a sickness can be determined as being characteristic of a certain age, you still have to do something about it.

However, many parents worry less when they recognize a certain illness as one which is especially characteristic of a certain age period.

Here are a few of the sicknesses which in the early years seem to have an age tie-up. (You will of course consult your pediatrician when any serious illness occurs, but your anxiety may be lessened by this information.)

18 months: Convulsions may accompany illnesses, especially those with high temperature.

21 months: Elimination difficulties; frequency of both functions; diarrhea common.

2½ years: Elimination difficulties. Long retention span; constipation more common in girls.
Frequent colds with ear complications, especially in slow-speech children.
Gets a bloody nose if falls.

3 years: Expresses marked fatigue.

4 years: May have one cold right after another all winter.
Stomachache in social situations.
Needs to urinate in difficult situations or at mealtimes.
May have "accidents" in emotional situations.
May knock out front teeth if falls.

5 years: Good or even excellent health characteristic. May have only one or two colds all winter.
Some increase in whooping cough, measles, chicken pox.
Occasional stomachaches or vomiting in relation to disliked foods or just prior to elimination.
Constipation in girls.

5½ years: Complains that feet "hurt."
Some have frequent colds. Headaches or earaches.

Stomachaches with some nausea and vomiting connected with school or other demands.

Somatic symptoms may appear after a week or two of school.

Whooping cough, measles, chicken pox the most common communicable diseases.

Hypersensitivity of face, head, neck region to washing, hair combing, etc.

Child may endure large pains yet fuss about a splinter or nose drops.

6 years: More susceptible to diseases and sicker with illness than earlier.

Frequent sore throats, colds, with complications (lung and ear); increase in allergies.

Chicken pox, measles, whooping cough. Diphtheria and scarlet fever, German measles and mumps.

Stomachaches and vomiting in connection with going to school.

Toilet "accidents" with overexcitement.

May break arm if falls.

Hypersensitivity of face, neck region if washed or touched.

Increased redness of genitals in girls.

7 years: Fewer illnesses than at 6, but colds of longer duration.

German measles and mumps frequent. Chicken pox and measles may occur.

Complain of headaches with fatigue or excitement; complain of muscular pain, especially of legs or knees.

Minor accidents to eyes, but fewer gross accidents; eye rubbing.

Extreme fatigue—yawning, stretching.

8 years: Improving health. Fewer illnesses and of shorter duration. Less absence from school because of illness.

Increase in allergies.

Headaches, stomachaches, and need to urinate in connection with disagreeable tasks.

Accidents frequent: falls, drowning, and in relation to automobiles and bicycles.

May break leg if falls.

9 years: Improving health and few illnesses, but marked individual differences.

Some have a prolonged illness or show marked fatigue.

Many minor complaints related to the task at hand (eyes hurt when tested, hands hurt when writing). Or may say, "It makes me feel dizzy."

10 years: Health much better in most. Many report, retrospectively, that there was a period of bad health around 6 with earaches, sore throats, contagious diseases.

A few worry about their own health.

Car Sickness

Car sickness! When the writers were young, this was the name of a dread malady which attacked young children on street cars— usually when they and their families were dressed in their Sunday best and out for an excursion.

Nowadays it more often strikes the victim when out in the family automobile. It is probably most common in the first 6 years of life, though in some it persists till adulthood.

This problem can loom large indeed. In fact, it can not only cause much discomfort to the child who suffers from it, but if severe, may even seriously interfere with the social life and vacation and visiting habits of the whole family.

The scientific literature on this subject is extremely scant. And in many cases not only is an effective remedy not found, but even the cause is difficult to determine.

Some years ago the analysts introduced a theory that car sickness resulted from antagonism to or hatred of the sufferer's mother. We ourselves do not subscribe to this theory, though it may be true of some isolated cases.

It has been our observation that more often than not a visual factor seems to lie at the basis of car sickness. Children with too peripheral vision (that is, those who are overresponsive to things in the distance or in the margins of the field of vision) frequently have this difficulty. If you can get them to lie down in the back seat of the car or even to lean against your shoulder with their eyes closed as you sing the time away, frequently their symptoms are relieved. Or you may interest them in some activity on the floor of the car. Or sometimes dark glasses with fairly wide rims will cut down the too strong dose of visual stimulation which they are getting.

Especially avoid having such children use their eyes to read or even to look at road maps while the car is in motion. Sometimes a correct prescription of glasses may do the trick. Or your eye doctor may, in extreme cases, suggest the wearing of a patch over one eye.

In any event, if your child does suffer from car sickness, a thorough visual checkup from a skilled children's eye doctor may help out. And in the meantime, you may find that some specific medicine for motion sickness—given of course at your pediatrician's prescription—may turn out to be all that is needed.

8 Fears

Different Fears at Different Ages

The children frightened Davey on Halloween night and he's been jumpy ever since. A baby-sitter threatened Joe with the "bogey-man" and he's suddenly refused to sleep without his light on. An unfamiliar dog bit Betsey, and now she's afraid of dogs.

Into any child's life can come frightening and unhappy incidents which set up special fears, and you as parents naturally do your best to protect your children from such specially frightening incidents.

But you cannot protect them from all fears. As children grow up, they seem to need to go through a series of fears which come in and then later drop out. Each child differs somewhat, but, in general, each age brings its own characteristic fears. A much abbreviated summary of some of the most common fears which are likely to develop in almost any child, from age to age, is as follows:

> *2 years:* Many fears, chiefly auditory: trains, trucks, thunder, flushing of toilet, vacuum cleaner.
> Visual fears: dark colors, large objects, trains, hats.
> Spatial: toy or crib moved from usual place, moving to a new house, fear of going down the drain.
> Personal: Mother's departure, or separation from her at bedtime. Rain and wind.
> Animals—especially wild animals.
>
> *2 ½ years:* Many fears, especially spatial: fear of movement or of having objects moved.

Any different orientation, as someone entering house
  by a different door.
Large objects—as trucks—approaching.

3 years: Visual fears predominate: old or wrinkled people,
  masks, "bogeymen."
The dark.
Animals.
Policemen, burglars.
Mother or Father going out at night.

4 years: Auditory fears again, especially fire engines.
The dark.
Wild animals.
Mother leaving, especially going out at night.

5 years: Not a fearful age. More visual fears than others.
Less fear of animals, bad people, bogeymen.
Concrete, down-to-earth fears: bodily harm, falling,
  dogs.
The dark.
That Mother will not return home.

6 years: Very fearful. Especially auditory fears: doorbell, tele-
  phone, static, ugly voice tones, flushing of toilet, in-
  sect and bird noises.
Fear of the supernatural: ghosts, witches.
Fear that someone is hiding under the bed.
Spatial: fear of being lost, fear of the woods.
Fear of the elements: fire, water, thunder, lightning.
Fear of sleeping alone in a room or of being the only
  one on a floor of the house.
Fear that Mother will not be home when child arrives
  home, or that something will happen to her or that
  she may die.
Afraid of being hit by others.
Brave about big hurts but fears splinters, little cuts,
  blood, nose drops.

7 years: Many fears, especially visual: the dark, attics, cellars. Interprets shadows as ghosts and witches.

Fears war, spies, burglars, people hiding in closet or under bed.

Fears now stimulated by reading, radio, cinema.

Worries about things: not being liked, being late to school.

8 to 9 years: Fewer fears and less worrying. No longer fears the water; less fear of the dark. Good evaluation, and fears are reasonable: about personal inability and failure, especially school failure.

10 years: Many fears, though fewer than in the ages which immediately follow. Animals, especially snakes and wild animals, are the things most feared. The dark is feared by a few. Also high places, fires and criminals, or "killers" or burglars.

A few are beginning spontaneously to mention things they are *not* afraid of: chiefly the dark, dogs, and being left alone.

Our studies of thousands of normal children have shown us that as any child matures, he or she is likely from time to time to exhibit fears of things which often seem quite harmless to parents. However—and this should be most reassuring to parents—these fears do not appear completely at random, nor are they different for every child.

On the contrary, we find that they appear, and soon disappear, in an ordered, patterned fashion which often shows great similarity from child to child. For example, as the preceding list suggests, 2-year-olds frequently fear any sudden loud sounds, like vacuum cleaners or locomotives. Two-and-a-half-year-olds are more likely to have spatial fears, or fears of moving objects. Threes most often fear things seen.

Each age brings its characteristic fears.

Withdrawal from Feared Stimuli Is Natural Response

In a large downtown department store a determined-looking mother pushed her crying 3-year-old into one of the waiting elevators.

"It's very embarrassing," she explained to another passenger. "But you see my little boy is terribly afraid of elevators and I know that the only way to get him over this fear is to make him ride on them until he gets used to them."

Actually, it is not the only way. It is not even a very good way in most cases. It is astonishing, and unfortunate, that this mother's notion is so widely prevalent.

Celia is afraid of heights. Take her up the highest hill! Joe is deathly afraid of cows. Take him out to the pasture! Even worse —Dave is afraid of water. Throw him in!

Too many parents for too many years have followed this unfeeling policy because, for some reason or other, they believe it is "the way" to cure fears in the child.

We do not say that it never works. In our years of clinical practice we have known the most unusual ways of dealing with children to work, on occasion. Child behavior tends as the child matures to proceed toward an optimum regardless of parental handling. But good handling certainly helps, and for the more sensitive souls it is essential.

The best handling of a child's fears is based on the realization that fear is not altogether a bad thing. In primitive or natural societies, the person or organism fears that which may harm him and withdraws from it as rapidly as possible. Often he thereby saves his life.

It is not so different with us. The child withdraws from those things which are or seem dangerous or harmful. This period of withdrawal may be long or short, depending on the child and the situation. But, unless you have strong reasons to act to the contrary, *you should respect* the child's natural tendency to withdraw from the thing that is feared.

In some situations this withdrawal may be short—only momentary. In others it may last for weeks or months. As a rule, even without your help, the child will get over his fear. As he grows older, things look different to him. He understands more about them. They seem less threatening.

If he does not spontaneously get over his fear in what seems like a reasonable length of time, you can help him gradually to overcome it. If he is afraid of large, fierce dogs, let him play with a puppy of his own. If he fears the ocean with its noisy surf, give him a chance to bathe in a small, warm pool or lake.

But don't try to do the whole thing at once. Don't be too impatient if he doesn't get over his fears as quickly as you think he should. Most important, don't use shock methods! Don't force him to face the thing he fears.

Above all—respect all fears. As a rule they drop out much more quickly if they are treated with respect. In fact, in the ordinarily stable child most fears are relatively short-lived. Not only short-lived, but often they are followed by a brief period in which the child may seem almost compulsively attracted to the thing or situation which he or she has formerly feared.

Overwithdrawal, then Overapproach

"Most contrary child I ever heard of," complained Jake's father to Jake's mother.

"Why, what do you mean, dear?" replied Mother. "I think he's a pretty good little boy. I know you're disturbed about his setting that fire in the backyard. But he didn't realize it would spread over to your tool house."

"That's just it. This business of setting fires. Six months ago he was so terrified of fire that he wouldn't even go near the fireplace, and now he goes around setting fires every time he can lay his hands on a match. That's just what I'm trying to point out—it doesn't make sense. He's just contrary."

Contrary he may be—but if this is contrariness, make the most of it, because Jake's actions are perfectly "normal" according to what we know of human behavior. We can learn a lot from analyzing these actions.

To begin with, when Jake was about 6 years old he had a spell of being afraid of fire, a not unusual fear at this age. And, as most people do, he just naturally withdrew when he could from the thing he feared. This did not alarm his family unduly.

But now, six months later, he not only no longer fears fire, but he seems to be almost compulsively attracted to it. He just loves fire and can never seem to get enough of it. So much so that if there are no fires at hand, he will often set one, sometimes with disastrous results.

This is within a predictable response for this child at around the age of 6. In the natural course of events a child will first withdraw too far from, and then later approach too closely, some feared object. Finally, in a third stage, he settles down to a more adaptive state. He is then in control of his fear. He can take the thing or leave it. With fire, for instance, he does not fear it unduly, nor is he unduly attracted to it. He will be in control of his reaction. If we were more understanding of this mechanism, we might even be able to help those who compulsively light fires.

Knowledge of these facts may help you to work out successfully your own handling of your child's fears. You will see that if a child's first reaction to a feared object is withdrawal, if you force him to face the thing before he is ready you are going directly against his natural tendencies. Withdrawal from a feared object is natural and should be permitted.

The natural period of withdrawal may be long or short, depending on the personality of the child and on how frightened he or she is. If the withdrawal period is short, the time of the child's approaching too closely will also be short. If it is long, the time of too closely approaching may also be long.

In general, you will do best if you permit the period of withdrawal without scolding, shaming, or forcing. Sometimes it is wisest to be on the sidelines, not making the child more aware of his fear, but protecting him from experiencing it before he is ready. At other times and with other children it may be wisest to discuss the fear. Tell him that there will be this period of withdrawal and that he can count on your protecting him during the period. This can relieve the tension so that he may be able to resolve his fear more quickly than if he were trying to resolve it alone. And then, when the child comes to the period of overapproach, find calm ways of dealing with this, too. Each situation, of course, varies in detail and has its own individual solution.

However, there are a few generally applicable *do's* and *don'ts* (though remember always that each child is an individual and that each case has its own special aspects which make any generalized advice of only limited value).*

What not to do when your child is afraid:

Don't ever make fun of his fears.

Don't shame him before others because of them.

Don't force him to "face" the thing he fears before he is ready unless you are very sure you are right to do so. (And you seldom will be.)

Don't become impatient and treat him as if he were babyish because he is afraid.

Don't assume that it is necessarily your fault, or his fault, that he is afraid.

Don't necessarily feel that it is bad or unnatural for the child to have some fears.

What to do when your child is afraid:

Respect his fears.

Realize that he will outgrow most of them.

---

*Books can't solve all problems, but they can surely help. One which we recommend for any fearful boy or girl is called *It's Scary Sometimes,* by "I and the Others" Writers' Collective, published by Human Sciences Press.

Allow him at least a reasonable period of withdrawal from feared things before attempting to help him adjust to them.

Give him a chance to become gradually used to fearful situations, a little at a time. If he fears great heights, accustom him first to small elevations; if he is afraid of dogs, let him first get acquainted with a puppy. (This gradual approach does not, however, work with all children. Some children need to take the plunge and get it over with.)

When and if he comes to the period of compulsively overapproaching a formerly feared object or situation—his natural method of tackling his fears—help him to have the experience he desires, but under your supervision. If he has first been afraid of fires, he may later have a strong desire to set fires and to play with fire. Let him light the fire in the fireplace or the candles for the table. Or let him help burn the trash, or help with a bonfire, of course under your most careful supervision.

Analyze his fears in relation to his personality. Does he characteristically fear strange sounds or sights? Does he fear movement? Try within reason to spare him situations which you know will cause fear.

Familiarize yourself with the kinds of fears which children naturally experience at different ages. You can take more lightly a fear which is common to the majority of children at some one age. It will usually not last long.

If your child seems to fear some large, general situation which he must nevertheless experience, as school, analyze the situation to find out what specific aspect of it has caused the fear.

But if your child's fear is excessive and troublesome and you cannot find out the cause, and time does not take care of it, you may wish to seek specialized help to solve the problem.

Fear of the Dark

One of the most common and most persistent of all the child's fears is fear of the dark. Starting in many at around 2½, it goes on in some, in one form or another, even up into the late teens. (Before 1 year of age many children seem completely fearless so far as the dark is concerned, though the 10–11-month-old child may shy away from a darkening room at twilight as he or she creeps about, or hurry past an open closet door where it is dark inside, making for the nearest window.) At around 2 years of age many can move about their own room in the dark with great deftness, especially if they are supposed to be in bed, as though their eyes were adapted to darkness and they could see in the dark.

Ways of dealing with this very common fear have been suggested on page 100, in our general discussion of fears related to sleeping. *Who's Afraid of the Dark?* by Crosby Bonsall (Harper & Row) may help the 4–8-year-old conquer usual fears of darkness.

Fear of Dogs

Some children never show any fear of dogs. For the majority of those who do exhibit this fear, it is fairly temporary.

Fear of dogs, when it is expressed, should like other fears be respected. It can usually best be overcome by allowing the child as much experience with dogs as he or she can accept.

Thus, small dogs or puppies can often be tolerated when large dogs cannot. Or dogs in the distance can be accepted even though the child does not like to have them too close at first. Or the child himself can approach a dog when he is still afraid of one which approaches him. He may be able to pat a dog which his parents are holding. Or better still, if he himself is safely held by his parents, he may then be less fearful.

Some have to start out even more remotely—with a toy dog, or with stories or books about dogs. Some can accept a small kitten at a time when they are still afraid of puppies.

With many, having a small dog or puppy of their own, planned for in advance, is the best way to overcome fear of dogs. However, even after the dog has been introduced into the family circle, the young child should not be forced to approach it till he is fully ready.

Even children who are not excessively afraid of dogs may quite normally show some fear of them as late as 6 or 7 years of age. And even some 10-year-olds will tell you spontaneously and proudly that they are *no longer* afraid of dogs.

Fear of the Water

The most common and earliest fear of the water appears in relation to being bathed. This may occur at any age but is most frequent from around 18 to 24 months of age. The child suddenly refuses to bathe and screams every time he or she is approached with a washcloth.

As a rule, when this kind of objection first comes in, it is best to respect it. The more times you force a bath on a resisting, screaming child, the stronger may become resistance to it.

Simply discontinue the routine bathing situation to which your child is objecting, for a few days. Put him on the set tub in the kitchen, or beside the bowl in the bathroom, and, until the period of resistance seems to be over, merely give sponge baths. Always approach with the washcloth from behind and not from the front. Reduce even this necessary sponging to a minimum.

With most, some such simple tactics are all that you will need. With extreme resisters, someone other than Mother may have to take over the bathing situation for a while. Some will accept bathing from an outsider better than from Mother. Perhaps they recognize the fact that an outsider is not quite so soft-hearted and vulnerable to their objections, or at least they haven't set up the same patterns of response as with the mother. Some will accept the idea of sharing Father's bath, especially if they are held in his lap or on his knee as they are being bathed.

Fear of the water at the beach or lake is a different problem, less difficult, in a way, because for most children it is not absolutely essential that they get into the water.

The old-fashioned notions of "throw him in and he'll get over his fear," or "shame him into it" are no longer much in vogue. As a rule we find that it works best with most to give a little encouragement—by word or example—but for the most part to avoid any real pressure. And know that interest in swimming and a real desire to tackle and overcome any fear of the water comes for many at 7 years of age.

In the meantime, let the child play on the shore till he himself feels the wish and confidence to get into the water.

This problem, if not exaggerated by adult mishandling, is in all but the most timid children a fairly temporary one. We know of one family who even went so far as to pay for their son's swimming lessons at a local pool with the understanding that he could watch and not swim for as long as he wanted. After seven lessons of just watching, this boy got into the pool and soon swam as well as, or better than, the other pupils.

Fear of the Dentist

Most children, unless their temperament is extremely sturdy and their experience fortunate, have at least some slight fear of having dental work done.

In many, this is a minor and reasonable fear (or dislike) of a potentially painful, or at least uncomfortable, experience. It presents no practical problem since these children can control their fear enough to go to the dentist and allow the necessary work to be done.

Others do express some resistance, but this can usually be overcome in simple, commonsense ways. With many children it is enough if parents simply take a firm stand—the work has to be done.

With others, a little preplanning, the offer of simple but meaningful rewards, sometimes having Father rather than Mother accompany the child to the dentist's office, will be sufficient to overcome resistance.

With still others, a preliminary (and paid for) get-acquainted visit to the dentist's office will do the trick. The child is promised that no actual dental work will be done on this occasion, but that he or she will have an opportunity to find out just what is going to happen.

Some children, however, in spite of any technique the parent may use, still violently resist the idea of having any dental work done. In times past, parents nevertheless insisted and dentists often used force. We have even heard of a dentist who had a policeman bring reluctant patients to his office.

Most dentists today take a very different attitude. As one young dentist commented: "You should never force a child, against his will, to have dental work done. Actually it should seldom be necessary if you let them see that you like them. If you don't like them, you can't expect them to like you. And it's important that they do like you—because it makes the whole experience easier for them."

However, he had found that in spite of reasonable preplanning, promise of reward, and efforts on the part of the dentist (by use of novocaine and such) to make the treatment reasonably painless, some children still resisted. In these cases he believed that some postponement of treatment was usually indicated, since he had found that a child who was bitterly and obstructively resistant in October might by January be more receptive.

There are a few cases where necessary dental work simply cannot be put off and when all reasonable commonsense efforts at overcoming the child's fears and resistance do not seem to be effective. Even in such cases the majority of modern dentists do not favor the use of force. Instead, many nowadays believe that the best method is to resort to the use of extensive anesthetic. Some dentists' offices are set up for this procedure. In other cases, the child can be admitted to the hospital for overnight, and the work done there.

Only in a minority of cases would one need to go so far. But most of today's dentists seem to agree that even this rather extreme procedure is preferable to using physical force to overcome a child's fear and resistance.

Fear of Hospitalization

The problem of how to prepare a child for necessary hospitalization in such a way as to avoid arousing unnecessary fears is a problem for which there is no one "correct" solution.

Children vary tremendously in the way in which they accept hospitalization—depending partly on the length of the stay, the severity of the illness, their own familiarity or unfamiliarity with hospitals. More, however, probably depends on the child's own temperament and the skill with which parents have prepared him or her for the experience than on these other factors.

The child's own basic temperament—the ease with which he separates from his parents and accepts new and unfamiliar surroundings and experiences—is probably the thing which makes the most difference in how he will adapt to hospitalization. This is something that you cannot do much about.

But you can, taking his temperament into consideration, do your best to prepare him as adequately as possible for the experience.

Whether you plan with the child a long time in advance or a short time, whether you plan in detail or superficially, depends on your knowledge of his personality. Some do better with a great deal of advance preparation. Others become too apprehensive and do best if things are more or less "sprung" on them.

In any advance planning, you can talk to the child about what a hospital experience is like. You can let him play doctor or nurse with the very adequate toy doctor and nurse kits now available for children. Some parents go so far as to have the child visit the hospital in advance of the operation.

Best of all, perhaps, there are now available numerous books which tell of children's experiences in hospitals. Among the best are *Curious George Goes to the Hospital* by Margaret H. Rey in collaboration with Children's Hospital Medical Center (Boston: Houghton Mifflin) and *Going to the Hospital* by Bettina Clark and

Lester Coleman (New York: Random House).

Actually, in most instances it is the unfamiliar aspect of the hospital rather than any specific thing that happens there which some children find so hard to accept. Thus anything done in advance which familiarizes children with what is going to happen to them there can be helpful.

Aside from this, the main thing to keep in mind is that you should always tell your child the truth, in this as in other situations. Don't promise that it won't hurt. It may. Don't promise that you won't leave him. You will probably have to. Don't promise that he will have a wonderful time. He may not.

Plan in advance for some nice thing which will happen after the child gets home from the hospital. This will give him something to look forward to.

And it will not be all up to you. Hospitals themselves are becoming increasingly aware that it is not only the child's physical welfare which is important during a hospital stay. They will therefore be more than cooperative in trying to make your child's hospital experience an agreeable one. A good many hospitals now provide a place for parents to stay with the child, either in his room or in an adjoining room.

9 Intelligence—Defect— Deviation

Intelligence and Maturity Level

In spite of the many and all too prevalent books which tell you *How To Raise Your Child's I.Q., How To Give Your Child a Superior Mind, How To Teach Your Baby To Read,* and (most recent and most ridiculous of all) *How To Teach Your Baby Math,* there is actually not too much you need to do along these lines in the early years.

Your baby does not need to read even if he or she could, and most certainly it is not necessary to learn math in the first years of life. Nor is there much that a parent can do to make a baby more intelligent than Nature intended.

That is, you can't, so far as we know, actually either speed up behavior growth or increase intelligence. But you can and very likely will do your best to play with your young child, talk with him, read to him, answer his many questions. We strongly recommend that you do not push your preschooler. But we would encourage you to spend as much time as practical with him and to provide an enriched environment.

When parents want to know, as many do, how "smart" their boy or girl is, they are, perhaps without knowing it, talking about two separate things. "Smartness"—at least as we think of it—includes both the child's total maturity level and his specific intelligence (I.Q.) as such.

These two things may or may not go hand in hand. A child who is ahead of himself in general ways—walking early, talking early

—may also be highly superior in intelligence. But he *could* be merely average (though probably not below average).

Conversely, a child who is highly superior intellectually might well be above average in maturity level. But he could be merely of average maturity or even below average. (In fact we have one special term which expresses one aspect of this possible discrepancy—*superior immature*. This describes the child who is very bright academically but slower than average in general development.)

However, certainly in the first year or two of life, there does tend to be a good correspondence between these two measures. The likelihood is that if a 1-year-old infant has reached a 1-year-old level of maturity, that child is of at least normal intelligence as well.

Maturity Level

Here are a few clues as to the ages when we have found that some of the common behaviors occur in the early years of life. These are, however, only clues. If you are worried about your child and really feel that he or she needs a developmental examination, you should of course have it done by a specialist.

16 weeks: Spontaneous social smile.
Laughs aloud.
Anticipates on sight of food.
Can sit propped ten to fifteen minutes.

28 weeks: Sits briefly, leaning forward on hands.
Held standing, takes large fraction of weight and bounces actively.
Grasps objects placed before him.
Transfers objects from one hand to the other.
Many vowel sounds.
Takes solids well.
Feet to mouth when lying on back.
Pats mirror image.

40 weeks: Creeps on hands and knees; cruises along, holding onto furniture.

Pokes at small objects with extended forefinger.

May be able to vocalize "mama," "dada," and one other "word."

12 months: Can walk with one hand held.

Has two words besides "mama" and "dada."

Cooperates a little when being dressed.

Plays peek-a-boo.

15 months: Walks at least a few steps alone.

Can creep upstairs.

Helps turn pages of a book. Pats pages.

Has four to six words and uses jargon.

May inhibit grasp of dish on tray.

Says "ta-ta" or equivalent.

Shows or offers toy to Mother, but wants it back again.

18 months: Walks well, seldom falls.

Can walk upstairs, one hand held.

Can seat self in a small chair or climb into adult chair.

Has ten words, including names.

Looks at pictures in a book.

Feeds self in part, spilling.

Pulls a pull-toy as walks backwards.

24 months: Walks up and down stairs alone.

Turns pages of a book singly.

Speaks in three-word sentences.

Inhibits turning of spoon when feeding self.

May verbalize toilet needs, in daytime, fairly consistently. (May be dry in daytime by 2½ years.)

Refers to self by name.

36 months: Alternates feet going upstairs.

Can ride a tricycle using pedals.

Uses plurals in speech.

Feeds self with little spilling and pours from a pitcher.
Can put on own shoes.
Knows a few rhymes.

48 months: Can imitate drawing of a square.
Can count, with correct pointing, four objects.
Can skip on one foot.
Can wash and dry face and hands, brush teeth.
Can draw a person with head, arms, and legs.
Dresses and undresses if supervised.
Laces shoes.
Plays cooperatively with other children.
Can go on errand outside home (without crossing streets).

60 months: Skips using feet alternately.
Can count ten objects correctly.
Can tell how many fingers on each hand.
Can name a penny, nickel, dime.
Can name colors correctly.
Dresses and undresses without assistance.
Can print first name.
Can write numbers 1–5.

Since individual differences in the rate of growth are quite normally tremendous, even fairly marked deviations from such standards should not necessarily be cause for alarm (or for undue rejoicing). Many perfectly normal children are late walkers or late talkers, or are late in staying dry all night, or in learning to read or write. Furthermore, the fact that all of these standards are only averages means that in the first year of life a variation even of several months from the average—at 4 or 5 years of age a variation of even a year—can be quite within normal limits.

Particularly we would like to say a word of warning about "late talkers." In this field, even more than in the field of motor behavior, individual differences are very great. Some children are already speaking in short sentences by 18 months of age.

Others, especially boys, are saying very little at 2½ years or even later.

If your child seems to understand clearly what is said to him or her, and if in other behaviors seems to be about up to other children of the same age, lack of spoken language should not be of too much concern to you before 3 or 4 years of age. After that age, you will probably be wise, if talking has not come in, to check with a child specialist.

In measuring child behavior we usually think of four fields of activity. These are: motor behavior (how the child uses his body); adaptive behavior (how he solves problems); language behavior (how he understands and uses words); and personal-social behavior (how he manages the tasks of everyday living and of getting on with others).

The fact that there are four fields of behavior to be considered will suggest to you, as is the case, that the human organism does not, as a rule, develop all of a piece. Most children are not uniformly advanced (or retarded) in all these fields.

Most are good in some things, less good in others. Thus one child may be above average in language and personal-social behavior, below average in motor and adaptive. So long as in most things he is around average or above, actually it is his pattern of strong points and weaknesses which should perhaps interest you more than just exactly where he rates on any given test.

"But What's My Child's I.Q.?"

Everyone has inevitably heard a great deal about the intelligence quotient. You know that in general it is a figure (100 for average I.Q., above 100 for above average, and below 100 for below average) which is supposed to indicate a person's basic intellectual endowment. You get it by dividing the child's "intellectual age" by his or her "chronological age."

Mostly intelligence tests deal with words—how you define them, how you compare them, how you understand them. Problems of fact and of arithmetic are included in most tests. Wooden puzzles and other performance tests of ability are included in some. Some tests give separate scores for each special kind of ability—verbal, numerical, perceptual, etc.—and all give an over-all total score which averages the child's abilities.

Though nowadays there is much objection to I.Q. tests on the grounds that they are not fair to the underprivileged (some cities have actually banned their use entirely), they can be of great value. They do give a good measure of at least a certain aspect of intelligence. They provide a reasonably good picture of how well a child may be expected to perform academically. In cases where the basic intelligence is low, it is important to know this fact when making our academic plans and determining expectations.

The intelligence quotient is a useful measure for sorting out groups of children and for gearing tasks set to the child's ability to perform.

As we have suggested, the child does not develop all of a piece. He or she may have a high I.Q. and still be very poor in social behavior, in motor skills and athletics, or in everyday practical living. A child may also have a high I.Q. but be extremely imma-ture. Thus, though we should not overlook the I.Q. as a very important measure of one kind of ability, we must always remem-ber that a high I.Q. alone does not guarantee all-round excellence of performance.

Defect and Deviation

It may be cold comfort to the parents of an already handicapped child, but it is a nevertheless encouraging fact that Society has, in the past few decades, made vast strides both in preventing defect and deviation and in helping the child who was born handicapped.

Mothers-to-be are increasingly aware of the importance of a proper diet during pregnancy. Pediatricians nowadays lay less stress on how much the pregnant woman eats and more stress on the quality of her diet. It is generally accepted that a pregnant woman should avoid alcohol, tobacco, and drugs, as well as foods and other substances to which she as an individual may be allergic.

And if any sort of abnormality is suspected in the fetus, the art of amniocentesis makes it possible to detect whether it does exist. Thus if need be, an unhealthy pregnancy can be terminated.

Once born, a baby today has an increasingly good chance of being breast-fed. Gone are the days when Dr. Spock and others assured the parent that "breast and bottle are equally good; it's up to you." Today it is generally accepted that breast-feeding not only gives the baby better nourishment and is more easily accepted, but also that breast milk provides immunities not found in cow's milk.

Thus an increasing number of infants are off to a good start. And in those instances where in spite of precautions a child is born with any kind of handicap either of body or behavior, more help is available than in days past.

Also many communities now, through their schools, provide a searching service which aims to identify boys and girls who for any reason whatever may be in difficulty. Such communities provide *preschool* facilities for these children in a nursery-school type of setting which helps the children with whatever problems they may exhibit, and also helps parents to understand and work with their children.

The theory behind these schools is that many preschoolers who might later on (for any reason whatever) exhibit learning disabilities may be able to avoid such difficulties if their problems are faced and dealt with early. This theory may be a bit overambitious, but certainly any care and attention a handicapped child may receive in the early years is all to the good.

Once a handicapped girl or boy has reached school age, even more widespread, in fact wholesale, help is available. It used to seem to us that Society did much too little to help its handicapped children and their parents. Now we have swung to perhaps the opposite extreme.

Public Law 94-142 requires that every community arrange to educate all children, regardless of the nature of their handicap, in the "least restrictive environment" possible. If the community cannot do this, it is responsible for providing such a situation for the child, at its expense, outside the community.

The cost of carrying out this requirement is often rather large. Many thousands of dollars a year are sometimes spent on one individual child.

And just what constitutes "the least restrictive environment" is often in question. Currently many educators, who seemingly believe that everybody would be or could be pretty much the same if everyone were treated alike, are pushing a policy called *mainstreaming*. This policy to a large extent does away with special classes for children with special problems and bunches everybody together in so-called regular classes.

Fortunately, those valuable special classes which teachers and parents together fought so hard to establish a few decades ago have not entirely vanished from the scene. And many administrators and educational planners are holding hard to the line that for the child with problems the least restrictive environment may indeed be the special class.

We strongly urge parents whose child's I.Q. is 80 or less to do their very best to locate one of those classes set up for just such children. This rather than permit their child to be mainstreamed into a situation where he or she will all too likely falter, fumble, and fail. And for parents with children having other kinds of problems we recommend that, if allowed to do so, you choose very carefully between mainstreaming and the special help that a special class can give a special child.

In addition to the help provided by the schools, all kinds of support groups made up of parents of children with special problems—hyperactivity, autism, retardation, emotional disturbance, as well as the various serious physical handicaps—are now available in many communities.

Some physicians are beginning to practice the kind of medicine described in Chapter 17. They recognize that many children suffering from what seem like very major handicaps can be helped substantially if one is careful about their diet and protects them from foods and other substances to which they are allergic.

Parents of children with handicaps are fortunate to be living today rather than thirty years ago, a time when psychoanalytically oriented psychologists and physicians tended to blame the parents' handling for many or most of a child's difficulties.

The climate today is far healthier for both parent and child. Today's specialists for the most part are willing to look at the child's own body and that body's reaction to the physical environment as the likely source of many of his or her problems.

We as specialists are now working with parents rather than against them, as we try to give help to a child in trouble.

What If Your Child Is Diagnosed as MBD, Hyperactive, Learning Disabled, Dyslexic?

Labels unquestionably serve a purpose in life. They may be especially helpful as one professional communicates with another. How helpful they are to you as a parent or to your child is open to question.

The practice of medicine in the past seems to have been designed, at least in part, for a labeling of the "problem" afflicting the patient. In some hospitals patients are referred to not by name but by the name of their disease.

Diagnosis *is* important, but even when correctly carried out it is not an end in itself. All too many educators and child specialists, perhaps inadvertently, give parents the impression that once their child has been labeled, something significant and important has been accomplished.

A few years ago dyslexia was one of the more popular labels which supposedly explained why a boy or girl had trouble with reading. "It's very big here this year," one school principal told us when we asked why there appeared to be so many cases of dyslexia in his small school.

MBD (multiple brain dysfunction) followed dyslexia as a popular diagnosis as the years went on, followed in popularity by hyperactivity. And now L.D. (learning disability) is having its day in the sun.

We by no means intend to ridicule those professionals who are struggling with the problems of children who have severe difficulty in learning or in living. However, it does seem fair to say that almost any one of the labels we have mentioned is vastly overused. It is true that they are reasonably descriptive in many instances, but many children who are merely having a little difficulty with reading material that is over their head are all too often labeled dyslexic. Many preschoolers who are, quite normally, extremely active are labeled hyperactive. And many children who are failing in school because they have been overplaced are labeled L.D.

Second, too many adults, parents and professionals alike, seem to feel that something has really been accomplished when a label is given. They ignore the fact that our remedies for any one of these customary classifications are often all too inadequate.

Our best recommendation would be that any parent of any child who is having serious trouble either at home or at school seek out an individual diagnosis of his child by a specialist who sees that child not merely as something to be labeled but as a person to be understood. We would hope that this child would then be treated both medically and educationally as an individual rather than as one of the currently popular group name for children in trouble.

Early detection, of course, is an even more ideal solution. Your very best bet, as mentioned earlier, if infant or child is less than comfortable in his total living or in any aspect of his functioning, is to try to find out right away, if you can, what about his body or environment is causing the difficulty. And then try, at least, to do something about it.

10 Sex Behavior and Sex Interests

How to Tell Your Child about Sex

"How shall I tell my child about sex?" parents ask time and time again. They seldom ask, "How shall I tell my child about war?"— though war, to our way of thinking, is much harder to explain than sex. Nor are most parents stumped about how to explain the nature of the universe, though that, again, seems a more difficult task.

So our first suggestion might be to try to think of sex as an unembarrassing, natural subject about which you are really qualified to speak. Realize that here is a field in which the chances are that you, as a parent, know the answer to any question your child may ask. Which is probably not true in the fields of relativity or atomic warfare, which as topics of discussion do not, we suspect, worry you half as much.

Feel, if you can, confident and unembarrassed. Believe in yourself. Not what you say but how you say it is what will really influence your child.

Second, let the child's own questions be your guide as to what you tell. There is probably no safer rule.

If you give only the information the child requests, and for the most part offer it only when asked, you will avoid that greatest error of all—telling too much too soon. You will also be fairly sure of a receptive audience, since children are not likely to ask unless they want to hear the answer. Their questions can be your guide as to how much they are ready to hear.

A third suggestion is not to read too much into the child's questions. Don't let your own more detailed knowledge of the subject lead you to believe that he or she wants to know all the details when often a very simple answer would suffice.

Lastly, do not make the mistake of thinking that you have given this kind of information once and for all. Perhaps here more than with any other topic, the child asks and asks again. And you will need to answer over and over again, with increased elaboration and detail as the child matures. It may not be so much that he forgets what you say as that, as he grows older, the same questions (and the same answers) mean different things to him.

Information which may have gone over the head of the 4-year-old may make sense to him at 5. So just because you have given a piece of information once, don't check it off your list. You may need to explain the same thing half a dozen times with further elaborations.

Giving Sex Information

"Why is it dark at night?"

"What makes the train go?"

"Where do babies come from?"

All these are among the questions 4-year-olds are likely to ask. And in all probability your children's questions about sex and babies are to them little different from their questions about other things. If we, as adults, could match our children's matter-of-fact, unembarrassed attitude about sex, we would find it easier to answer their questions and would probably do a better job of it.

Typical of the average child's matter-of-factness about sex is the answer one 5-year-old girl gave to a friend who asked her, "Are you old enough to have a baby?"

"Oh, no," replied the little girl. "I can't even tell time yet."

It is important when giving sex information to avoid bewildering the child. Often in our embarrassment we find ourselves talking around the subject and confusing more than we clear up.

When 5-year-olds ask, "Where do babies come from?" what they want to know is that babies grow "in Mommy's tummy." If we use such words as "seed" and "egg," we may make children think of gardens and chickens and merely confuse them.

"What was your mommy telling you about just now?" a little boy asked his friend.

"Oh, some wild story about the birds and bees," the friend replied.

For the majority of children, simple, direct answers to their direct questions are most effective. But there are some parents who find it hard to give direct answers, some children who find it hard to ask direct questions. If you find it too difficult to discuss matters of sex with your child, it may be best to provide him or her with books on the subject.

A Baby Is Born by Milton Levine and Jean Seligmann, *Making Babies* by Sara Bonnett Stein, *How Was I Born?* by Lennart Nilsson, and an extremely amusing presentation, *Where Did I Come From?* by Peter Mayle, are among the good books now available.

Many authorities feel that you should give this kind of information yourself personally and not leave the child to read it from a book. Better, however, for him to read it clearly from a book than to hear a confused story from an embarrassed parent.

"And what if he doesn't ask?" you say. The chances are that if you have answered his questions about other things adequately, and have not adopted a hush-hush attitude about sex, he will ask. But, if you feel that your child is way past the age when he should be asking, check up. You will very likely discover that he has already found out what he wants to know elsewhere, especially from his friends. Then it is wise to check up on the correctness of his information. Many children harbor misconceptions when their "sources" are not adequately informed.

If he is not already informed, tell him what you want him to know, directly if possible, through books or other people if you cannot comfortably do it yourself.

When to Tell about Babies

How can you best tell your child about babies, their source and production? Obviously, in as straightforward and unembarrassed a manner as you can muster.

What to tell? Well, you know the facts. And the child's own questionings will give you clues as to which bits of information are needed and desired.

But when to tell may puzzle you a bit. We have found certain usual stages in the child's interest in and understanding about babies (as reported fully in our publication *The Child from Five to Ten*, by Gesell, Ilg, and Ames.). A brief summary of these usual stages may help you with the timing of information.

3 years: Beginning of interest in babies. Child wants family to have one. Asks, "What can the baby do when it comes?" "Where does it come from?"

Most do not understand when Mother says the baby grows inside of her. But they can understand the idea that babies come from the hospital. Many spontaneously believe that you purchase a baby from the store the way you buy groceries.

4 years: Asks where babies come from. May believe Mother's answer that baby grows inside her "tummy," but may also cling to notion that baby is purchased.

Asks how baby gets out of mother's tummy. May think the baby is born through the navel.

5 years: Interest in babies and in having own baby; may act this out in play.

Again asks, "Where do babies come from?" Most accept "mother's stomach" as an answer.

6 years: Strong interest or reinterest in origin of babies, pregnancy, and birth. Vague idea that babies follow marriage.

Interest in how baby comes out of mother and if it hurts.

Some interest in knowing how baby started. Accepts idea that baby grows in mother's stomach and started from a seed.

7 years: Intense longing for a new baby in the family.

Knows that having babies can be repeated and that older women do not have them.

Interested in mother's pregnancy. Excited about the baby's growth. Wants to know how it is fed, how big it is, how much it costs.

Interested in books about babies, such as *That New Baby,* by Sara Bonnett Stein.

Associates size of pregnant women with presence of baby.

Satisfied to know that baby came from two seeds (or eggs), one from mother and one from father.

8 years: Understands slow process of growth of baby within mother.

Wants more exact information as to where baby is in mother's abdomen. Confused by use of word *stomach.*

Some girls may ask about father's part in reproduction. Their questions can be very searching.

9 to 10 years: The majority, though not all, do know about menstruation.

There is, in some, mild interest in the father's part in reproduction. Especially interested in the "seed-planting" aspect.

Your child's ability to understand about babies may be a little ahead of or a little behind this "schedule," but this will give you an idea of the approximate rate at which his or her understanding will develop.

Sex Play

The child's interest in sex may be embarrassing, but it usually is not particularly devastating to you so long as it remains in the realm of pure theory. Questions about babies and the relations of the two sexes to each other may embarrass, but they usually do not really disturb you.

When that interest takes the form of actual sex activity, however, your reaction may be less calm and much more emotional. There is probably nothing which disturbs the mothers of young children more than to discover them taking part, with other children, in sex play—or to hear of their activities along this line from other, indignant, mothers.

A knowledge of the customary stages of sex play which we have found to take place in perfectly normal, well-brought-up children during the first ten years of life may help you to meet neighborhood sex-play situations calmly and without too much horrified surprise:

2 ½ years: Child shows interest in different postures of boys and girls when urinating and is interested in physical differences between the sexes.

3 years: Verbally expresses interest in physical differences between sexes and in different postures of urinating. Girls attempt to urinate standing up.

4 years: Extremely conscious of the navel. Under social stress may grasp genitals and may need to urinate.

May play the game of "show." Also verbal play about eliminating.

Calling of names related to elimination.

Interest in other people's bathrooms; may demand privacy for self but be extremely interested in the bathroom activity of others.

5 years: Familiar with but not too interested in physical differences between sexes.

Less sex play and game of "show." More modest and less likely to expose self.

Less bathroom play and less interest in unfamiliar bathrooms.

6 years: Marked awareness of and interest in differences between sexes in body structure. Questioning. Mutual investigation by both sexes reveals practical answers to questions about sex differences.

Mild sex play or exhibitionism in play or in school toilets. Game of "show." May also play "hospital" and take rectal temperatures.

Giggling, calling names, or remarks involving words dealing with elimination functions.

Some children are subjected to sex play by older children. Or girls are bothered by older men.

7 years: Less interest in sex.

Some mutual exploration, experimentation, and sex play, but less than earlier.

8 years: Interest in sex rather high, though sex exploration and play is less common than at 6.

Interest in peeping, smutty jokes, provocative giggling; children whisper, write, or spell elimination or sex words.

9 years: May talk about sex information with friends of same sex.

Interest in details of own organs and functions; seek out pictures in books.

Sex swearing, sex poems, beginning.

10 years: Considerable interest in "smutty" jokes.

It is very important to keep in mind that usually none of the children who take part at any of these ages in recurrent neighborhood sex play are to "blame." Sex play often just naturally occurs if several children are left together unsupervised and with nothing better to do. Giving them more supervision, or providing ideas for other activities, will often prevent such behavior, or at least keep it within certain confines.

And, as you will note from the gradient, this interest in sex play tends to go in fits and starts. Ages when such interests are intense alternate with ages when there is relatively little such interest.

Individual Differences

Not only are there ages when sex interest is strong, but there are also children who are, by nature, much more interested than others in the whole subject of sex.

There are the highly sexed children who show an early and intense interest, not only in asking about sex, but in trying things out for themselves. There are others who show a very lukewarm interest in the whole topic and ask practically no questions. There are the intellectual children who want much information early. There are the more practical ones who ask few questions but find out for themselves.

There are some children who prefer the direct approach in all things. Such children want and need clear, direct answers to their questions about sex. Others are not able to approach anything directly. They do best with a little information given late, and may be able to accept information about the sex activities of animals better than such information about people.

There are the aware and the unaware children, the observant and the unobservant. This is not just a matter of intelligence. Some extremely intelligent children are quite unobservant about sex. Other less intelligent, or younger, children are quite alert. The two Jones boys—Eddie aged 6, Peter aged 4, who had a baby sister Patty—had just been told about cats and kittens. Eddie was amazed, but Pete said matter-of-factly, "Always that way. Same thing with people too. Don't you remember that Mommy carried Patty in her stomach before Patty was born?" Pete, by nature, not by training, was interested in and observant about matters of sex. Eddie, though older, was not.

In regard to sex interest and sex behavior, as in regard to other things, children vary. You will do well to study your own child, find out what his or her response to sex is, and be governed accordingly.

Try to accept all the different stages through which children pass as they learn about sex, and as they react to the opposite sex, with equal calm.

Interest in the Opposite Sex

This does not mean that you need welcome the occasions when your child indulges in sex play. Most of you, in our culture, will prefer your children to avoid such activity. But at least attempt to regard this behavior as calmly as you do other undesirable behavior—swearing at 4, lying and cheating at 6. Make no more and no less of it than you do of other lapses from the standards you choose to set up. Try to realize that it may be better for the child to show too much than too little interest in sex. Sex play at 6 is at least a sign that your child is developing "normal" sexual interests.

Similarly, when the child reaches the age of making smutty jokes, again you have the right to discourage such activity. But you should not be unduly shocked and distressed about it. Generation after generation, it appears to come in, and subsequently in most children to drop out, as regularly as do the usual childhood diseases. Eleven and 12 seem to be a high point for smutty joking. It may seem unfortunate to you that the child's first strong interest in the opposite sex sometimes takes this seemingly unattractive turn, but there it is.

Sex play and smutty jokes may seem to you to have little relation to the young person's first demand to use the family car. Actually, however, all of these things are part of a general growth gradient through which most children pass. First they are interested in the facts of sex and sex differences. Later they are interested in the opposite sex. But even here, in their interest in the opposite sex, they go through alternating periods of interest and indifference or repulsion. And even these latter are a cause for worry to some parents.

Most, however, are calmer about this matter of interest in the opposite sex than they are in the matter of actual sex behavior. They view quite calmly, or even with amusement and pride, the heterosexual activities of their 3-year-olds, some of whom even in the nursery school set up strong crushes. We remember one little boy who, at the age of 3½, grew tired of his first "girl" and got another, and then didn't dare to turn up at nursery school for fear of what the jilted damsel would think.

Through 6, 7, and sometimes 8 years of age, twosomes continue to be frequent. And then comes a more subterranean period. Even here, interest in the opposite sex may be strong, but it is expressed in an interesting way. Girls and boys, beginning at 9 years, draw away from each other and profess to hate the opposite sex. A little boy of 9 told us the other day, "Your book is all wrong. It says here that boys of nine don't like girls, but that they will like them again when they are fourteen. Well, all the boys in my class say they will *never* like girls again, and we treat them just as bad as we can just to be sure they will never like us."

This period, in its intensity, is extremely amusing to observe. Amusing because as adults who have once gone through it, we realize that if all goes well, your boy and your girl will emerge from it and many of them will go to the opposite extreme. "All she thinks about is boys," say the parents of teenage girls. "All we talk about at the table is boys," says another parent. "Sometimes, though, we change the subject and talk about a different boy."

And here again, calmness on the part of the parents, especially on the part of fathers, is necessary. Growth does not proceed evenly, and often it does not proceed gracefully. Too much at one age, too little at another. But the knowledge that other parents are also suffering from this too-much and too-little, and a knowledge that it is the common lot of mankind to develop mature sexual abilities and interests through a long, complex, and sometimes difficult series of stages, may help you to accept tolerantly what goes on. Accept and perhaps even welcome. Accept so calmly that by your very calmness you can help your child through this difficult series of stages toward a well-adjusted maturity. Such an attitude can also bring enjoyment. Bringing up children shouldn't be all work and control.

11 The Parent-Child Relationship

Things have changed considerably in the American home in the past few decades. Time was, and not too long ago, when mothers stayed at home and cared for their children and fathers worked outside the home in order to support their families.

In that not-too-long-ago time, in probably the majority of households, mothers, who were at home with their children all day long and day after day, as a rule understood their children better than their husbands did. Mothers' demands thus tended to be the more realistic.

It was generally Father who insisted, "Now it's time that child was toilet-trained" (or came when you called, or told the truth, or whatever behavior was in question). It was Mother who knew that all too often the child was not ready to meet these demands and who therefore stood up for and protected the child.

In the majority of families today, even though many mothers work outside the home, the infant's and child's closest relationship is still with his or her mother. As we have noted earlier, most children are at their best and worst with Mother. They love her the most, want her love and approbation the most, and yet demand the most of her or "take things out on her" most.

There can be exceptions to this rule. In those cases, increasing in number, in which in a so-called "single-parent family" the father is the one and only responsible parent, he can easily attract and thus of necessity take on the responsibilities of motherhood. He will then become the "mothering" parent. (When a mother works outside the home, assuming that *she* is the single parent, she still tends to remain the mothering person.)

In most two-parent households today the mother—whether she works outside the home or not—is the person most likely to be responsible for the child's welfare and the person most intimately involved with son or daughter. Thus in this chapter we shall discuss primarily the mother-child relationship. And we will follow with comment on the father's relation to the child to the extent that it differs from that of the mother.

Mother-Child

The mother-child relationship cannot, no matter how skillful and gifted and kindly a mother may be, always go smoothly. But fortunately the problems she will meet are not all unpredictable. Despite individual differences, there are many similarities in the development of children. Thus the 5-year-old tends to be loving, docile, and obedient in relations with Mother. The 5½–6-year-old tends to thrust out against her and to resist her strongly. And the 7-year-old may feel that she is mean and cruel.

Behavior changes, even in something as complex as the mother-child relationship, tend to be patterned and somewhat predictable. How you get along depends not just on how well or skillfully you treat your child. It depends a good deal on the changes which occur in the growing organism. Understanding may help keep you from being too surprised or worried when certain undesirable but normal changes in your child's behavior take place. It can also help you not to blame yourself or the child for the unattractive but apparently necessary disturbances which do occur at some ages.

You will feel differently about certain resistances to you which the child may show if you know that he or she shares these resistances with most other children of the same age. Here are some of the high points:

Two Years

"Jackie, come here dear," calls Mother; and Jackie patters over to where Mother is sitting and climbs cozily up onto her knee.

Six months earlier Jackie, who was then 18 months old, would at a similar command either have run in the opposite direction or have shouted "No" and stood stock still, refusing to budge.

Has a miracle taken place? Or has his parents' good discipline taught Jackie that he must mind immediately when spoken to? Probably neither. Our own interpretation, arrived at after watching hundreds of 18-monthers turn 2 (we were not always right there on the spot—sometimes we watched simply through the mother's eyes), is that the average 18-monther does not obey direct commands too easily—in fact, he or she is inclined to be a bit mulish. The average 2-year-old, on the other hand, often finds it easy and pleasant to obey.

And so, if you have been relatively calm at your 18-monther's inevitable resistance and, knowing what seeming miracles age can bring about, have waited more or less patiently for him to get a bit older, and abler—you will have been rewarded. You will find that much of the time your 2-year-old will mind you nicely.

Jackie has just taught his mother an important lesson, if she but looks at it that way. He has shown her that readiness for many important behaviors—coming when called, and later being able to read the printed word or to write his name, or being able to admit wrongdoing when faced with the evidence—develops in the human at its own pace.

If parents can know approximately what that pace will be, they can fit their demands to the child's capabilities. And can be successful.

This does not mean that you should make no demands. It does mean that it is most effective to make reasonable ones. Two is ready to "Come here, dear" when Mother calls.

Two-and-a-Half Years

"Me do it myself," clamors Two-and-a-half as his mother, in the interests of speed and efficiency and of getting through her morning chores before lunchtime, tries to dress him. But if she should give in and leave him to dress himself, the demand would change to, "Mommy do, Mommy do." If Mommy then comes to the rescue, but Daddy is still on the scene, we will soon hear a chorus of, "Mommy go way. Daddy do it."

The 2½-year-old lives in a world of opposite extremes: "I will— I won't . . . I can—I can't . . . Yes—No." He thrives by shuttling from one extreme to the other. His choices are all multiple choices; he wants both of any possible alternatives. And if alternatives are not offered, he sets them up himself.

No matter what his mother wants him to do, he wants to do the opposite. Opposite extremes are to the 2½-year-old like magnetic poles pulling him in two directions at once so that he may, if not prevented, shuttle endlessly from one to the other. "Don't want spinach." (Mother throws it out.) . . . "Want spinach." (Mother opens a fresh can.)

It is therefore the mother's problem to keep the child, so far as possible, on a one-way street. Streamline daily routines; don't give choices; take over the direction of activities; talk glibly of the next thing (the walk you're going to take) while you steer him rapidly through this thing (putting on his outdoor clothes).

And at all costs avoid direct questions which can be answered by "No," such as, "Do you want to go for a walk?"

Avoid choices to which, even if he makes them, he cannot stick: "Do you want to go for a walk or play in the yard?" "Do you want a brown cookie or a white one?" Recognize his opposite extremeness and try to give his behavior the one-way direction it lacks.

All of his activities, all of his demands and commands, are carried out with an imperiousness which would befit a Roman emperor. No wonder that some mothers, in mock despair, rechristen their children at this age "King John" or "Queen Mary." Thus the wise mother may, instead of worrying about keeping the upper hand and making the child "mind," give in on unimportant matters—"Certainly, your majesty!" A little humor on Mother's part can do a great deal toward making things go more smoothly.

And remember, mothers, that Two-and-a-half is at his best and at his worst with you. He is most loving with you but also most demanding. His most remarkable new abilities he expresses in your presence (and often cannot repeat them when you later try to get him to show off for others). But also he is most contrary and demanding when you are with him. Therefore, if you find yourself becoming too exasperated with your child, take a few hours off on occasion, and you can return with renewed patience and enthusiasm.

Two-and-a-Half to Three Years

From 2½ to 3 years many children go through an odd period of wanting to relive their babyhood. Emotionally they may relive their whole previous lives, with help from their mother. They demand that their mothers treat them as if they were little babies. When tired, they want to be carried, rocked, even fed from a bottle. The more verbal children talk about their feelings. "I'm a little baby. I can't talk. I have no teeth and I have no hair," one little boy told his mother.

Another, a bit more accurately, reported, "I'm a little baby. I have to have a bottle. I sleep out in a carriage. But I can talk!"

The wise mother, appreciating the child's need to thus relive his babyhood before giving it up (once and for all?) to become a big boy, helps him to do so. She does not punish him for his babyish ways, or try to shame or laugh him out of them. Nor does she blame his behavior just on jealousy of the new baby (if there is one in the family). And she does not worry that he is "regressing to an earlier phase."

Once he has had enough of this experience of reliving his babyhood, he will be ready to go forward, more independent and more grown up; to look forward rather than backward; to think of himself in relation to the future rather than the past.

Three Years

Three is an age period when the mother-child relationship is characteristically smooth and satisfactory to both of the people chiefly concerned.

It is for many children a "we" age, and for many, Mother is the especially favored companion. From 2½ to 3 years the average child progresses through a concentration on "I" and "me" and personal needs, and on "you" and his or her demands from "you" (both of which were so strong at 2½)—and arrives at a friendly and sharing "we."

And so, not only does the child give considerable pleasure to Mother as a friendly companion, but Three is easier to "manage" —daily routines go more quickly and with less friction than earlier.

The 3-year-old, for example, does not get lost between opposite extremes—trying to choose both at the same time. Rather, he can make a choice. If he is hesitating about coming into the house (when you want him to do so), you can say, "Do you want to come in the front or the back door?"—and he can usually choose one and stick to that choice.

Furthermore, you can often bargain with a 3-year-old—if you are not above using such tactics. The younger child had such a strong sense of "now" and of wanting what he wanted when he wanted it that bargaining was apt not to work. But the 3-year-old can often be persuaded to do something distasteful "now" if "later" he can look forward to an attractive reward.

The 3-year-old, as we have told you, is increasing tremendously his ability to use language effectively and to respond to verbal approaches. He not only will respond with gratifying pleasure to being allowed to share a "secret" or a "surprise," but he can often be persuaded to do what you want him to do in return for a "surprise" reward.

And the 3-year-old will, on occasion, listen well when you try to reason with him. Sometimes he may even do things he does not like to do if given a good reason for doing them.

All in all, Three is much less demanding of the adult than was his younger self, easier to get along with, and more fun to be with.

Three-and-a-Half Years

Dinner is for the moment taking care of itself on the stove and Jennifer's mother has sat down, just for a minute, in the living room, to talk over the day's happenings with her husband.

Father has had a good day, Mother is feeling relaxed, and 3½-year-old Jennifer is looking very angelic as she sits in her little chair.

Mother, with part of her mind on the dinner and part on what her husband is telling her, still spares a thought for the total scene. What a nice family! What a pleasant picture!

And then, without warning, Jennifer spoils the picture with a most unexpected outburst. "Don't you talk," she shouts bossily at her parents. "Stop talking."

Jennifer's mother doesn't know what to make of this. But since the dinner is calling her anyway, she just skips the whole problem by going kitchenward. Her husband, also surprised at his daughter's outburst, picks up his evening paper and starts to read it.

"Don't read your paper, Daddy," whines Jennifer. "Play with me."

After Jennifer is safely in bed for the night—looking once more her usual angelic self—her parents discuss her recent odd behavior.

"Do you suppose she is what they call insecure?" Mother asks Father. "She seems to feel so unsure of herself lately. She asks me a dozen times a day, 'Do you love me?' and she seems to want to have everybody's complete attention right on her. If I talk to anybody else while she's around and leave her out of it, she makes a terrible fuss, just as she did tonight. Do you think we've done something wrong to make her feel so uncertain?"

Jennifer's father said he didn't know. He, too, had read a lot about "insecurity," and like many parents was often worried that he might, without knowing it, be making his child feel insecure.

What could have helped both of Jennifer's parents, and relieved them of their worry that something they had done had caused her to act the way she did, would have been a little more knowledge about child development. The knowledge that many 3½-year-olds go briefly through a stage when not only are they uncertain and badly coordinated in motor ways—that is, they stutter and stumble—but they are uncertain and insecure in their emotions as well. They fear that people do not love them. They demand extra attention and reassurance. They are excessively demanding of their parents' love and attention.

This is a natural stage of growth and behavior. The parents have not caused it, and they do not have to cure it. Growth itself will, in the normal course of events, do that.

Four Years

"My mommy says so!" The 4-year-old, with this statement, has quoted the highest authority. He has proved his point beyond all dispute. He has said the last word.

"My mommy says I have to have four cookies!" The nursery-school child gives the teacher what he genuinely believes to be a foolproof reason for having four cookies.

He will go even further. "My mommy says you have to do so and so," he will tell his playmates. And they may even obey—unless they are quick enough to cite their own mothers in rebuttal.

But the 4-year-old is not an entirely consistent creature. If Mother is such a tremendous authority, you would almost expect that he would on all occasions mind what she had to say to him.

Not at all! The child of any age may have moments of resistance, but the 4-year-old's vocabulary fairly bristles with "No, I won't!" or even "Try and make me!"

At some ages the child resists because he does not want to do the thing in question. Four often seems to resist simply for the sake of resisting. Mommy (or Daddy) is the authority, but he can resist (or can at least attempt to resist) that authority.

Four has been described as an out-of-bounds age in which the child seems to feel a real drive to go against any established bounds. And one of the boundaries which he tries hardest to go beyond is that of parental authority. He will usually succumb (and obey) in the long run but will often put up quite a fight first.

This kind of behavior does not apparently occur just in "bad" children who have been "badly" brought up. We have seen it crop up too often, as batch after batch of children whom we have studied have turned 4. It seems almost as inevitable as growing pains. It gives way at 5 to behavior that is contrastingly more docile and agreeable.

Four revolts and delights in the revolution. Five obeys and enjoys the obedience. The same child but a different age!

Deal with it as you personally choose, but do not take Four's resistance too seriously.

Five to Six Years

Five-year-olds are characteristically, in relation to their mothers, so docile, friendly, helpful, so willing and even anxious to obey and carry out instructions, that the mother may think of herself as, briefly, in paradise—in fact, many a mother has in our presence described her 5-year-old as "just like an angel." Mother seems to be the center of Five's world, and the child frequently seems to put her welfare ahead of his or her own.

Not so at 6. The 6-year-old is once again, as when he was younger, the center of the world himself, and he wants to be first, to be loved best, to have the most of everything. Why should Mommy have more money than he has? Why should Mommy stay up later than he does?

He not only competes with his mother, but he is extremely resistant to her commands. He defies her with, "I won't. Try and make me."

Six takes things out on her—she is to blame for everything. "Finish your dinner, Joanie dear," says Mother to her daughter, who sits with arms folded, staring stonily at her plate.

"I can't. I have no fork," replies Joan coldly. What else can she do, she implies, but sit there and wait till her mother brings her a fork?

Six is an emotional age, and emotions are violent and often contradictory. Perhaps they are most often expressed toward and against the mother. "I love you, Mommy, most of anybody in the world," says the 6-year-old, giving Mother a crushing bear hug. Mother is delighted. "My child really loves me," she thinks.

"I hate you, Mommy, I wish you were dead." Mother is in despair. "What have I done to deserve this?"

Actually, neither of these expressions represents a reasoned judgment. They both mean merely that Six is an emotional little creature and that he is, in his immature fashion, taking out his emotions on the person nearest at hand, and the person who means the most to him. If things go well, he loves her. If they go badly, he blames her.

His disobedience may mean that he is tired and things are going wrong with him. Or it may mean that he is trying his wings. What's more natural than that he should try them by disobeying his mother, whose word was law a few short months ago. Disobeying Mother may be the most daring and grown-up thing he can think of to do.

We see this in the child who is sent back to the dining room till he has finished his milk. Mother, in the living room, hears loud gulping sounds, then a little figure comes in with sparkling eyes and milk-rimmed mouth. "I didn't finish it!"

"What! You didn't drink your milk!" says Mother—but, of course, he did, and both are delighted with the joke. His delight in such a pretense shows us how daring disobedience seems to him, and yet how pleased he is to do things right.

Seven Years

Seven-year-old Cynthia was feeling very sorry for herself. Nobody liked her, she insisted. The other kids teased her. Her teacher was mean to her. And even her mother and father weren't treating her right. Everybody was picking on her all the time.

Cynthia's complaints may seem to you unreasonable—and they actually did not fit the facts. But they are extremely typical of the 7-year-old child. Seven is very likely to feel that he or she is getting the bad end of things, that everyone is mistreating him.

In fact, some children of this age become so resentful and unhappy that they may complain, "I don't even want to be a member of this family!"

The 6-year-old tends to be an aggressive little creature. If he thinks people aren't treating him right—as he frequently does— he just fights back. With words or fists, or both.

But Seven's tendency is just the opposite. Six approaches trouble aggressively. Seven withdraws, complaining.

And his parents are among those of whom he complains most. They are mean to him. It is even possible—he figures—that they don't like him.

Most stop there. But a few vigorously imaginative ones go even further and develop what has been called the adoption fantasy. The child figures first that his parents don't treat him right. He goes from there to the conclusion that they really aren't his parents at all. And from there he goes on to the fantasy that he actually comes from some rich and powerful family and that his present mother and father just "got hold of him" somehow and are now mistreating him.

Marvel at the fertility of the 7-year-old imagination! Sympathize with his discouraged mood. Don't make fun of him. But on the other hand, don't take such complaints too seriously. The mood— we can practically guarantee it—will pass.

Eight Years

"Ever since her father died six months ago, that child has simply haunted me. She just doesn't let me out of her sight for a minute, except of course when she's at school. She won't go to the movies with anybody but me and won't even go out and play with her friends very much. She just hangs around the house and talks to me."

This was Mary's mother's complaint, and she went on to say that she was afraid that Mary was getting some sort of an attachment or fixation on her, and it seemed unhealthy. She wondered if it would not be wise to take Mary to a psychiatrist to get her over this attachment.

"How old is your Mary? About eight?" we hazarded a guess.

"Why, yes, she is, but how could you know?" replied Mary's mother, quite surprised.

We were not too much surprised at the success of our guess because it had not been at random. Mary's mother had given a brief but accurate description of what we have come to know as typical 8-year-old behavior.

A typical 8-year-old child may literally haunt his or her mother. The child's need for a real relationship at this time is deep and demanding. And it is not only the mother's actions which are important to the 8-year-old, but her very thoughts as well. The death of Mary's father may well have accentuated this behavior, but it still would have occurred in any event.

The 6-year-old wants his mother to do what he wants her to, but the 8-year-old wants her even to think in a way that pleases him. And he is so sensitive to her approval and disapproval that he is quick to notice the slightest change in her facial expression.

In fact, his wish for closeness is so great that it often leads to his being "embroiled with" his mother. It seems to many mothers that their 8-year-olds prefer even fighting with them to being left out of a relationship.

If this excessive demand for attention, affection, and response from the mother should go through the years unabated, it might well be considered a danger signal. But we do not consider it a danger signal when it occurs only around 8 years of age, as it appears to in many children, in the normal course of growth. This is, in many children, the first demand for a deep, close relationship with another person, and if it is fulfilled, it may well pave the way for other successful personal relationships in the future.

Nine Years

"Jack! You come straight home from the movies, now mind. They get out at five o'clock, remember, and I'll expect you home promptly at five-thirty. And be sure you wear your rubbers. It looks like rain. And you'd better take your cap along. I don't want you going bare-headed in the rain. And don't forget your gloves."

"Aw, Ma, let me alone. I'll be all right. I don't mind a little rain," mutters Jack.

Even Jack's father is moved to chime in. "Dear, let the boy alone. He can look out for himself."

This scene, quite typically, takes place in many homes on a Saturday afternoon, but it probably takes place most often in the homes of 9-year-olds, judging from our experience. And the frank reporting of many of the mothers we see has taught us that it is often preceded by another, also typical, scene:

It is almost movietime and the 9-year-old son comes out to the kitchen and comments casually—almost too casually—to his mother, "I'm going to the movies now, Ma."

"Oh, fine. Just a minute, dear, and I'll get my things on."

Her son shuffles his feet, ducks his head, looks embarrassed, and mumbles, "Well, the thing is, I'm going with Bill."

"You mean you don't want your own mother to go along with you?"

This is one of the hardest lessons that many mothers have to learn. The 8-year-old child is as a rule "all mixed up with" his mother. He wants her attention and he loves her company. She is often his favored and chosen companion for the movies, for playing games, just for company. Some mothers find this a little exhausting. But at least it is flattering. It shows that your child likes you and appreciates your company.

And then, often quite suddenly, when he is nine or so, the child comes to a point where a friend is more important to him, at least as a companion, than his mother. This is actually a sign that he is developing normally—he cannot stay dependent on Mother all his life.

But it often comes as a shock to a mother who, without realizing it, has come to count on her starring role in her child's life.

Most mothers do not come right out and say, like the mother just described, "Don't you want your own mother?" What they do is say, "All right. Run along. But—wear your rubbers. Come home early." Etc., etc.

What they are saying, though they may not realize it, is, "I may not be the most important thing to you any more, but I can still boss you around." Much of the trouble that mothers have with their 9-year-olds comes from this giving of too many directions, this overinsistence on complete conformity.

If you are giving your 9-year-old too many orders and he is rebelling, just check to be sure whether all the commands you give are really essential—or whether you may be just trying to convince yourself, and your child, that you still have the upper hand.

Ten Years

"When Mummy and I are shopping, if she likes a dress and I like it, we get it. But if she likes it and really wants me to have it and I don't like it, she gets it for me. And if I like it and she doesn't, we don't get it," explains 10-year-old Betty calmly. There is no tone of complaint in her voice. That is just the way things are— "If she likes it, she gets it for me."

"Mommy usually can argue me out of things because she argues best," reports another 10-year-old.

Others say, "I don't have a chemical set yet. Mummy thinks they are too expensive"; "I'd like to have a gear-shift bike, but Mummy doesn't want me to have one yet"; "I just started taking music lessons this year. My mother says I'm as good as I should be, but not too good. I usually do scales four or ten times, depending on what she tells me."

All of these comments reflect the gratifying docility of the 10-year-old which makes him, in many families, a thing of joy (more or less) in the household. He is still accepting Mummy (or Daddy) and their directives as ruling forces which he just naturally lives by. In little ways he may disobey—he does not always mind the minute he is spoken to; he may on occasion argue and tease. But basically he accepts, and cheerfully, the idea that mother's commands are reasonable and are to be obeyed.

Ten marks a happy period in the mother-child relation, somewhat reminiscent of Five. The child obeys Mother cheerfully and seemingly with the feeling that it is right and reasonable for him to do so. Ten is docile, and it might seem at first glance desirable that he or she should remain so. But it would not really be desirable. We would not want our adolescents to be guided entirely by their mothers' demands.

The adolescent, if he is to grow into a mature capable adult, must learn to think for himself; must grow beyond the place where he is completely guided by what "Mummy says."

Father-Child

Father's role has changed vastly in the last forty or fifty years. Today many fathers share in parenthood, in addition to their initial procreative role, even before the baby is born. They attend preparental classes with their wives.

And while Baby is being born, many no longer pace in the hospital waiting room. Instead they are very often actually in the delivery room, acting as "coach" to their wives who are delivering the baby by so-called natural childbirth.

Once the new baby is brought home, fathers now diaper and burp them. If Baby is bottle-fed it may be Father who provides at least the night bottle.

In some instances, a "househusband" is the person who stays at home with infant or preschooler. Or if, as is sometimes the case, Father is the only parent, he may indeed take on all the responsibilities of parenthood.

However, regardless of circumstances, the father-child relationship as a rule is less variable and less vulnerable to the passing whims of the child's own age changes than the mother-child relationship.

It is true that preschoolers tend to worship Father as they do Mother. Later, from 6 to 10, the child tries himself out against Father in little ways, though he still thinks Father is pretty wonderful. (From 11 to 16 he tries himself out in bigger ways and sometimes doesn't think Father is as wonderful as he used to be.)

But the little year-to-year variations do not seem to affect the child's behavior toward Father as much as they do his behavior toward Mother. (Unless, of course the father has had to assume a mother's role and is the one to supervise daily routines and chores.)

This is perhaps because the mother-child relationship seems to be more sensitive, delicate, intense, but more easily upset than the relationship with the father. Three-and-a-half whines most with Mother. Four boasts and defies Mother more. Five clings hardest to Mother. Six battles against her authority more vigorously. Mother attracts the child's best behavior too, but she certainly does attract his worst.

Feelings about Father are not as intense, not as mixed up, not as variable. Father tends to represent stability and firmness. He is the one to whom Mother reports extra-bad behavior. He is the court of last appeal. He is the person who gives out important rewards as well as important punishments. He is the prized companion on those welcome occasions when he can spend time alone with son or daughter.

Thus fathers should not under ordinary circumstances expect to attract from their children the same kinds of responses which mothers attract. Father's role in bringing up the children is perhaps, as in their production, an essential but a supplementary one.

Above all, it should ideally be Father's role to back up Mother's policies. If he disagrees with her methods of handling the children, he should *always* express that disagreement in private—not where the children can hear or observe.

We don't mean that Mother will always be right and that Father should just agreeably go along with her decisions. We mean simply that if there are differences of opinion about child raising and disciplining, they should not be discussed in front of the children. Even very young children can learn to play one parent against the other if they sense disagreement. In such instances, discipline really flies out of the window.

Of course each family differs in its own way—in some, parents agree completely; in others it is Mother who is firm and Father who is soft-hearted. The most common situation, however, appears to be that in which Mother pleads for tolerance—"He's just a baby"; "It's just a stage he's going through." Father is most commonly the firm one: "You and your stages! He's just got to learn to mind. It's time he found out that he can't get away with that sort of thing!"

Now Father may be quite right. Especially if when he says, "It's time that," he is sure that he knows that children of his child's age and temperament quite normally are able to do the "good" thing (or to refrain from doing the "bad" thing) in question. Most often, however, he simply means that he's tired of waiting for the desired behavior to appear.

Mother's "just a stage" is not as a rule simply spinelessness on her part or a weak giving-in to the child. It most often represents an objective realization that this child at this time can't seem to do any better and that this stage, like others which have preceded it, will probably be short-lived. Mother's hopes and wishes as to the way her child should act have been, more often than not, cut down to size by the actual daily living reality of the child himself. Father, being away from home more, clings to his illusions.

However, all of this doesn't mean that Father should be afraid of clamping down when necessary. Mother's gentleness and understanding, Father's firmness but also, we hope, understanding, are both essential ingredients for a stable family life.

Three to Five Years

Three is an easy age for most children in all respects, the father-child relationship included. The 3-year-old is less rigid and demanding than he or she was at 2½; and now, though Mother tends to be the favored parent, Father can frequently take over in many situations. In fact, he can often do so most effectively. If snags have crept into the going to bed, or other routines, things often go much more smoothly for Father than for Mother.

At 3½ many children change from favoring Mother to showing a great favoritism for Father. Girls may even go so far as to propose to their fathers, who may at this time be their idea of utter perfection.

And at 4—that exuberant, out-of-bounds, rebellious age—many "No I won'ts" can be turned to relatively docile obedience by a word from Father. Not only is he respected in the home, but he is often quoted outside. "My father" is for many the ultimate authority. And even the boldest, most bossy and boastful 4-year-olds can be quite gentle creatures when Father turns an eye on them.

Excursions and times alone with Father are greatly prized, and his word is often law even when Mother's has temporarily ceased to be. Name-calling 4-year-olds seldom call their fathers names, no matter what they may call their mothers.

Five is, as a rule, fond and proud of Father and may obey him more promptly than he does Mother. But most Fives are at heart mothers' boys (or girls), so that though relationships with Father are generally smooth, pleasant, and undisturbed, Five is usually more casual with Father than with Mother. It is Mother, not Father, who is the center of the 5-year-old's world.

Six Years

"Sometimes I think I'm the cause of all his difficulties," mothers of 6-year-olds often admit to us. "He's certainly at his worst with me."

They are, unfortunately—at least more often than not—correct. For the 6-year-old (who was so much of a mother's boy at 5) is now fighting to be free of his mother. Mother is the center of the world for many 5-year-olds. Most children are—or would like to be—the center of their own world at 6. The shift is not always accomplished without bloodshed.

So the 6-year-old is traditionally defiant and violent. He defies his mother. He will not mind. He shouts, "I hate you, Mommy!"

And what is Father's role here?

Most commonly, we're afraid, he steps into the fray and makes things worse, either by bringing vigorous physical punishment to bear on the erring 6-year-old, or by explaining to Mother what a poor disciplinarian she is to have allowed things to come to such a pass.

Other fathers follow a more constructive program. We would like to recommend their policy to all.

Two general, very simple principles are involved. The first is that at those ages when the child is at his very worst with Mother, he is, fortunately, often at his best with Father.

This means, in actual practice, that the worst trouble areas in a 6-year-old's day—dressing, eating, going to bed—can often be gotten through with relative speed and a minimum of confusion by a patient and even moderately inventive father. A visit to the doctor's or dentist's office is far more successful with Father than with Mother. Needles will be accepted with less emotion. Teeth can be filled without too much fuss or fear of pain.

This is partly because the child of this age doesn't seem to be having such a struggle for power with his father as he has with his mother. It's partly because most Sixes have more respect for Father's authority than for Mother's, and don't dare to be as bad with him as they are with her. In fact, Six organizes under the firmer rein of the father. Fathers may well realize this and profit by it.

So any father of a 6-year-old who will, even on occasion, be willing to take over some of the child's routines, can contribute a very great deal to the harmony of the household.

The second general principle which the father of any 6-year-old might usefully keep in mind is this: It is far more effective to step in and prevent trouble before it occurs than to try to pick up the pieces afterward.

Don't wait till mother and child are completely embroiled to lend a hand. Step in before that tantrum occurs! It will save wear and tear on everybody.

Seven to Ten Years

There is in most families great need for the father to step in and stabilize things when the child is 6. By 7, this need has become much less intense. Worrying Seven may be quite unhappy within himself—you would be too if you figured as he often does that everybody hates you! But he isn't as a rule too hard to manage. Mother can usually provide what discipline is needed. Seven, with his tendency (stronger at 8) to go to extremes, may now "worship" his father; but for many children the father-child relationship is not intense at 7.

At 8, the intensely demanding emotional relationship of the child with Mother often quite overshadows any other personal relationship. Father may feel a trifle left out at this point, but he is actually fortunate. Eight may love him less intensively, but is also usually less demanding of him. Father can make a mistake and get away with it. But not Mother. She has to do and say and even think just the way her 8-year-old son or daughter wants her to. And trouble comes when Eight is too aware of the mother-father relationship. Some parents of 8-year-olds have to be careful of exposing either their affection for each other or their disagreements before a jealous son or daughter.

On the whole, however, Father can go his own way. And what is more, Eight—increasingly bold with Mother—usually will mind, and quickly, when Father speaks. Father's role at this point, as so often, is in many ways easier than Mother's.

At 9, many children are less interested in and less demanding of either Mother or Father than they were earlier. Friends are the big thing, and what Bill or even Bill's mother or father says may be much more important than anything said at home.

However, many boys do at this time enter into a new relationship with their fathers. Children are now quite old enough to be interesting to those fathers who may not have enjoyed them much at an earlier age. And they are old enough, themselves, to respect Father's technical knowledge and abilities. Children now share real interests with their fathers; and boys and their fathers may group together against feminine interference.

The relationship may be largely in the things they *do* together —but many boys are extremely sensitive to any criticism from Father and think highly of his good regard. Some, especially at this age, may feel great superiority and pride in relation to Father's occupation.

Ten is one of the happiest ages from the point of view of the father-child relationship. You don't even have to be an exceptionally superior or expert father for things to succeed now.

For at this age most boys and girls just naturally think their fathers are wonderful. Mothers tell us, "He thinks his father is the end answer to everything"; "He idolizes his father"; "Thinks his daddy is wonderful"; or, "To her he is the shining light."

Ten-year-olds themselves make approximately the same report: "I think he's just about right," they tell us. Or, "I think he's the best father in the whole world." Or, "He's just right. He's strict, of course, but he has to be. You can't be too patient with your children."

We suggest that you make the most of this golden age. In the years that follow, you may not feel that you are changing very much. But unless yours is the very exceptional child, his or her wholehearted approbation and adoration will very probably diminish. Because, as we have commented before and as most of you realize, one of the biggest tasks of adolescence is getting free of the parent. And to do this, most children seem to have to go through at least a stage of running you down.

Most 10-year-olds, however, still in the admiring stage, love to spend time alone with their father. It doesn't matter too much what you do, so long as you are together. Ballgames, movies, walks, playing games, reading, wrestling—Ten is ready for almost anything.

Companionable is the word which mothers often use in describing the father-child relationship. And children themselves use this same word about their father—"He's very companionable; we get on very nicely."

So even though, like many fathers, you're pretty busy and don't have much spare time—we still suggest that it is a good idea to enjoy your 10-year-old's company and to let him enjoy yours. Don't make the mistake of waiting until your child is a little older (and more interesting, you may think). By the time you get around to it, if you do wait, you may find that your son or daughter does not have time for *you!*

12 Brothers and Sisters

"Birds in their little nests agree" was an aggravating statement that parents used to make to their children in the early part of this century. Perhaps they did agree, not daring to behave otherwise.

At least one must admit that nowadays brothers and sisters often do not agree. We all know that. However, the extent to which actual physical violence between siblings occurs is probably not common knowledge. At least it is probably not usually admitted.

When it does happen, most of us tend to shrug it off with excuses about the special provocation which led Jim to slug Joan, Billy to kick John, Mary to pull out swatches of Matthew's hair.

Current research, notably that of Professor Murray A. Straus of the University of New Hampshire, is causing many of us to take a second look at family life in America.* It may even be giving a certain amount of comfort to those who feared that the fighting which went on in their own family was drastically atypical.

In an extremely comprehensive survey of acts of violence in a nationally representative sample of over two thousand American families, Straus determined that child-child acts of violence occurred annually in 79 out of every 100 American families.

Thus, the most common type of the all-too-pervasive family violence which occurs is attacks by one child in a family against a brother or sister. According to Straus:

---

*Murray A. Straus, "A Sociological Perspective on the Causes of Family Violence," paper read at the American Association for the Advancement of Science, Houston, Tex., January 6, 1979.

Eight out of ten American children get into a physical fight with a sibling each year. Not only are children more violent to each other than to anyone else, in addition they are the ones most likely to attack in ways that could cause serious injury. Over half of American children do one or more of the following to a sibling each year: kick, bite, punch, hit with objects, beat up a sibling or attack with a knife or gun.

Though their violence rate goes down as children grow older, it far from disappears. According to Straus's figures, if just major acts of violence are counted the rates go from 74 per hundred 3–4-year-olds, to 64 per hundred 5–9-year-olds, to 47 per hundred 10–14-year-olds, and to 36 per hundred 15–17-year-olds.

He points out, probably correctly, that within the confines of the family we accept a great deal as normal, or at least as inevitable, which we would absolutely not tolerate outside the family. We tend to accept the fact that violence in the family is just a part of life—not necessarily a good part, but one that is to be expected. He notes that

> parents react differently than if it were someone else's child who had been punched or kicked by one of their children, or someone else's child who had done this to one of their children. If it were someone else's child there would be cries of outrage and possibly even legal action if the violence persisted. But between their own children parents, in effect, tolerate such behavior for years.

And unfortunately this violence continues into the late teens. In one of his samples, 62 percent of the high school seniors had hit a sibling during the year, but "only" 35 percent had hit someone outside the family during that same year.

What Can You Do to Improve Matters?

Assuming that your family is one of the lucky ones where brother-sister relationships are not quite all that violent, chances are there is still a great deal of disagreement and even fighting between your children. As one mother put it, "They fight all the time. I used to try to stop it, but I don't any more. It would be like cutting off their breathing if I stopped their fighting."

Some believe that the main cause of disagreement between siblings is that they all want to be their parents' favorite child, to be the one who is loved best.

Others feel that competitiveness with one's peers is natural, regardless of how a child feels about his or her parents. It seems to be, except in the most angelic, a natural wish to get the most of everything and to come out on top.

Still others think that children fight because it is fun, because it fills an emotional need, and that later on friendship—first with one's own sex and later with the opposite sex—will take its place in giving emotional satisfaction. Certainly most parents know that even the child who screams the loudest and always gets the worst of things, once a given quarrel is settled and he has been rescued from his older or stronger sibling, will get right back into the fray. He will do again the very thing that got him into trouble in the first place.

So, since fighting between sibs seems to be more or less inevitable, what can you do about it?

Because it is usually easier to tell people what *not* to do than what *to* do, we'll give you some *Don'ts* first.*

Don't act as a referee; at least don't do it any more than is absolutely necessary. What every child longs to hear is your verdict that "You were right and your brother [sister] was wrong"; "You were right to do what you had to to protect your property"; "He was the one who started it. No wonder you hit him back."

Don't intervene in "normal" bickering. If somebody is getting murdered, you will usually know it by the violence of the cries (or by the loudness of the silence). The more you can manage to stay out of things, the more ingenious and self-reliant your children will become in settling their own squabbles.

---

*These *don'ts* and *do's* are adapted from a forthcoming book by Louise Bates Ames and Carol Chase Haber, *Sisters and Brothers.*

Even if one of your children does seem to you most often to be the cause or center of quarrels, don't if you can help it give him the poor self-image of feeling that "everything" is "always" his fault.

Don't insist on getting to the bottom of things in the hope of finding out who was "really" to blame. There are rare instances when it is absolutely necessary for you to know how the whole thing started, who did what to whom, and when. But much of the time the whole story will be so convoluted, and often only slightly related to the truth of the matter, and each of any two or three combatants will be so dedicated to proving that he or she was the innocent victim, that your most skilled efforts in getting at the true facts will be doomed to failure.

Don't allow your children to draw you into a pattern of spending a vast amount of time and energy discussing and trying to straighten out their disagreements. Keep such sessions as few and brief as possible. Don't be a patsy.

Don't set yourself up by allowing repetition of situations which you know aren't going to work. For instance, if your 6-year-old, like most, absolutely cannot stand to lose a competitive game, don't permit him (or her) to play such games every day with, let's say, a demanding 8-year-old. Fighting, blaming, and name-calling are almost certain to result.

Don't bemoan loudly, often, and in the children's presence that they "fight all the time" and you just cannot stand it or do anything about it. Most children are ready and eager to live up to advance billing, especially when it is negative.

Any child in your family is likely to feel that you "always" favor the other(s). This can't be helped. Don't add fuel to the fire by allowing yourself conspicuously to favor one or the other even though your heart may urge you to do so. You very likely will have a favorite, but try not to make this grossly obvious.

Don't ask unanswerable questions: "Why can't you be nicer to your little brother?" "Why do you kids have to fight all the time?" "Why are you always so selfish?"

Don't allow your children to play you against your spouse for favors. In all likelihood, one of you will be a little more lenient, one a little stricter than the other. This is natural and not necessarily harmful. But do your best not to let the children capitalize on it.

If you, the mother, are the home-bound parent, don't take all the blame for the way the children behave. Though many children do behave a little better for their father (they are usually more afraid of him), if Dad feels that you are doing a "lousy" job with them and their bickering, arrange things so that he is the person in charge at least for a while.

Don't set up unrealistic goals with regard to the degree of family harmony which you expect. Start where you actually are and then try, little by little, to improve matters.

DO'S:

To begin with, keep in mind that most children do fight. A lot.

Unless children are vastly ill-matched, try to encourage them to work out their own solutions to problems. There will inevitably be times, often many times a day, when you will be called upon to settle some dispute. Sometimes you can get out of it by saying, "You settle it yourselves." Or when some ill-doing on the part of a sib is reported you can say, "Well what are you going to do about it?" (Admittedly there will be times when you will be confronted with a situation which you cannot weasel out of with all the good techniques in the world. Then, indeed, you will have to give a verdict.)

Although we've warned you not to try to get to the bottom of every quarrel, *do* try to find out why they fight. (The reasons may be so deep-seated—basic hatred, desperate jealousy—that they will be hard to deal with. But the reason might be a small or specific thing that you can do something about.)

Try making need rather than complete fairness the basis for decisions. Don't try to always have things come out utterly fairly. They won't; and even if they did, the children wouldn't think so. So get whatever it is for the child who needs it, not for every child in the family.

Separate your children more. Break up bad combinations so far as you can.

Many children, especially preschoolers, are absolutely snowed if you tell them that something is "the rule." To make this work, make rules simple and specific. Do not make a big rule such as "You must be good to your sister." Instead state specifically, "You are not to hit your sister."

Do what you can to make each child feel special. Spend as much time as you can alone with each one.

Help children protect their most prized possessions. You can't necessarily keep siblings from *looking* at them, but at least try to keep a child's very best things from being destroyed.

Try to help your child find other outlets for emotions, so that fighting with siblings will not be the primary pleasure.

Help (older) children not to let others get a rise out of them. Teach them that if they ignore behaviors these may not be repeated.

If you know that a certain kind of situation always turns out badly, try to step in before the lid blows off.

Try using behavior-modification techniques. That is, reward behaviors which you wish to have repeated. So far as you can stand it, ignore the bad.

Do all you can to reduce tattling by making it unrewarding. Unless the behavior reported sounds definitely serious say, "Oh is that so?" and show the child by your indifference that tattling isn't going to get him very far. On the other hand, if the report demands some action on your part, say something like, "Thank you for telling me that Bobby broke the glass. I'll pick up the pieces."

Check your child's health. An allergic or otherwise unhealthy child tends to be irritable and to get into more trouble than one who feels well.

If things are really horrendous, don't be afraid to get outside help. Family therapy has saved many a family's sanity.

And for yourself, take some time off from your family each day or at least each week. You will be much better able to handle sibling quarreling if you yourself have an occasional rest from it.

That New Baby

And now back to the beginning of things, when the first sibling is about to be added to a family group which up till now has consisted, presumably, merely of mother, father, and child.

Each generation of parents asks rather much the same questions about their older child or children and the new baby: "How do I tell him [her, them] about the coming baby? How do I prepare him for its arrival? What arrangements should I make for him while I am in the hospital? What do I do if he *is* jealous?"

The answers to all of these questions seem to us to involve good sense more than anything especially psychological. They also depend to a great extent on the temperament of your own child or children.

A child's basic personality or temperament combines with the way life has treated him to determine the way he will feel about a new baby (and potential rival). Some are delighted and excited about the new arrival. Others are not so friendly. One little boy is reported to have pressed his nose against his mother's protuberant abdomen with the threat, "Come on out and fight."

So, the joy and enthusiasm with which you announce the coming event will be tempered by your own knowledge of your child and your evaluation of what his or her response is likely to be.

Preparing a Child for the Arrival of the New Baby

Telling a child about the prospective arrival of a new baby, like telling him or her about sex, should not be too difficult. You know the facts. The trick is to give this information calmly, coolly, clearly, in an unembarrassed manner, and not to tell too much.

The secret of success may lie not so much in what you do as in what you do not do. It is extremely important not to give this information too soon. The very young child has a very different time sense from the adult. A month can seem forever, so if you tell him about the new baby, say six months in advance, he may get very tired indeed of the long wait.

So unless the child asks questions, best delay the announcement till the last few months. Though we once knew a 10-year-old boy who seemed quite oblivious to the fact that his mother was very shortly to have a baby, many quite young children do notice that mother is changing in form and feature and, often, in her behavior. When the child inquires is an ideal time to give needed information. If he does not ask, however, you will have to bring up the topic yourself. (One can hardly spring a baby on an entirely unprepared child.)

Do your best not to get the child's hopes up too much. Talk about the baby in simple, clear, uncomplicated terms. And by all means avoid giving the impression that the new arrival will be a barrel of fun. Be quite honest about a new baby's smallness, lack of motility, and do mention the fact that the baby will cry a lot and will need quite a lot of care and protection. Also of course do not promise specifically that it will be either a boy or a girl unless amniocentesis has revealed this to you.

Try not to tell too much. The entire story of how a baby is conceived need not be shared with the very young. Fortunately almost every public library or bookstore has many fine books to help the expectant mother tell the main and necessary facts about a new baby. One of the best, if appropriate, is *Betsy's Baby Brother* by Gunilla Wolde. This book shows very nicely how helpless and demanding a new baby can be. It discusses the fact that an older child might on occasion feel jealous and even wish the family could give the baby away. And then it shows that a little girl can help her mother in caring for a new baby and that will make her feel better.

Another very dear book about new babies is titled *When the New Baby Comes, I'm Moving Out* by Martha Alexander. Oliver is *not* happy to learn that his mother is going to have a new baby. But his mother helps him to see that there are many advantages in being a big brother.

Two more books (you will see that we are very strong on the use of books in a crisis) which should prove very helpful are *Making Babies: An Open Family Book for Parents and Children Together* and *That New Baby* by Sara Bonnett Stein. These charming picture books cover almost any question that might come up, either before or after the baby is born.

Reading such books to your child not only presents the information needed, but hopefully gives him or her a good chance to ventilate feelings as well as to find out the facts.

In addition to all the talk which may or may not be involved, many mothers do find that some preschoolers enjoy short shopping trips for the purpose of buying things for the baby. Quite obviously such trips must be planned with the stamina and staying power of a youngster in mind. The trip should be short, undemanding, fun. And most certainly there should be some purchase or purchases for the child himself. We do not believe that everything in a family has to be fair or to come out even, but when a new baby (a rather large unknown) is descending on the family, it is only fair to go out of one's way to make the soon-to-be-displaced young person feel that he is still of major importance.

Other arrangements around the home will very likely be going on in the weeks or months preceding the birth of the new baby. It is very important here that the child not be given the impression that his crib, high chair, powdering table or any of the rest of his paraphernalia are going to be ruthlessly taken from him and handed over to the new arrival.

We prefer that a child not be moved from crib to bed much before the age of 4. If your child is around 4 years of age, it would be possible to first buy his new bed and then make plans with him to have the new baby sleep in his old crib (if that is to be the case). Arrangements about rooming should be made with equal care. Whatever the new plan is to be, it is essential to do everything within your power to prevent the older child from feeling displaced.

Probably your very best clues, in conversation, book reading, shopping, or making plans for the new baby, will come from the child himself. If the whole matter appears to be of special interest, devote considerable time to it. If he really doesn't seem to care, it may just be that the time is not right for this kind of concern, so don't dwell on it.

What Arrangements for the Older Child While Mother Is in the Hospital?

In those days when mothers stayed in the hospital with their new babies for a good two weeks, what to do about the older child or children in the family used to pose a serious problem. Some parents felt that there was less disruption if the child could remain at home with some trusted and familiar caretaker. Others believed that going to Grandma's (if Grandma was available and if the child was accustomed to visiting with her) might be the most comfortable solution.

Nowadays hospital stays are so short, and new-baby leave for fathers so much more easily obtainable than in the past, that in many families it seems to work out best if the child remains at home, with Father or some familiar baby-sitter or housekeeper in charge.

Though some very advanced thinkers believe that not only Father but a sibling should be permitted in the delivery room, this seems a most questionable gambit as far as the child is concerned. In fact with the hospital stay currently so short, many experts feel that any visiting by the child at the hospital might best be omitted, and that the introduction to the new baby is best accomplished in the safety of the child's own home.

What about Jealousy?

Much everyday, sensible advice has been written about what to do when you bring the new baby home. The old wisdom is still good. Most young children are, rightfully, apprehensive when this new member of the family first makes its appearance. Common sense tells you not to make too big a deal of the event.

Downplay the baby. He or she absolutely will not care. Play up the fact that here you are at home and very happy to see your big boy or girl.

Then in the first days and weeks, busy as you will be and tired as you quite surely will be, do whatever you reasonably can to make your older child feel that life is not too entirely different from what it was before. Spend as much time with him as you reasonably can. If there is outside help, have the helper tend the baby when possible while you spend time with your older child.

Some people advise not having the older child watch you breast-feed the baby. But even though this event may arouse some rather peculiar feelings in your son or daughter, most agree that the more natural you make life seem, the better. Admittedly some children when they first see the baby nursing behave in ways intended to take your time and attention from this process. They get into trouble, break things and whine, have a bowel movement which (they feel) needs immediate attention.

However, by the time you have a second child, chances are that the breast-feeding will not seem all that big a deal to you and that you will be able to combine it with a reasonable amount of attention to your oldest. The majority of children do accept this function with relative calm. As one 2½-year-old explained to Grandma as Mother nursed the baby, "He's just having his lunch."

One of the biggest helps we have observed is for Mother and Father to refer to the newcomer as New Brother or New Sister. Calling the infant Your Baby, as some do, seems a masterpiece of overstatement. New Brother or New Sister as the case may be, seems to state in a matter-of-fact way that this is just a new and accepted family member.

But though you do your very best, some jealousy still will raise its ugly head. It comes in different forms and at different times. Some children are quite unaccepting of a new arrival from the very beginning: "Why don't you take him back to the hospital?" "Why don't you give her away?" "I don't like her." Others seem friendly and even loving early on, only to take a turn for the worse when the baby becomes mobile and therefore more of a nuisance and more of an attention-getter.

Some jealousy takes the form of too-hard hugs, too-devouring kisses. Or it may come right out in the form of biting, hitting or straight-arm slugging. We have known a preschooler to approach her baby brother with a large, sharp knife and obvious intent to harm. That is, some jealousy disguises itself but can still be hurtful. And in other cases there is absolutely no question about the older child's intention. He or she wants to do the baby in.

In any event, it is never wise to leave an untended, unprotected infant with an older sibling under the age of 6 or 7. This may sound extreme, but best to err on the side of overcautiousness. A family rule that "We do not hurt anybody and that includes the baby" is fine to make. But if you're not on the scene, you won't be available to enforce it when enforcement may sorely be needed.

A baby doll for brother or sister, a doll which the child can dress and undress, powder, change, put to bed, and pretend to feed, often helps. Once the baby is mobile, a fairly safe place for the older sibling's "things," a baby-proof place, will also help. Your time and attention and anything you can possibly do to make a child feel important can help even more.

There are many who consider a so-called geographical cure, that is removing a child from a possible trouble spot, a weak solution. Not so in the present instance. Sending your older child to nursery school, if a good one is available in your community, can be one of your very best cures for jealousy. Nursery school can solve, or at least help with, so many problems—poor eating, poor sleeping, fighting among brothers and sisters. And of course not only nursery school. Keeping older children happily occupied, providing for them as rich and full a life as possible, reduces their need to obtain emotional satisfaction by feeling and expressing jealousy of any brothers and sisters, and especially of a new baby.

13 Television

"Mass communication, in a word, is neither good nor bad. It is
a force and, like any other force, it can be used either well or ill."
ALDOUS HUXLEY

Parents who have been led to believe, by television's highly vocal
critics, that the medium is the road to ruin might do well to keep
in mind this thought that television itself is presumably neither
good nor evil, any more than is literature or the theater good or
evil. It is indeed the way in which it is used that primarily influences our children.

Every generation seems to need a whipping boy or scapegoat.
Thirty years ago it was radio and comic books. A well-known
psychologist, Frederic Wertham, wrote a rather frightening book
called *Seduction of the Innocent.* In it he made very strong claims
about the supposedly horrendous effect that these media—especially comic books—exercised on our vulnerable young.

Today it is television which many consider the root of all evil so
far as children are concerned. As James Halloran, Director of the
Centre for Mass Communication Research at the University of
Leicester has commented:

> The attack on television does not really represent a new phenome-
> non. Throughout history, technological innovations in communica-
> tion have been received with hostility. It is convenient for us to find
> a scapegoat, a single explanation for the ills of society, since this ab-
> solves us from examining our own possible involvement in them.
> Admittedly, there are some who regard television as being entirely
> different in nature (and therefore in influence) from print and sound
> media. But what people are saying now about television has been

said before by their forebears about films, comics, magazines and the press.*

Certainly critics make what seem to us like exaggerated claims as to the amount of time spent viewing television; the adverse effects which viewing has on character, disposition, sense of values, imagination, and family living; the amount of violence it leads to; and the extravagant buying it stimulates.

According to the Spring 1980 issue of a newsletter titled *The PreSchooler:*

> Elementary level students who watch a great deal of TV tend to be hyperactive, nervous and anti-social. The ability to sustain a train of thought, to work concepts through, is perceptibly weakened in students whose thoughts and impressions are numb from bombardment by TV. In addition to causing fatigue, television also contributes to tension, suspicion and aggressive behavior in social relations among young children.

That is one of the milder criticisms.

This chapter will discuss the following issues:

1. Does the average child spend an exorbitant amount of time watching TV?
2. Is television actually, as so many claim, primarily harmful in that it teaches children to be violent?
3. Does television watching cause fatigue, contribute to tension, dampen spontaneity, and reduce the imagination?
4. Does it necessarily lead children into unwise buying habits?
5. On the other hand, can television, as a few claim, actually make children smarter and more mature?
6. Do the average parents have any control over their children's television watching?
7. What might parents do to render television not only harmless but even useful?

---

*Halloran, James, "Television in Focus," *The Unesco Courier*, (March, 1979).

1. *How much time does the average child actually spend in television watching?*

Among what seem to us the more unrealistic criticisms of television are the figures which some give concerning the amount of time the supposedly average child spends watching TV. Thus well-known reading specialist Nancy Larrick is quoted as stating that research shows preschool children spend an average of 54 hours a week, or nearly two-thirds of their waking time, in front of the television set.*

From what we have observed of children's behavior this is a gross exaggeration. In an admittedly rather small survey which we ourselves recently conducted on preschoolers, weekly viewing times ranged from 4 to 34 hours. In one group of our own nursery school children the average was 9 hours a week.

As to older children, we recently conducted a survey of a minimum of 100 girls and 100 boys at each of the ages from 10 through 17.† For girls, the weekly number of viewing hours ranged from 20 at 10 years of age to 10 at age 16. For boys, the range was from 25 hours a week for 10-year-olds to 15 for 17-year-olds. These boys and girls were from highly varying socio-economic levels and lived all over the country, from New Hampshire to Oregon.

2. *Does TV viewing lead to violence?*

This is one of the most hotly debated issues with regard to the effect of television on the young. Though a great deal of research has been carried out in this area, and hundreds of thousands of words have been written, so far few if any solid conclusions have been reached. This is probably due to the fact that it is difficult if not impossible to set up a truly scientific experiment which would reveal the actual relationship between violence observed

---

*Interview reported in *The Preschooler*, Spring 1980.

†Frances L. Ilg and Louise B. Ames, *The Years from Ten to Sixteen* (New York: Harper & Row, 1982).

on the television screen and violent behavior in real life. A humorist has suggested that about the only way to make a reliable determination of the effects of TV violence would be to divide the United States into two halves and make a rule that nobody could move out of his or her half. Then for ten years or so permit violence on the screens of homes in one half of the country and forbid it in the other half. And at the end of the ten years compare the behavior of the children in the two halves of the country.

Summarizing the vast body of research which has been done on the effects of TV violence on young people's behavior, Dr. Ruth E. Hartley, a member of the American Board of Examiners in professional psychology, charged in a full-length technical volume that this research in toto is flawed by "semantic confusion, verbal obscurantism, experimental slovenliness, challengeable premises, unjustifiable extrapolation, evasion of internal contradictions, evasion of external contradictions, slanted reporting . . . and other offenses against reason."*

At any rate, we know of no research which actually proves conclusively that television watching leads to violence.

Though some may feel that young people's own evaluations of the effects of television violence on them may not be entirely valid, we took the opportunity while recently interviewing boys and girls between the ages of 10 and 17 to ask them whether they thought such shows of violence actually did affect them adversely. The number of girls who believed it did *not* affect them adversely ranged from a low of 68 percent at 10 years (that conscientious age) to a high of 87 percent at 15. The low for boys was 67 percent at 15, and the high was 88 percent at 17. That is, by far the majority at every age believed that television violence did not affect them adversely.

---

*Ruth E. Hartley, *Children Vis-à-Vis Television and Filmed Material*, Archives Division of the Library of the University of Wisconsin (Green Bay, Wisc.: Joint Committee of Research on Television and Children, 1968).

3. *Does television watching cause fatigue, contribute to tension, and reduce the imagination?*

The answer to this question is very "iffy." We can only comment that for some children, at least, television viewing can be more restful than fatiguing and it does not necessarily interfere with spontaneity when the set is turned off. (That is, it does not have a lingering or hidden effect.) And some evidence indicates that playing with imaginary companions, a good clue as to imagination, has increased rather than decreased in the years since we first wrote on the subject.*

4. *Does "false and unfair" television advertising cause children to insist that their parents buy them food and toys that are too expensive or even worthless?*

There seems to be little question that many children do tease, excessively, for things they see advertised on TV. However, when products such as toys are clearly overadvertised and turn out to be disappointing when purchased, even quite young children grow wise rather quickly.

An encouraging book on children's buying habits summarizes the author's findings as follows:

> Our data show that only among kindergartners do appreciable numbers of children believe that commercials *always* tell the truth. . . . Children who explicitly stated that commercials tried to sell products were assumed to have a "cognitive filter" in that they clearly understood advertisers' selling intent. Only 18% of the kindergartners were filters, but 73% of the third-graders and 90% of the sixth-graders could be so classified. That is, nearly three-fourths of the third-graders have an understanding of the persuasive function of commercials.
>
> Parents can have a substantial impact on the young child's understanding of commercials by talking with them about commercials and

---

*Louise B. Ames and Janet Learned, "Imaginary Companions and Related Phenomena, *Journal of Genetic Psychology,* 69 (1946): 147–167.

about products they request. For older children such interaction would probably do little to increase their already-developed understanding. . . . Many kindergarten mothers appeared to be missing an opportunity to teach their children to understand the intent of commercials, an understanding that can help them to begin to function as effective consumers.

These analyses have shown that children can "filter" advertising messages and that this ability extends even to children in the youngest age groups. Most importantly, the data suggest that this ability can be taught by parents even to kindergarten-age children.*

5. *Can television, as a few claim, actually make children smarter and more mature?*

The occasional claims made by some that television can actually make children smarter and more mature seem almost as excessive as the claims that it will be their ruination. Outstanding among such promises was that of the founder of *Sesame Street.* This lady predicted that the schools would not know what hit them when the first generation of *Sesame Street* graduates reached kindergarten. (That is, these children would be so superior to and so much better prepared for school than other children that schools would need to beef up curricula in order to meet their academic demands.) The schools withstood this onslaught nicely and the earth remained on its axis. The *Sesame Street* generation performed no better and no worse than those who had come before.

Television undoubtedly does, through its better programs at least, provide boys and girls with considerable useful information as well as enlivening their days. But it does not increase intelligence or speed up the maturing process.

6. *Do the average parents have reasonable control over their children's television watching?*

The amount of supervision which parents wish to give, and the

---

*Scott Ward, Daniel B. Wackman and Ellen Wartella, *How Children Learn to Buy* (Beverly Hills, Calif.: Sage Publications, 1977).

amount which they succeed in giving, varies tremendously from one family to another. To quite an extent it is determined by the age of the child, and to quite an extent by the socioeconomic standing of the family. The newsletter *Behavior Today* for June 2, 1980 reported:

> The children of better-educated or more affluent parents are more likely to confront rules about TV viewing, and much more likely to get suggestions that they watch certain types of programs. The higher the class position, as indicated by the mother's education or family income, the more the balance shifts toward positive encouragement. . . . The less parents watch TV themselves, the more likely they are to try to guide as well as limit their children's use of TV.

Our own rather modest research on the subject indicates that the television watching of the majority of preschoolers can be reasonably well controlled by their parents. Any fussing, arguing, complaining tends to be related to discipline in general rather than specifically to TV.

From 5 through 8, most of the girls questioned by us *claim* that they themselves decide what and when they will watch; many boys say that they and their parents decide together. At 9 years of age the majority of both sexes claim that their parents do not object to the amount of time they spend watching, though the parents may object to certain programs.

Results of our own questioning of over a thousand boys and girls between the ages of 10 and 16 indicate that, according to their own reporting, at 10 years of age about half the girls do have at least some arguments with their parents about either the amount of watching they do or the kinds of programs they watch. From 11 through 15 only about one-third of the girls claim to have arguments. At all of these ages, right through 15, approximately one-third of the boys admit to having difficulties with their parents about television viewing.

Conflict is obviously sometimes good and sometimes bad, depending on how it is handled. If parents merely nag at their children without doing anything further, this reported disagreement is clearly not useful. But if after disagreement there is positive action, it would seem to be all to the good.

7. *What might parents do to render television not only harmless but actually useful?*

Since television definitely is here to stay, we strongly suggest that parents try to look at it as a resource and not as a menace. As James Halloran, mentioned above, has commented:

> Clearly a medium which attracts so much attention and takes up so much time cannot be ignored. In fact we have to be prepared to accept the possibility that television should be regarded, along with family, school, church etc., as an important agent in the development of socialization of the child. Additionally, in some countries, most schools have the necessary facilities and equipment and, consequently, many children are also able to view (even if what they watch is somewhat different) in the school as well as in the home.

At any rate, television is presumably here to stay. So how can parents manage the television viewing of their children, especially perhaps of their younger children, so that it can be a plus rather than a minus in the family situation?

With preschoolers and with children of early school age it would be desirable if parents took control of television viewing. Though some mothers claim that they have "too much to do" to supervise television, it should be quite possible to make a simple but firm weekly plan as to what programs will be permitted and also how much time may be spent viewing.

Any child's weekly schedule normally involves a certain amount of time for school, naps (for the youngest), outdoor play, and indoor play other than television. A clever mother should be able to arrange her child's schedule so that he or she will not be confronted with tremendous amounts of unfilled time.

Second, and this is very important, watch with your children when you can. Preschoolers often ask their parents to watch with them and explain what is going on. Older children enjoy sharing their pleasure at a program.

Share at least some of their viewing and then discuss what you have seen. You might ask, "Is that reasonable? Do people really act like that? *Should* they behave that way? With older children, many good discussions about manners and morals—discussions which otherwise might not interest them tremendously—can be initiated.

Most important, try to demonstrate by your own viewing that television is a medium to be used selectively. A family which keeps its set on, routinely, all evening—or worse, all day as well as all evening—is not sending any message of selectivity to its younger members. It can be especially useful if by your own viewing you steer your children to the enjoyment of informative (and one can hope also interesting) educational and news programs. There is a lot there for everybody if one uses a certain discretion in making choices.

A very old lady who came to TV only in her 80s, once remarked to her daughter, "It's just like the Arabian nights." Perhaps if we could think more about the wonder of it and its potential, and less about our dissatisfaction that it cannot be all things to all people, our children might share this appreciation of its actually quite remarkable possibilities.

However, uncritical as we may seem about the entire television scene, we must admit that perhaps the majority of programs shown today do seem less than impressive. Though some criticize as simplistic the notion that the public gets what it wants, it seems reasonable that programs would not succeed if nobody watched them.

You as parents can certainly make known your own feelings about undesirable programs by discouraging your children from watching them and also by writing to your station or to the program's sponsors. The public does have a voice. The main problem is that perhaps the most critical viewers by no means represent the majority.

Fortunately, common sense makes us realize that not all programs need please everybody. We do have a choice of programs; and we also have a choice, for ourselves and at least for our younger children, of watching or not watching. There is an "Off" button on every set.

14 School Success

Every Child in the Right Grade

If somebody offered you a formula which in all likelihood would increase your child's chances of school success, would you welcome it? Well, here it is.

It is the Gesell Institute position that at least half of the school failures now experienced in the early grades could be prevented or cured if children started school only when they were fully ready. We recommend starting all children in school, and subsequently promoting them, on the basis of their behavior age rather than their birthday (chronological) age or their level of intelligence.

Thus a child could be 7 years old and could have an I.Q. of say, 120, but if he were behaving like a 6-year-old we would like to see him placed in first, not second, grade.

State laws which permit children to start kindergarten when they are 5 (and in some states when they are only 4½), and first grade when they are 6, are dealing only with averages. Common sense tells us that not all 5-year-olds have actually reached a normative 5-year-old level of behavior.

Thus it is our recommendation that before any child starts kindergarten, he or she should be given a behavior test, or developmental examination, which would indicate exactly how far he or she had come in behavior, and thus was, or was not, ready for the grade which the law might indicate.*

---

*There are several behavior tests now available. We, quite naturally, prefer our own Gesell Behavior Tests, described fully in both *The Gesell Institute's Child*

What we recommend, and something that is being tried in many communities, is a so-called Developmental Placement Program. In carrying out such a program, all children who will be ready, agewise, for kindergarten in the fall, would be tested in the preceding spring by means of a shortened developmental examination.

Such an examination does not test intelligence or personality but merely reveals the age level at which the child is using eyes, hands, body. Among the tests which we use are copy forms (the child merely copies a circle, cross, square, triangle, divided rectangle, and diamond), and completing the figure of what we call an Incomplete Man. The child's response to these simple tests indicates whether he or she is behaving at an age level of 4, 4½, 5, or perhaps 5½ years.

If the child's behavior age fully matches his chronological age, the likelihood is that he would be permitted to start kindergarten in the fall, with the expectation that he would move on to first grade the following fall.

If his behavior age is somewhat below his chronological age so that he would not be expected to be behaving like a 5-year-old by fall, we would recommend that he be placed, come fall, in a pre-kindergarten, with the plan that he would spend two years in kindergarten.

If behavior is far below chronological age expectations, it might be recommended that the child spend an extra year in nursery school, or at home, before entering the public school system.

In addition to all of this caution, we would like to see schools provide a pre–first grade, or readiness class, for those who having finished kindergarten are still not ready for first grade.

All of this may seem overcautious to the uninitiated. However, experience has shown that if a child is fully ready for first grade by the time he is placed there, chances are excellent that school

from One to Six by Ames, Gillespie, Haines, and Ilg, and *School Readiness* by Ilg, Ames, Gillespie, and Haines.

from then on will be a success. Experience has also shown that by using the Developmental Placement Program schools can sharply reduce the number of children who fail and thus require special remedial help. It can also cut down the number who do poorly in school and thus are labeled "learning disabilities," and again require special help.

Our clinical service has demonstrated that many children who are failing and who are thus labeled L.D. could actually be successful IF they were placed in a lower grade where they could do the work, not in a grade just a bit above the place where they were functioning.

Our research has shown that in typical public schools not more than the top third of the children in any class, when grouped according to their chronological age, are fully ready for the work that the grade demands. Others are questionably ready or simply unready.*

Though in our opinion chronological age is not a good criterion for deciding when a child should begin school, if developmental examining is not available, parents will do well to follow the path of caution. If birthday age must be the criterion, we like to see girls at least 5 *before* they begin kindergarten, boys fully 5½. We prefer girls to be at least 6 before they begin first grade and boys fully 6½.

Repeating

Let's suppose, however, that as will be the case for many of you, your child is already in school, is not doing well, and seems quite clearly overplaced. Should you have him repeat? Our answer would be a resounding "Yes." In years past, some parents, supported by some child specialists, voiced the fear that requiring a child to repeat would be emotionally harmful. Experience, sup-

---

*"School Readiness as Evaluated by Gesell Developmental, Visual and Projective Tests," by Frances L. Ilg, Louise Bates Ames, and Richard J. Apell, *Genetic Psychology Monographs*, 71 (1965): 61–91.

ported by research, shows that such fears are largely groundless.

In actual practice we have found that the majority of children will accept the notion that they must repeat rather calmly if parents and school convey this information in a calm, unemotional way. Do not talk about failure. Instead present the position that parents and school *made a mistake* by starting the child in school before he was ready. Point out that *no wonder* he finds school so hard and doesn't like it and doesn't do well. Say that *isn't it lucky* you all found out in time so that now he can be in first (second, third, or whatever) grade again and this time it will be easy and fun.

These promises will not turn out to be false. In nearly every instance in which a child is permitted to repeat a grade (assuming that immaturity and overplacement were, as so often, the root of the problem), repeating does bring success. Obviously, repeating cannot solve all possible school problems. But if other causes of failure have been ruled out and thus if as is so often the case overplacement is the main cause of difficulty, repeating a grade can do the trick.

The chorus is growing louder, over the years. From the hundreds, very likely thousands of families whom we have encouraged to permit their overplaced children to repeat a grade during the last twenty-five years, the story is always the same:

"He's a different boy," "She's a changed child." "Except that he's in the same skin I wouldn't know my son, he's so tremendously improved." "Now she goes around the house singing; it's as if the weight of the world had been lifted from her shoulders."

Perhaps even more impressive are the thanks we receive from boys and girls (now young men and women) themselves, who tell us, "You changed my life. I was floundering and failing till you persuaded my parents to let me repeat a grade. It was all roses after that."

Research supports these personal testimonials. Among the most impressive data are those reported by psychologist Verne Lewis, now of La Mirada, California. The research, a questionnaire study of parents of over four hundred repeated children, was carried out in Jefferson, Iowa. Of these parents, 88 percent reported that the good effects of repeating outweighed the bad; 90 percent felt that retention had been justified; 80 percent said their child had done better academically after repeating. Ninety percent said they had never regretted having their child repeat, while 86 percent said they would make the same decision again.

A further study by Joan Ames Chase checked on the success of retention of sixty-five first-, second-, and third-grade repeaters as judged by teachers and by the children's parents.* Teachers felt that repeating had met the needs of 75 percent of the children and had produced no emotional upset whatever in 78 percent, with only temporary upset in 16 percent more. Of the parents, 95 percent expressed themselves as being in favor of having their children repeat. The majority reported that after repeating their children liked school better, felt more confident and successful in school, were happier and easier to live with at home, and got on better with their friends.

Reasons for Failure Other than Overplacement

"He could do better if he would!" What teacher doesn't say this about at least one of her pupils during the course of the school year?

"She could do better if she would only try. She has a perfectly adequate intelligence but just doesn't seem to care."

"He could do better if he would only concentrate."

"She could do better if only she wouldn't daydream."

The teachers (and parents) who make these statements all speak as if the pupil in question *could* pay attention and stop fooling around and stop daydreaming and get better grades if only he or she would *try*. As if it were just a matter of students' exerting will power, and disciplining themselves into more effective behavior.

---

*"A Study of the Impact of Grade Retention on Primary School Children," by Joan Ames Chase, *The Journal of Psychology*, 70 (1968): 169–177.

Yet our experiences with the many children who are brought to our Institute because of poor schoolwork have led us to reverse the key statement. We say not, "He could do better if he would," but rather, "He would do better if he could."

All these behaviors which parents and teachers complain about seem to us danger signals which tell us that something (or often many a thing) is wrong with the school situation for this particular child at this time. The secret, of course, is to obtain a clear-cut, differential diagnosis from a clinician knowledgeable not only about child behavior in general but about school behavior.

There are, of course, many, many different possible reasons why children fail in school. Those we run into most often in our clinical practice are the following. Though overplacement seems to be the outstanding reason for school failure, some sort of visual problem is nearly as prevalent. Another chief reason for school difficulty is just plain inadequate endowment. Though it is popular to believe nowadays that almost any child could make it if only somebody (parent, teacher, society) just did the right things, we must admit that many children are underendowed intellectually or academically and need very much the special help that a special class or special school can provide.

Though not as prevalent as some people once thought, there are some children who fail in school because of their own individual emotional problems—children who would indeed be helped by some degree or kind of psychotherapy.

And finally, there are a good many children who do poorly in school for reasons of health. Either because of inadequate nutrition or because of debilitating allergic reactions either to foods or inhalants, many children are just not physically and behaviorally well enough to succeed in school.

We shall discuss briefly the problems of vision and of health.

Vision

One special aspect of the child's behavior which should always be carefully checked when there is trouble in school is his or her vision. We should always ask ourselves: Is this 5-year-old visually mature enough for kindergarten? Will this immature 5½-year-old who can read at a third-grade level be visually harmed by excessive attention to materials seen at near point? Is this 6-year-old visually ready for first grade? Does this 7-year-old have the visual sustaining power demanded in second grade? And so on, right up through the various grades. Our clinical experience indicates that many children are not ready visually for the demands of the grade in which they are placed.

One reason for overlooking the child's visual problems has been a lack of understanding by some educators and even by some eye specialists as to what constitutes a *visual* problem and how it may differ from an *eye* problem. Many children have a visual problem but not an eye problem. That is, the interior and exterior parts of their eyes are healthy, they have the ability to see small letters clearly at twenty feet (20/20 vision), and there are no obvious errors in the optical systems of either eye. Therefore the diagnosis is healthy eyes and no eye problem.

But in a proper visual examination more than healthy eyes is involved. In a visual examination we should be concerned with the child's visual *abilities:* whether or not he can focus and point his eyes together as a team; his speed of perception; his accuracy in looking from one object to another. We must find out whether he can keep his eyes on an object moving toward him, in a circular direction, from side to side, up and down, and at an angle.

We must check on his ability to sustain focus at the reading distance; on how he uses his eyes and hands together; and on many other visual skills that are necessary within the school environment. A child lacking some of these essential visual skills may find himself classed as a reading problem, a behavior problem, or more often as just a lazy child who could do the work if he would only try. When we speak of "vision," we must be concerned with the child's ability to get meaning and understanding from what he sees by the skillful and efficient use of both eyes.

As parents or teachers, you will want to know what can be done to prevent visual difficulties in the child who is visually immature and/or lacking in some of the necessary visual skills mentioned above. If it seems to be a question of overall immaturity, then the question of correcting grade placement as mentioned earlier should be seriously considered as a first step. For many other children, visual therapy—that is, being taught how to move, focus, and fixate the two eyes so that they coordinate properly—is essential for efficient visual development.

One 7-year-old boy was brought to us because he was failing in second grade and was unhappy in school. The boy had complained to his mother for several months that he kept getting the words wrong that the teacher wrote on the blackboard. A routine eye examination indicated that there was no eye problem. However, our visual examination showed that he had very poor ability in moving his eyes from one point in space to another and in keeping his eyes on a moving target. After this boy was taught, through visual training, how to use his eyes efficiently, he began to improve in his schoolwork, took real interest in his studies for the first time, and was no longer unhappy in school.

Sometimes when visual therapy is not available, it is possible to rearrange the school environment to get around the problem. For example, one very intelligent 8-year-old girl was forever disturbing the class with her childlike antics, which necessitated her being sent home from school, until it was discovered that she couldn't see to copy her daily assignments from the blackboard. When she couldn't succeed, she just blew off steam. The problem was solved by having her copy the assignments at her desk— something that was well within her visual ability—rather than from the board.

Sometimes glasses that allow the child to focus his eyes more easily when he reads or works at his desk are used as an aid to visual development and to prevent certain types of eye problems. Many visually immature children in first and second grade have not developed their focusing ability at near range to a degree where they can read or do deskwork for any length of time. This kind of glasses makes it easier for them to work without fatigue. Without such glasses, some of these children avoid reading and other near work as much as possible. Others, particularly 7-year-olds, may force themselves to achieve perfection and to finish their near work to such a degree that they lose their ability to focus their eyes at distance. The result is the development of myopia (nearsightedness), and now the child has a visual problem and an eye problem, too!

The visual difficulties of many children are not even suspected. Probably more boys and girls than one realizes have rather severe visual problems. Even something as drastic as seeing double is often not suspected till it is discovered almost by accident.

For this reason, if for no other, we strongly recommend annual visual examinations for every child from 3 or 4 years of age and after. If a visual problem is discovered early enough, it can in many instances be dealt with either through lens help or visual training before it develops into something more serious and more difficult to treat. Early and frequent visual examinations are one of a parent's best ways of preventing serious visual problems in school or at home.

Specific evidence that early intervention can markedly decrease many of the visual problems which develop in the early school years because too much is demanded too soon comes from a project carried out by Dr. John W. Streff, formerly of our visual staff. National norms have it that not more than 10 percent of first-graders are nearsighted. But by sixth grade the figure ranges from 25 percent to 30 percent. In Cheshire, Connecticut, where we were working when we first checked, the figure was 25 percent nearsightedness in sixth grade, close to the national average.

However, after we and the school had conducted several years of a program of proper school placement plus visual training given in the schools, only 2 to 18 percent of sixth-grade children (depending on the school) were nearsighted.

Early examination, proper placement, visual training, all three can be used effectively to prevent many visual problems before they occur.

Health and School Performance

Admittedly, by no means every case of visual difficulty is diagnosed or treated. Even in situations where parents complain about their child's visual performance, all too often school and specialist assure them, incorrectly, that there is nothing wrong with the child's vision because he or she has 20/20 acuity. Acuity is certainly not the only aspect of vision which needs to be checked.

However, in theory most people do at least admit that poor vision can indeed be a cause of inadequate school performance. They also agree that a "really" sick child might have trouble in school. Fortunately nowadays we have come a long way beyond this commonsense acknowledgment. Today many people—parents, doctors, teachers, child specialists—are aware that a poor diet can also lie at the root of much academic malfunctioning. This poor diet may consist of a merely inadequate diet, or it may involve foods to which the child has an allergic reaction.

In the past, even when allergy was obvious—and often it is not —schools were all too unaware of its effect on behavior. But in just the past decade tremendous strides have been made in our awareness of the all-important role which both poor diet and/or allergies can play in influencing not merely a child's health but also his or her school behavior for the worse.

One of the first to emphasize this close connection between allergic reaction to foods or inhalants and school behavior, or misbehavior, was pediatrician Ray Wunderlich who, in his groundbreaking book, *Allergy, Brains and Children Coping*, pointed out that we must all pay more attention to the health aspect of the child's body. He emphasized that one important consideration is the possibility that the schoolchild in behavior difficulty might be allergic. According to Wunderlich:

It works both ways. Allergy can interfere with the function of the brain and the brain that doesn't work properly can bring on allergy. . . . There is a growing realization that the adjustment problems of children are more often biologically based than was commonly recognized in the past.

Wunderlich stresses that the child who falls asleep over his desk may not necessarily be one who has not gotten enough sleep. He may be one who is allergic to something in his diet (especially in his school lunch) or something in the atmosphere.

Wunderlich's book was followed closely by the now well-known *Why Your Child Is Hyperactive* by Ben Feingold, whose thesis is that a poor diet, especially the ingestion of artificial colorings and flavorings, has a very bad effect on behavior. These substances can especially cause hyperactivity and resulting learning disability.

Then came Lendon H. Smith's useful pair of books, *Improving Your Child's Behavior Chemistry* and *Feed Your Kids Right,* and William Crook's *Tracking Down Hidden Food Allergy.*

Both these factors—the importance of proper nutrition and the devastating effects of allergy—have been discussed earlier in this book. We mention them here simply to remind parents that if a child is having difficulty in school, health factors rather than the so-often-blamed emotional factors may be at the basis of the difficulty.

Education Policies of Concern to Parents

Space does not permit a comprehensive review of all public policies with which parents might well be concerned. We shall mention simply a very few major considerations of which we think you should be aware.

All-Day Academic Kindergarten

There is always somebody out there, unfortunately often somebody in power, who is pushing to have young children spend longer periods of time in school than they now spend. These same people want more emphasis put on highly academic instruction in the very early grades. The present push is for all-day kindergarten, in which reading, writing, and presumably arithmetic will be strongly stressed. (We have even heard of one kindergarten in which the children are "taught," early in the year, to underline nouns in blue and verbs in red.)

Research by John Mulrain and others supports the notion, long held by us, that a full-day school session is too much even for first-graders, let alone for kindergarteners.* If, as is often the case, mothers need somewhere to leave their children while they work, the question of need for day-care should be squarely faced. Kindergartens should not be used as substitutes for day-care centers.

If the idea, as some insist, is that kindergarten children need all day to "get ready" for first grade, if first-grade curriculums could remain as modestly demanding as they should, then there would be relatively little "getting ready" needed.

As for pushing reading in kindergarten, we and many others believe that even many 6-year-old first-graders are not ready for formal instruction in reading, let alone 5-year-old kindergarteners. There is little to be gained, and much to be lost, by pushing the academic aspects of school before young children are ready.

Mainstreaming

A currently very popular method of grouping boys and girls in school is so-called mainstreaming. As present laws are currently interpreted, many schools believe that the "least restrictive environment" required by law means the regular classroom.

Thus in all too many communities, students who formerly would have had the privilege of being in special classes (classes which one hopes would have met their special needs) are now pushed into the mainstream. The argument for this seems to be twofold: first that special classes are bad because they discriminate against the

---

*"Half Days for First Graders," by John Mulrain and Louise Bates Ames, *The Instructor* (February 1979): 116, 118.

less able students, and second that the less capable students will in some mysterious way "benefit" from being in the same class as the brighter students.

Well-known educator Marianne Frostig has this to say about mainstreaming:

> The beautiful uplifting phrases we hear about mainstreaming, such as "All children have the right to the best education," or "All children must learn in the least restrictive environment," may drown out the less enthusiastic, more pragmatic voices of teachers who realize that integrating children into regular classrooms after they have been attending segregated (special) classrooms will not be easy. *I would like to object to the dishonesty and hypocrisy found in some school systems, which the mainstreaming edict has spawned or at least reinforced.*
>
> Exceptional children need highly individualized treatment. Such individualized treatment may be a burden on the teacher who is in charge of the total classroom. . . . About 15% of the children in today's schools have difficulties in keeping up with other children in the classroom. . . . Any special child mainstreamed possibly takes up as much of a teacher's time as three normally endowed children without special problems. . . .
>
> Although Public Law 94-142 and the law for protection of the handicapped are humane and could be models for laws in many countries, our habit of over-bureaucratizing and undertaking what we are not ready for works counter to our good intentions. *We should realize that we do not have enough well-trained teachers and should not attempt to mainstream all children as a matter of course.**

Learning Disabilities

One last educational concept, very big these days and very confused, seems worthy of comment—the concept of learning disabilities. Disagreements in this field are many. People disagree as to whether more children today have trouble in school than

---

*"Meeting Individual Needs of All Children in the Classroom Setting," by Marianne Frostig, *Journal of Learning Disabilities,* 13 (March 1980): 51–54.

once did or whether it is just our massive interest in them that makes it seem so.

They disagree as to how much of a problem a child has to be before he or she can be designated as having a learning disability. They disagree as to just what a learning disability is. And they disagree about how, and under what circumstances, such children should be taught. They even disagree as to what kind of a professional organization should be the official representative of people who work in the field.

One of the main problems in this area seems to be the unwillingness of those who work in it to associate themselves, or their charges, with older groups who work in the entire area of retardation. There seems to be a strong need among learning-disability specialists to be special and unique. And yet virtually everything in the field is borrowed.

According to Samuel A. Kirk and John Elkins, a review of three thousand children enrolled in Child Service Demonstration Centers for Learning Disabilities in twenty-one states shows that most of these children were general underachievers to a moderate degree in reading, spelling, and arithmetic.* These writers raise the question of whether such generalized underachievement constitutes a specific learning disability.

All of this is said not to disparage the field of learning disabilities. There are many dedicated people laboring vastly in this vineyard. Rather, it is said as a warning to parents who may be told that their child who is having trouble in school has a Learning Disability.

That may indeed be true. Your boy or girl may indeed have some very special difficulty which cannot be blamed on any usual diagnosable problem or treated in customary ways. And he or she may be located in a school district which has specially gifted teach-

---

*"Learning Disabilities: Characteristics of Children Enrolled in the Child Service Demonstration Centers," *Journal of Learning Disabilities*, 8 (December 1975): 630–637.

ers trained to work with such children and highly suitable classes into which they can be placed.

However, if such a label is given, here are a few warnings. Do your very best to obtain a careful diagnosis which will tell you just exactly what your child's problem is. For instance, is he of a low enough intelligence to warrant placement in a special class for such children? Does your child have special visual difficulties which may account for school problems? Is something about your child's diet contributing to his academic ineffectiveness?

Most important, may he or she simply be overplaced? There are all too many children in our schools today who have been placed in a grade above the one where they can do the work. They fail. Then they are kept in this inappropriate grade but sent out each day to a learning-disability laboratory where they are given special help in the vain effort to permit them to keep up with the work of a grade in which they didn't belong in the first place.

The whole concept of learning disabilities may not be the panacea it has been thought to be.

Conclusion

It is important to remember that much school difficulty can be prevented entirely by not starting the child in school too soon. Proper grade placement might eliminate as much as 50 percent of the difficulties which children experience in school.

Second, do not be too quick to condemn a poor student by saying, "He could do better if he would." A good many school "failures" are, nevertheless, doing the best they can in a situation which is, in one respect or another, too difficult for them. Remember that a high I.Q. alone is not enough to guarantee good school performance.

And lastly, if your child is experiencing school difficulties which simpler efforts cannot clear up, a careful physical examination, and a thorough visual examination if possible, can often reveal the source of difficulty.

PART THREE

15 What to Tell about Death, Deity, Adoption, Divorce

This chapter will discuss four important though perhaps somewhat unrelated topics and situations—death, deity, adoption, and divorce. It will cover what children commonly think about, how they react to, and what you may wish to tell them about three major events and one significant concept. Children vary in their reaction to all four of these topics, as well as in the interest they feel about them. But here, as elsewhere, certain basic age-related changes do occur, and certain basic suggestions as to how a parent can help, apply to nearly all.

Death

What one tells a child about death, and how when necessary one helps him to face the fact of death, depends chiefly on two things. One is your own personality and your interpretation of your child's and of what works with him. The second is the child's age.

The very young child has an extremely limited conception of death, and unless it is a much-loved pet that dies or a parent whose absence he naturally misses, his reaction tends to be minimal. Even by 4 years of age the child's notions of death are extremely limited. As a rule, no particular emotion is expressed, though the child may verbalize some rudimentary notion that death is connected with sorrow or sadness.

By 5 in many the concept becomes more detailed, accurate, and factual. Many recognize that death is "the end." Many recognize the immobility of the dead. They may like to avoid dead things— like birds or animals.

With some exceptions, most preschoolers are not ready for anything but the most simple explanations of death. Unless it is someone very close to him and someone much loved who dies, concern about the event may be mild. Most 5-year-olds have a notion of themselves as always living; only other people die. At 5 we get the beginning of concern that Mother will one day die, a concern that becomes much, much stronger at 6.

Five may utilize the facts he or she has about death falsely. For instance, one little girl, told about how Abraham Lincoln had been shot, asked at the time of her grandfather's death, "Who shot Grandpa?" Another child, whose grandfathers both had died but both of whose grandmothers were still alive, inquired, "Do daddies always die first?"

Some at 5½ believe in the reversibility of death—you're dead for a while and then you come to life. One such boy expressed this attitude in a threat to a friend: "Always have you been bad. Never have you been good. Now I will make you dead. Never will I make you alive again."

By 6 years of age a new emotional awareness and a much clearer concept of death is coming in. Though most children still do not realize that they themselves will one day die, many are beginning to get the idea that death is often connected with old age and that the older people often die first. As one child remarked to her mother, "You will be an old, old lady. And then you will die. And I will have babies." At 6 as well as just earlier, the notion of the reversibility of death tends to be strong.

Seven, with his often morbid and moody personality, tends to be strongly interested in death and its causes: disease, violence, old age. He now begins to suspect that he himself may one day die. Some strongly deny this. Others view the possibility quite calmly, like the little girl who remarked to her mother: "If Granny dies I shall cry, but not for long. I shall be unhappy for you because you have no mother. I shall be extra nice and be your mother. I might die next year when I'm eight. Or I might die before Christmas and get no presents."

Seven's complaint, "I wish I were dead," is quite typical of many of his remarks and should not, as a rule, be taken too seriously. The 8-year-old, less morbid and more expansive than Seven, has usually progressed from an interest in graves and funerals to an interest in what happens after death. He may make some such comment as, "After you die, you get buried. You don't feel it. If you're good you go to Heaven. God takes you out of the box and brings you to Heaven. God makes you alive. If you're bad you go to Hell and the Devil burns you up."

By 9 and 10 most are ready to face the notion of death quite squarely. They no longer concentrate on funerals or on what happens after. Many now can make reference to the logical or biological essentials: "Not living," or "When you die you have no pulse and no temperature and you can't breathe." Most 9- and 10-year-olds are ready for as full an explanation as you may wish to or be able to give.

In telling your child about death you will be governed in what you say, and especially in how much you say, by his questions and attention, or lack of attention. If you are talking over his head or telling more than he wants to know, you will be alerted to this very quickly by his waning interest.

Fortunately we can recommend a beautiful book which will help almost any parent in the telling. It is titled *Talking About Death: A Dialogue Between Parent and Child* by Rabbi Earl A. Grollman. This book consists of wonderful illustrations, almost like finger paintings; a clear, factual honest test; and a discussion of questions which may arise as you share the book with your child. The story starts out:

> When you die, you're dead. Try saying that word, DEAD. It is a hard word to say, isn't it? Not hard to pronounce, really, but hard to make yourself say. Maybe because it's a sad word, even a little frightening. Now let's say another word: DIE. That's what happened to grandfather. Grandfather died. He is dead . . . DEAD is DEAD. It is not a game. It is very real. Grandfather is gone. He will never come back.

The book continues through an analogy with plants which bloom and then fade. But we can remember how beautiful they were, and we can remember the person who has died. . . . This is a story which can be meaningful to old and young alike.

A few basic suggestions which Rabbi Grollman gives include:

1. Always tell your child the truth. Never tell anything he or she will have to unlearn later.
2. Be prepared to calmly meet a child's emotional outbursts or denials of what you are saying.
3. Do not expect to tell this story once and for all, or all at once. It will need repetition.
4. Make it very clear that the person's death (if it was someone near to you) was not in any way the child's fault.
5. Don't feel that the young child needs an elaborate, theological explanation of death or of what may happen after death, even if you feel qualified to give it. As the child grows older, share any honest religious convictions, but do not lean too heavily on the concept of Heaven.

Adults sometimes try to shield their child from their own grief at the time of death. Most of us feel that you do children no kindness by shutting them out. This holds true for funerals. To include a wiggly preschooler in a funeral may serve little purpose; but by 6 or 7, if your child is one who as a rule behaves reasonably well in public places, inclusion in a funeral can be meaningful to him and a possible source of comfort to the grown-ups. Your own understanding of your child's predictable reactions can be your best guide in making a decision.

Deity

Religion is a very personal and a very individual thing. We would not presume to advise parents as to what they should tell their children about the deity.

We might, however, comment that the child's interest in and

concept of deity to some extent follow the same path as his interest in and concept of Santa Claus.

Both, to begin with, are believed in thoroughly and uncritically. They are thought of in highly anthropomorphic terms. Both are seen as having the form of human men—almighty, all-powerful, and kind, taking a highly personal interest in each little girl or boy.

The typical 4-year-old asks very specific questions about God: "Who is God?" "Does he like candy?" "Does he look like my Daddy?"

The usual 5-year-old continues Four's markedly practical interest in God: "Where does he live? Can you call him up on the phone?" The related concepts of Santa Claus and God are suggested by the comments of one little girl who explained to her family: "You know God? Well he has two names: God and Jesus. You can call him either. I prefer 'God.' Some people don't believe on God. Some children don't believe on Santa Claus. The ones that don't don't get any Christmas presents. I believe on Santa Claus."

The 6-year-old loves to think about religious matters. He loves to pray. He loves to hear stories about God "Our Father," and he especially loves to hear about "Our Little Lord Jesus." Six is apt to take all of this very personally, and it tends to be extremely meaningful to him.

And then comes skepticism. Children of 7 begin to ask rather probing questions about God. They require more proof than they did earlier. Thus the same boy or girl who at 6 came home from Sunday School bursting with lively accounts of God and Jesus, is not quite so certain at 7. Asked about God, a 7-year-old is apt to reply, "Well, I have never seen him." Seven's approach to religion has turned from the emotional to the intellectual.

Now his questions become more "appropriate" than they were just earlier. Now he asks, "How can he see everything and be everywhere all at one time? Why don't people come back from Heaven? Is it so wonderful that they don't want to?" Seven's skepticism is not simply rebellion or the expression of an irreligious attitude. Rather, it means that these matters concern him and he is now attaining the maturity of wanting to find out for himself.

By 8 some have already reached a stage of believing that the soul but not the body goes to Heaven, though others persist in the notion that the body, too, goes to Heaven or Hell, depending on your behavior on earth.

And from here on, responses to religious matters vary tremendously from child to child, depending on temperament, exposure, and family beliefs and practices. Of the 10-year-olds we studied, exactly half told us that they did believe in God. But the others admitted that they either did not believe, never had believed, questioned God's existence, or were less interested in religion than formerly.

Those for whom religion remains an important concept tend to think of the deity increasingly as an abstraction, instead of in the concrete terms which characterize the younger child's thoughts on the matter.

What to Tell about Adoption

In this past century parents have come a long, long way in their attitudes toward adoption. Families have always taken in children, especially relatives, who were left homeless. But adoption as such is relatively new, and parents' questions about adoption are rapidly changing.

Back in the 1930s and 1940s the question parents asked most frequently was, "Shall I tell my child that he [she] is adopted?" Our own answer was always "Yes," though not everybody agreed. The accompanying question, in those days, was, "When shall I tell him?" The answer to that was "As soon as is practical."

Clearly it's not going to mean much to an infant or even to a 2-year-old to be told that he or she is adopted. But as soon as questions about where babies come from are asked, the concept of adoption can be slipped into the answer. Thus one can explain, without too much detail at first, that babies grow inside their mothers.

The child almost inevitably will then ask if he grew inside *his* mother. And here one can say, quite simply, that all babies grow inside *some* mother. Some stay with that mother, and others find a different mother. The fact that this adopted child was *chosen* by his present family seems to give comfort and security to many. Some even feel superior because they were chosen, and the book *The Chosen Baby* by Valentina Wasson has long been a favorite in its stress on this comforting theme.

Through the 1930s and '40s, however, very little, in fact usually nothing, was said about the child's own natural parents. Adopting parents, as well as children's books on the subject, tended to slide over that aspect of the matter. This is no longer the case. Though this topic is usually not introduced when the child is very young, even a preschooler may ask why the woman who bore him didn't keep him.

Today we have a typically frank and helpful book on this aspect of adoption. *And Now We Are a Family* by Judith Meredith tells how babies are born and families are made. It also points out that sometimes a man and woman do not create their children. They adopt them. And it explains that "Adopting a baby means doing the mothering and fathering for a baby that was born to someone else." Then it asks if the child wonders about the man and woman he or she was born to. It goes on to discuss, in a most sympathetic way, some of the many reasons a man and woman might not have been able to keep their baby. It is an extremely comforting book.

Now other books for children are keeping up with this shift in frankness and in addition are taking care of the question of racially mixed adoptions. Thus *Is That Your Sister?* by Catherine and Sherry Bunin, a child's own story of what she tells her friends about why her biological mother couldn't keep her and also why her skin is a different color from that of the rest of the family, may help an adoptive mother feel secure about explaining the situation when these particular questions arise. It certainly could be supportive to any young adopted child whose background differs from that of his adoptive family.

Needless to say, as with the matter of sex, this isn't something that one can tell a child about once and for all and then be done with the subject. Questions recur and become more penetrating as the child grows older. But as with sex, you have the advantage of knowing the answers. Your strongest weapon here is frankness, a lack of self-consciousness, and a wish to make your child feel secure.

As young people move on into their teens and beyond, a further problem arises which, though it presumably has always been there below the surface, has remained submerged until just the past few years. Till, say, the 1960s or even later, most social agencies *insisted* that all adoption records remain sealed and that any effort whatever on the part of adopted persons to find out something about their natural parents be thwarted at every turn.

Largely due to the insistent demands of the adopted, this situation is changing. Many now insist that it is their right to know something about their true origins. One of the first to push this demand was an extremely dedicated and determined woman named Jean Paton, herself an adoptee. Her first publication along these lines was titled *Orphan Voyage*. She has spent a lifetime in efforts to help adopted individuals discover their true origins.

More recent, and more publicized, is a book by Florence Fisher titled *The Search for Anna Fisher*, subtitled, *The Dramatic Story of an Adoptee Who Was Determined to Find Her Natural Parents—And After Twenty Heartbreaking Years, Did.* Her work and that of others has led to the formation of a support group called Alma, whose purpose is to help adoptees locate their natural parents.

Public opinion, and especially opinion among parents who themselves have adopted children, is still sharply divided between those who feel that it is desirable for people to locate and get acquainted with their natural parents, and those who feel it best to leave well enough alone. This, clearly, is a highly individual matter. Some—adopted individuals, adopting parents, and natural parents—very much favor discovery. Others, perhaps the majority, feel skeptical toward or even threatened by the whole idea.

Heredity vs. Environment

Whatever the topic, when one discusses human behavior, the question arises: Is a child's behavior determined more by heredity or by environment? Though in theory reasonable persons admit that actually neither can function without the other and that it is the *interaction* of the two that determines what we are and will become, in practice most of us tend to see one or the other as the primarily determining factor.

And so with adoption. There are those who insist that the way an adopted boy or girl turns out depends almost solely on how he or she is treated by the adopting parents. Others, and we among them, respect the fact that environment can do a very great deal but that it must always work within certain limits—limits prescribed by hereditary factors.

Thus it has always been our advice that before you adopt either an infant or a child, you obtain a careful behavior examination in addition to a careful medical examination. This former will tell you, within reason, whether the child in question is or is not of normal intelligence and what in all likelihood you can expect of his or her behavior.

Once you have this information, of course it is up to you to decide whether or not you wish to go ahead with the adoption. Some people have the capacity to love and take care of an adopted child who is not only physically handicapped but of less than normal intelligence. But our position is that you owe it to yourself to know—so far as one can predict the future—what you are getting into.

With the relative shortage of adoption candidates these days—caused by increasing knowledge of birth-control methods, the increasing availability of abortion, and the increasing trend for unmarried girls to keep their babies rather than to put them up for adoption—many couples become rather desperate for *any* adoptable child. Right at the time of adoption they may think they really don't care if the child's physical, intellectual, or emotional potential is below normal. As the years go by, however, some regret not having been a little more cautious.

One final comment about adoption. A seemingly strange but very common experience of couples who have felt that they could not themselves reproduce, is that after adopting, often very shortly after, they do conceive a child of their own. Scientific data on this phenomenon are largely lacking, but almost every one of us knows a couple who has had this experience.

Divorce.

Divorce—a subject mostly whispered about just a few years ago. In our lifetime one of the authors of this book was refused a college teaching post because she had recently been divorced. Now a discouraging number of marriages do end in divorce, with its accompanying problems for both parents and children.

It is undoubtedly helpful to many children of divorce to know that they, as individuals, are no longer the only ones. There is hardly a child of a divorced couple who does not have friends, or at the very least classmates, whose parents are also divorced. Uncomfortable as it may be to be a child of divorce, at least one is no longer unique.

Fortunately, in spite of dire predictions, current data seem to show that children of divorce in general turn out no worse, and themselves have no less successful marriages when the time comes, than children of intact unions.

The important thing for parents who are divorcing is to do their very best to be supportive of their children while they are getting their divorce and in the months and years that follow.

No one can give foolproof rules as to what to do to make this whole process as painless as possible for the children involved. But here are a few suggestions generally offered by those who are concerned with the problem:

1. Confused and unhappy as you may be while a divorce is being contemplated, carried through, and digested, do your very best to put your children first.
2. No matter how unhappy and confused you yourself may be, try to keep their daily lives as normal as possible.
3. Make efforts not to take out your hostility toward your deserting spouse on the children. Don't run the other parent down. You don't need to lie about his or her virtues. But try not to express to your children any venom you may feel.
4. If at all possible or practical, both of you, together, should tell your child or children about the coming separation.
5. Do your very best to make it completely clear to your children that the divorce is not their fault. It is not occurring because of something they have or haven't done.
6. Assure your children that parents may divorce each other but they do not divorce their children. Make it quite clear that their father (or mother, as the case may be) will still be their parent even though not present in the home.
7. Do your best, without cutting them down completely, to discourage their notions that this will all blow over and that soon they will have both parents together again in a united and happy home.
8. Do make it clear to your children that good provision will be made for them no matter what happens. If one parent leaves, children quite naturally fear that "everybody" will leave and then they will be left with nobody to take care of them. Assure them that this will not be the case (as in all probability it will not be).

Once the divorce has been accomplished, here are a few suggestions that might help:

1. Do your very best not to take out any hostility and anger you feel toward your now absent spouse on the children.

2. Absolutely do not make the children feel that they must take sides with you against their father (or mother).

3. Do not use your child as a go-between or spy between the two of you. After the child visits the absent parent, do not quiz him or her about the other person's life. Don't send messages back and forth (about nonpayment of support and related topics).

4. You don't have to praise your departed spouse, but now and then throw out hints that he or she was not a total monster, without virtue.

5. Expect that after your child has visited with the absent parent there will very likely be a period of readjustment. Accept this. Don't make things worse with questions and tart comments.

The probability is that you, the custodial parent, will remarry within a reasonable period of time. The majority of divorced parents do. And so, inevitably, your child will acquire a stepparent (two, if you both remarry).

Advice on stepparenting is not within the scope of this book. It is just too big a story.

Being a stepparent is tricky and hazardous—a mine field to be crossed very carefully, a bomb just waiting to explode. Perhaps the best advice one can give is this: Before you put yourself into the position of being a stepparent, ask yourself, "Do I really like this child [or these children]? Can I put up with weeks, months or even years of hostility directed at me because I have 'taken' their mother [or father] and replaced their absent father [or mother]? Can I put up with the fact that this child would often like nothing better than to break up my marriage?"

In other words, do you have the character of a saint and the patience of Job?

Fortunately, many ghosts are out of the closet these days. Several excellent books by stepparents who have stayed the course are now available. We especially recommend *The Half-Parent* by Brenda Maddox, and *Making It as a Stepparent: New Roles, New*

Rules by Claire Berman. If anybody can help you, these experienced individuals can. Your chances of success as a stepparent are good if you are really determined, and if your eyes are open in advance to the Herculean difficulty of what you are undertaking. Just don't think it is going to be easy.

16 What to Do about Discipline

"How can I make my child mind?" is one of the more common questions that parents ask.

Many who ask this question seem to be looking for some very simple recipe, or perhaps a neat list of suggestions which will solve their problems. We can give a few practical suggestions, but in truth the answer is much more complex than people often realize. Good discipline is like a giant jigsaw puzzle made up of many, many different pieces.

It depends primarily on your own philosophy of human behavior. Do you believe that you can make any child do almost anything you want if only you go about it the right way? Or do you respect the fact that the human individual is by no means clay to be molded? Do you believe, as we do, that to a very large extent behavior is a function of structure, and that we must recognize and respect that structure (the child's own body) before we can work with it effectively?

Are you authoritarian by nature, permissive, or somewhere in between? The authoritarian parent will lay down firm rules and will punish if they are not obeyed. The permissive parent will allow the child to do almost anything he or she wishes, for fear that any restraint will harm its psyche.

The parent who, with us, uses what we call *informed permissiveness* will make every reasonable effort to determine what kind of demand is reasonable for this particular child at his particular age. And then will make demands which in all likelihood can be met with.

However, if your discipline is to be successful, it is important to separate the concept of discipline from the concept of punishment. Certainly some punishment will be needed in almost any normal family. But really good disciplinarians will set things up in the household so that as far as possible it will be easy and comfortable for their children to behave in ways which at least do not substantially detract from family harmony.

Levels of Discipline

The easiest way of disciplining for many, and possibly the least desirable, is the emotional level. You slap, shout, and threaten. Some mothers even go so far as to cry or to complain, "You don't love Mommy or you wouldn't act that way."

No mother need blame herself if she descends to this level on occasion. But if these are her customary methods, chances are she will not have a well-disciplined child.

The second level is the rational or reasoning level, which involves mostly talking. You explain to the child why bad behavior gets bad results. You urge him to behave better. You tell him how bad his behavior makes you feel. You "isolate" him (nowadays people tend to call this "time out") and tell him he is too tired to play with the other children. In short, you reason with him. With some children this method works well. With some, it is just so many wasted words.

The third level, we believe, is the most effective but probably the most difficult because it requires the most knowledge. It is simply to adapt your techniques of discipline to the child's abilities, interests, and weaknesses at whatever stage of development he has reached. We call this using *developmental techniques*. This implies understanding the mechanics of behavior at every age level so thoroughly that you know how to motivate or encourage your child toward the kind of behavior you desire. That is, if you understand how a child's organism works, you will understand how best to move him in the direction you choose.

Developmental Techniques

Using developmental techniques can be an exciting adventure, particularly when it works. It involves, however, considerable knowledge of the growing organism and what it is like at different ages. Here are some examples of techniques which may be effective through the early years.

18 months: Keep in mind that the child of this age walks down a one-way street. His favorite word is "No" and his favorite direction "away from." You must expect these reactions and will need to use tricks and techniques to move him in a more positive direction.

Avoid direct commands such as, "Come here!" Instead, lure the child by offering food or a favorite toy, or by playing with some interesting object just out of his reach. Or pick him up and carry him.

Wherever possible, simplify the physical environment to prevent overstimulation and to reduce the number of possible danger areas. So far as you can, keep things he isn't supposed to touch out of reach.

If you use language with him, keep it very simple.

Consult him as little as possible. Streamline routines to avoid opportunities for him to say "No."

2 years: Two is much more positive and docile than he was at 18 months. He will be much more ready to obey. He can modulate his behavior. Help him by keeping situations simple and especially by keeping language simple and direct.

Two is likely to dawdle. Break into this by talk of the next activity, by telling him to "Say good-bye," or by leading him by means of an enticing toy.

Warn in advance of a proposed transition: "Pretty soon we'll wash our hands and then have lunch."

Do not expect him to share out of generosity. He may share if you say, "Johnny *needs* that wagon."

2 ½ years: Two-and-a-half is characteristically an age of opposite extremes. Remember this and try as much as possible to avoid giving the child choices. However, you can sometimes use choices effectively when the choice does not matter: "Do you want the red one or the blue one?"

It is hard for the child of this age to share. Help him to find "something else for Billy to use," but do not expect him to share out of generosity. Two-and-a-half is frequently both aggressive and selfish.

Environmental handling is most important. Shut and if necessary put high bolts on doors. Remove things not to be touched. This is more effective than trying to govern with words.

Except when compliance is essential, give face-saving commands: "How about——?" or, "Let's——."

Use words and phrases which are meaningful to the child: "needs," "has to have," "it's time to," "you forgot."

Avoid questions which can be answered by "No," as, "Can you hang up your coat?" Instead ask, "Where does your coat go?"

Don't be afraid to use humor (if it works). If he says angrily, "No, no, no," you say laughingly, "Yes, yes, yes."

3 years: Since this is a "me too" age, you can often motivate children positively by pointing out some other child who is doing the thing "right."

Give suggestions positively. Thus say, "We stand on the floor," rather than, "We don't stand on the table."

Children of this age will do a good deal if motivated by promise of a "surprise."

They respond very well to use of stimulating language. Adjectives such as "new," "different," "big," "strong." Nouns—"surprise," "secret." Verbs—"You could help," "You might try." Adverbs—"How about?" "Maybe."

Many can now listen to reason. "Let's pick up the toys so that we'll have more room for building, after dinner."

Some respond well to imaginative suggestions as, "Can the lumberjack pick up those big logs [blocks]?"

The indirect approach often works well. For instance, get a child to take off his outer clothing by your guessing what color his socks are—of course guessing all the wrong colors first.

4 years: Respect the fact that the 4-year-old quite naturally and characteristically behaves in an out-of-bounds manner. Realizing this you can perhaps let it go, part of the time, when he or she is a little rude, noisy, boastful, and rebellious. At other times, employ Four's own love of exaggeration in giving directions.

This is an age of tricks and adventure and new ways of doing things. Utilize this. Say, "Let's *skip* out to the dining room."

Use the child's waking interest in numbers to motivate him: "Can you get your suit off before I count to ten?" Or, "When the big hand gets to three, you may get up."

Giving commands in a whisper is surprisingly effective.

Many at this age are still very interested in their imaginary companions. This interest can be used in getting them to comply.

5 ½–6 years: Recognizing that the initial response of the child of this age tends to be "No I won't," or "Try and make me," wise parents build this knowledge into their planning. When a child does respond this rudely and this negatively, instead of jumping on him, remain calm.

Say something like "Well I guess you're going to need three chances on that one." This allows the child to rebel, which he does so naturally, and yet a few minutes later to comply.

Or, as you give a command, as you may have done at Four, add "And let's see if you can do it before I count to ten [or twenty or thirty]." Also, if the child is very rebellious, you can count very slowly.

A bedtime chatting time is much appreciated by most 6-year-olds. At this time, even a very naughty child tends to become gentle. Then, with some, you can have a little discussion of what you and he could try to make the next day go better.

7 years: Seven is by no means the rebellious little person he was just a year earlier. Much of the time he has no special objection to doing what he is told. It's just that he doesn't always quite get it done.

Since Seven finds it hard to stop what he is doing—reading, watching television, whatever—many parents of 7-year-olds have told us that they get best results if they warn their child in advance of a task to be done. Thus say, "When you come to the end of your chapter [or when your program is finished], I want you to take out the trash."

Then when the chapter is finished (or the program over) you *remind* them, because otherwise they are likely to forget. And then you may need to check up on them to be sure that they didn't get sidetracked halfway through the task.

So warn, remind, check up, and chances are your child will carry out all or most of your requests without too much objection.

Household Engineering

A different method of improving the child's behavior is one which requires little more than good common sense and a certain flexibility and willingness to try things which may be a little outside your usual routine.

This method has been called (though the name of it actually doesn't matter too much) *household engineering*.

Household engineering as we use the term means trying to arrange your household with regard to both the spacing and timing of necessary events in such a way that much of the disruptive behavior which bothers you simply does not take place. Thus you set up your daily schedule, or arrange your household physically, so that the worst danger points simply do not occur.

The possibilities are of course endless. It is probable that you yourself actually employ household engineering much of the time. Here are just a few somewhat random suggestions for the kinds of things we mean. There is nothing especially scientific about these suggestions. They are merely intended as examples. You yourself, knowing your family and your own household, can undoubtedly think up many others.

For instance, suppose two brothers or sisters cannot be together for any length of time without fighting. You may, if you wish, try to deal with this problem by warning, scolding, punishing. Simpler and more effective is to separate them physically. If you don't have the space to do this, you can often work wonders by rearranging their schedules. Naptimes can be shifted. It may even pay to have children eat separately. Some schools, in the early years, give a choice of morning or afternoon attendance. This might help. Or the baby-sitter can take one for a walk while the other uses the playroom. Or you may find that quarreling doesn't usually begin until after half an hour of play—so you can let them enjoy this much togetherness and no more. Sometimes a playroom can be sectioned off. Some children need real gates or partitions. Others will respect an imaginary line across the middle of the room.

Or consider the following parental complaint and our suggestion for solving the problem presented.

"My two-year-old gets into everything! Nothing in the house is safe from her!" What to do? Either fence in the 2-year-old or fence in your possessions. Specific warning and admonition will work in some special situations. The average child of 2 can be taught not to touch some special and important things—ash trays, Mommy's or Daddy's desk. But if he is the kind who is "into everything," this requires too much watchfulness from the adult. Locks and gates are easier for everyone. Be sure that there is a place for him and his toys in each room of the house. Then he can relate himself to his things. Each room brings change and surprise. He hasn't been forgotten. He is living in a child world in the midst of all these adult things.

Or take another example. Suppose your 4-year-old always behaves badly when company comes. Instead of bribing, threatening, cajoling, or punishing, try to arrange it so that child and company do not see too much of each other. Arrange for your child to be out of the house or pleasantly occupied in some other part of the house when visitors are present. Or include your guests in your planning. Allow one at a time to spend a few minutes with your child in his room if they like. Thus a social occasion can be salvaged by each guest being willing to give up just a slice of his social time for the sake of a child. This isn't really asking too much.

Rearranging your family's life just to avoid some difficult area, rather than just "making the child mind," may sound dangerously like giving in to the child. But we don't think of it that way. In our experience, trying to adapt the situation to everyone concerned rather than simply trying to fit the child into our notions of how children *ought* to act can help untangle a lot of snarls. A factory manager doesn't simply tell his workers that they *ought* to produce more. Instead, he tries to arrange things so that higher production is possible. Similarly, a little creative thinking about some of the most ordinary household routines can often result in improved behavior on the part of the child.

The Destructive Child

Unfortunately, regardless of how well you understand the different ages and how constructively you plan your household arrangements and routines, there are some children who just seem to get into trouble anyway. These are the children generally described by their parents as "destructive" (a not unusual appellation).

If your child is unusually destructive, the best discipline may involve finding out *why*. As with other undesirable behavior we have discussed, destructiveness may be caused by actual physical, bodily discomfort. The irritable, destructive child may be an uncomfortable child, one who is suffering from an allergic reaction to some aspect of the environment, most especially something in his or her diet. At least check this possibility.

Or destructiveness may be caused by some personal unhappiness, as for instance, by jealousy of a sibling. If so, be sure that the child realizes fully that he is loved, wanted, important to you. Destructiveness may be caused by the fact that the child is frustrated, either by your restrictions or by his own failings or inabilities. Try if you can to be less restrictive, and to help him work or play more successfully.

Here are some special things that you can try to reduce destructiveness:

1. Check your whole house to see what things you can move or put away so that the child won't get mixed up with them.
2. Lock all doors with high, complicated locks.
3. Give your child a large, fenced-in backyard where he can run and climb, play with messy things (mud, water, clay), and also hammer and saw, *under supervision.*
4. Try to stop situations which are likely to end in accidents—such as bouncing a ball in the living room—*before* the accident occurs.
5. Have as many different adults as possible take turns taking care of him. Mother alone will be absolutely exhausted with full-time care of such children. Men often can actually control them better than can women.
6. Above all, try to avoid taking him to public places, especially stores, where his destructive behavior will particularly cause trouble.
7. And lastly, start out by expecting a good deal of wear and tear, at least in all parts of the house which are used by the child.

If, however, his destructiveness seems intentional, you can try things like the following:

1. If your child crumples his father's newspaper or is careless with your books, give him a paper of his own to crumple.
2. If he tears up his own books, give him durable cloth books until he is old enough to manage the other kind.
3. If he gets into your bureau drawers, try locking them and also giving him some drawers or a cupboard of his own where he can keep his things.
4. If he draws on the walls, give him a wall in his own room, covered with beaver board, plain paper, or something of the sort that he can mark on.

5. If he pounds on your best furniture, try giving him other things to pound. A Bingo Bed if he is very young, or, if you have a place for such things, a hammer and boards.

6. If he gets at your scissors and uses them destructively, give him blunt scissors of his own and paper or cloth which he can cut.

7. If he gets into your pocketbook on every possible occasion, give him (or her) a pocketbook of his own to carry around. He may prefer a discarded one of yours to a new one of his own.

8. If he loves messes, give him messy things like clay and sand or finger paints to play with under adult supervision.

9. One of the best remedies for the child who is constantly doing destructive damage is to provide him with materials which you are willing to have him take apart.

Behind all of these suggestions you will see that there lies one main theme: Give the child permissible outlets for his destructive energy until he has matured to the point where added maturity permits him to handle materials constructively, not destructively.

General Suggestions

In conclusion, here are a few brief general suggestions about discipline. You may or may not agree with them. Discipline is an extremely individual and personal matter. Each parent knows best what "works" for her and for her child. No outsider can make up your mind for you as to just how you will discipline your children. But the following are suggestions which many have found helpful.

Stick by What You Have Said

Generally, the most successful parents are those who are able to maintain a firm and consistent policy of discipline, and who can be counted on to stick to what they have said. If on occasional second thought you do change your mind, it does no harm to tell the child of your changed verdict and your reason for changing. But in general, life is much simpler for the child if he or she knows that you can be counted on to do as you say.

Mother and Father Back Each Other Up

Though there are of course many exceptions, it is quite customary for mothers and fathers to have somewhat different ideas about discipline. Fathers as a rule are stricter—mothers are more likely to feel that the child is "just going through a stage and you might as well give in for a while." It is important for the child to feel the consistency of each parent's discipline. Then he or she comes to know how to expect each one to act.

Whatever your differences may be, it is extremely important to discuss them in private and to present a united front before the children. And to back up each other's directions. Discipline almost inevitably fails if one parent fails to support, or worse still, criticizes, the other parent's handling in front of the child.

To Spank or Not to Spank

We'd like to quote here from Dr. Arnold Gesell, who once recommended that if you plan *never* to spank your child, you'll probably end up by spanking about the right amount.

Physical punishment is by no means disastrous to the well-constituted child. But it is not a constructive method of discipline. It tells the child that you are displeased with what he has done, but it doesn't tell him what you would like to have him do. Nor does it show him how to behave in a way that will be more satisfactory.

More than that, according to Professor Murray A. Straus, physical punishment unfortunately is the foundation on which the edifice of family violence rests.* It is the way most people first

---

*Murray A. Straus, "A Sociological Perspective on the Causes of Family Violence," in Maurice R. Greer, ed., *Violence and the American Family* (Washington, D.C.: American Association for the Advancement of Science, 1980).

experience violence, and it establishes the emotional context of associating love with violence. The child learns early that those who love him or her are also those who hit.

Also, since physical punishment is used to train children or to teach them about dangerous things to be avoided, it establishes the moral rightness of hitting other family members. A further unintended consequence of spanking is the lesson that when something is really important it justifies the use of physical force.

Disciplining More than One Child at a Time

This chapter so far has for the most part discussed disciplining one child at a time. When more than one is concerned, obviously the task is harder. Here are what we consider excellent suggestions, from Andrew and Carole Calladine's very practical book, *Raising Siblings.**

1. Try to eliminate physical punishment in your household, whether you have one child or more. It merely teaches that if you are bigger, you can hit.
2. If there is trouble, try setting the kitchen timer for a calming time when siblings must sit apart from each other. The timer successfully takes your nagging voice out of things. If the bickering continues after play is resumed, a stronger disciplinary tool will have to be used.
3. Try taking away a relevant privilege from the children when house rules are abused. (Of course this means that you will have to set up house rules to begin with.)
4. Remove any fought-over object for a realistic period of time.
5. Securely hold from behind any physically attacking sibling.
6. Give suitable work assignments to all angry siblings to channel their aggression and to make some constructive use of this powerful energy.

---

*Andrew and Carole Calladine, *Raising Siblings* (New York: Delacorte, 1979).

7. Learn to ignore and stay out of sibling power plays for parental attention.

8. If problems arise about turns, have the children pick a number from 1 to 10 to see who is closest to a chosen number and therefore gets the first turn.

9. If at all possible, stop a growing struggle before it snowballs completely out of control.

10. If quarreling is vigorous, isolate the children until they can indulge in good group play.

11. Isolate yourself if you find that you are becoming irritable. Disciplining siblings works best when you are in control and can use a calm voice.

12. Praise and praise and praise, whenever you suitably can.

13. Change the activity that is causing dispute. Give them something better to do.

14. Role-play a sibling scene. Have children change places to discover how the other sibling feels.

15. Try to teach your children the power of words to work out agreements, compromises, contracts.

Discipline to Fit Your Temperament and that of Your Child

And last of all, to be effective, the type of discipline you use should fit both your own temperament and that of your child. If you are basically a "kiss and slap" type of parent, your handling will always, inevitably, be more emotional than that of the parent whose approach to child-rearing problems is more intellectual. If you are very quick-tempered, you will at times shout before you think. If you are more even-tempered, you may find it easy to have a quiet discussion with your child, or even to overlook much that goes on.

There are advantages and disadvantages to every approach. You will have to respond within the limits of your own individuality.

And the same consideration needs to be given to discovering what works with your child. Some can respond to a lengthy explanation of just why you are making certain demands. Others need the stronger force of verbal expressions of disapproval, isolation, deprivation of privileges. And a relatively small group do not respond until they have pushed their parents into the dead end of spanking.

As we have commented, disciplining a child is something like putting together a gigantic jigsaw puzzle. All too often the parts don't quite fit, or some may even seem to be missing.

This can be especially true when your child is in a stage when everything about living may seem hard for him or her. In your favor is the fact that any stage of marked disequilibrium tends, with any luck at all, to be followed by one of equilibrium, so that just as you are about to despair, growth forces themselves do come to your aid.

More than that, as each child grows older, if all goes well, he begins to make demands on himself. His own wish to conform, to do right, to please others begins to emerge. In the long run the ultimate aim of any disciplining you do with your child is to enable him to one day take over his own self-discipline. If your methods are anywhere near successful, that is the way the story should end.

PART FOUR

17 Behavioral Illness

Stress and Looking for the Causes of Behavior

Three-year-old Tommy had just been on a two-week-long car trip to visit relatives. His parents were worried about his "clingy" behavior on the trip home and for the first two days back. He seemed irritable, he was reluctant to let his parents out of sight, and he soiled his pants twice for the first time in a year. He didn't seem "physically ill," and his parents called to ask about the effects of all the changes in schedule that Tommy had experienced during two weeks of constant attention from uncles, aunts, cousins, and grandparents; as well as strange beds, unaccustomed baby-sitters, sleeping in his parents' room, and long car rides.

When his father brought him in to be checked, he didn't seem ill, but his left eardrum looked like a pizza instead of a translucent, delicate, gray membrane. Even when questioned, he denied that his ear hurt. Twenty-four hours after treatment of his ear infection with an antibiotic, his "behavioral problem" resolved and he became himself again.

There are several lessons to be learned from this story:

First of all, stress affects the whole person. The trip away from home may or may not have been a factor in Tommy's earache. His parents were ready to believe that his behavior had been affected by the stress of the trip, but they did not consider that the trip could "cause" a physical illness. They felt that picking up a cousin's germ was a more likely cause for the earache than the subtle combined effects of the child's getting out of kilter on a visit to relatives.

It is important to remember that stress, linked to the idea of kilter or balance, is a very general concept and any factors that tend to get children disorganized, tired, or worried can weaken their systems, causing one or more problems to surface.

Secondly, the obvious may blind us to the hidden. It seemed not only reasonable, but obvious, that Tommy's behavior resulted from the changes in routine and parenting that happened on the trip. One of the most important causes of mistakes on the part of doctors and parents is the finding of something wrong that blinds our search for other factors—in Tommy's case, an infected ear. Especially in the psychologically oriented culture of today, the "obvious" effects on a child of loss or of illness in other family members should not keep us from a thorough search for all other contributing factors.

And finally, we should realize that children do not localize or describe inner feelings as well as adults do. An ear infection in a grown-up would not be as mysterious as Tommy's. In the first years of life many children act out inner feelings such as pain, anger, fear, or sadness in ways that make it difficult to tell exactly where it hurts. By age 7 or somewhat earlier, most children learn to express their feelings in words. Even then a wide variety of feelings can come out in ways that make the causes of the behavior far from obvious. Every thorough diagnostic search should pay careful attention to the whole of the child's inner world—emotional and biochemical—in an effort to find all the factors that may give rise to a certain form of behavior.

The rest of this chapter describes the factors that should be considered and how to look for them.

How to Know When Your Child Is Ill

One of the most difficult decisions for a parent to make has to do with knowing when a child is "really sick." One of the problems is recognizing the signs of sickness, but another is knowing what it really is to be well. If you figure that wellness is the absence of some particular disease, then it should be relatively easy to take your children to the doctor and have them found free of disease. It can be comforting to find that "nothing serious seems to be going on." But it can be frustrating if your child acts irritable, tired, spacey, is unable to focus on a task, is sad or angry at home, and still "checks out okay" at the doctor's. If that is the case, giving a more complete description of your child as you see him or her at home will help you communicate with your doctor. The doctor's office is frequently a difficult environment in which to detect the kinds of changes in a child which sometimes are associated with severe behavior problems. Communicating with your doctor will be much easier if you organize information about your child along the lines detailed below.

Organizing Your Thinking

After exploring the following questions with a child and his or her parents, we and they have a better idea of how well the child is. You may find it helpful to organize your thinking in this manner even if you are not seeking professional help. If you do go for help, it will be of value to you and your doctor if this information is in order.

Problem	If a problem exists, what name have you or others given it? In order of importance, what are the main things that worry you about your child's behavior? Describe the onset, frequency (constant, daily, weekly), and duration of each episode. What seems to make it worse or better?
Home	Who lives at your house—including pets? Any recent changes?
Work	What is each person's occupation?
Care	Who are the main adults who take care of the child and how is the child care divided?
School/ Development	What is the child's experience with learning and development? Strong areas? Weak areas? What

was *your* experience with school, and how does it affect your attitude toward your child's work?

Religion

What is your religious background, and how does it help you understand your child's problem?

Sleep

When does your child go to bed? To sleep? How long does he sleep? Does he awaken in the night? Does he share his room? His bed? Does he awaken refreshed? Any nightmares?

Intake

Name everything your child eats in a typical twenty-four-hour period. Breakfast, lunch, dinner, snacks. How much sugar (candy, soda, pastries, gum, sweetened cereals, "junk")? How much refined flour? Are there any foods you know now bother him in any way? If so, how do they affect him? Were there ever any foods that bothered him in any way? If so, how? Does he crave any foods, or has he ever had any big intake of any particular food? Has he ever eaten dirt, paint, paper, or any other nonfood? Does he have any strong aversion to a food or to perfumes, tobacco smoke, auto exhaust, paint, or other chemical odors? Do you have a record of his height and weight? Does it follow a normal growth curve? Is he very thirsty? How much milk does he drink? Was he breast-fed? If so, for how long? When were solid foods introduced, and were there any difficulties at that time? Do you give your child vitamins—if so, what amounts of each one? Did you notice any change in him when you started the vitamins?

Bowels

Does he have a bowel movement at least once daily? Has he been constipated? Had diarrhea? Is he very gassy or does he have frequent abdominal pain? Was he a colicky baby? If so, did you identify any foods that were associated with the pain?

Urine
Is there any problem with urination? Too frequent? Bedwetting beyond age 5–6? Burning with urination? History of urinary infections? If so, was the infection proven by culturing the germs in the urine?

Activities
What are his favorite activities? Sports? Games? (If a baby, how does he spend most of his waking time?)

Friends
How many friends does he have and how do they get along?

Operations
Has he had any operations or procedures requiring anesthesia? Has he needed any dental work other than checkups?

Illness
What, if any, illnesses has he had that laid him up in bed or required hospitalization? How did they affect his attitude toward doctors?

Injuries
Have there been any major injuries? Cuts needing stitches? Head injuries—especially involving loss of consciousness?

Visual
Perception
Is there any indication that he has trouble with vision? Does he squint, tilt his head, or seem unable to relax while doing close work or reading? Did his behavior as an infant give you the idea that he was sometimes experiencing something quite different from what you experienced in terms of your visual perception of the surroundings? Does he describe alterations in his visual perception such as people's faces changing, things seeming too small or too far away? Does he have difficulty judging distances? Are colors too bright? Do bright lights sometimes bother

him? Does he say that the world sometimes feels as if it's moving around him or under him or that things appear blurry?

Hearing

Does he give every evidence of being able to hear well out of both ears? Does he describe any roaring, whistling, buzzing, or other noises in his ears, including voices?

Taste, Smell, and Touch

Does he seem to have normal ability to taste and smell foods and other odors?

Does he say that he feels as if he is either too big or too small to fit into his body, or that he is outside of it? Does he ever feel empty or nonexistent?

Allergies

Are there any substances known definitely to produce any kind of allergic reaction? Any history of chronic or recurring itching of the ear canals, eyes, nose, roof of mouth, skin, scalp, anus, or vagina? Any history of congestion (stuffiness) in the ears, eyes, nose, throat, or lungs? Wheezing? Sneezing? Any history of mucousy bowel movements for more than a few days?

Family History

Describe the history of both parents, brothers, sisters, aunts, uncles, grandparents, and cousins. Any allergies? Any conditions that seem related to your child's problems? Think of where the family is coming from and where it is going and how your child's illness affects the flow of your family river. How is it interpreted by family members more distant than parents, brothers and sisters?

Physical Environment

What is your source of water? Is the air quality good in terms of odors or chemicals from factories, farms, molds (mildew), dust, or tobacco smoke? What is the fuel for home heating, cooking, hot water? What is in the child's room (curtains, bedding, toys, stuffed animals, carpets, animals, other furniture or belongings)?

Once you have answered these questions, you may have a better notion of the scope of the problem, and you'll have a rather complete description of it instead of a simple name. Using this information, you and whatever professional person may help you will find it easier to avoid simple labels or explanations that fail to account for various parts of the problem. In attempting to solve the problem, all possible abnormalities should be considered and dealt with. Some children's problems are very difficult to explain even when they are easy to label. There is no childhood behavior illness in which only one factor needs to be considered in treatment.

An Illustrative Case—A Boy Named Sandy

Sandy was a 9-year-old boy who had the following problems: slow development, difficulty in school, slow speech, soiling in his pants, severe headaches. The headaches, soiling, and speech difficulty were getting worse; he was tearful, frustrated, and lonely. He snapped his fingers and made a variety of odd gestures and expressions, especially when under tension. Many parts of the problem were lifelong, made worse by school, better when tension levels in the home were lower.

Responses to our suggested questions were:

Home	Lives with his mother, 4-year-old sister, and two cats. His father recently separated from the family, and Sandy visits him on weekends.
Work	Sandy's mother operates a pastry shop and his father is a teacher.
Care	His mother; father on some weekends.
School	In a special class until this year. Now in regular class. Getting by in his work but very unhappy because he cannot control his bowels at school and is humiliated. Both parents were successful in school.

Religion   Not practicing.

Sleep   8 P.M.–7 A.M. Own bed in own room. Occasionally in room with mother and sister. Frequent nightmares.

Intake   (foods often eaten)
  Breakfast: toast made with white bread, pastries, cereal with sugar, milk, orange juice, occasionally eggs.

  Lunch: tacos, school lunch, cookies, pastry, soda, chocolate milk at school.

  Dinner: soup, peanut butter, rice, chicken, vegetables, pastry, white bread, milk.

  Snacks: pastry, soda, and cookies.

Foods that are known to bother him: 1) artificial color—known to have made it difficult for him to sleep in the past and was eliminated; 2) milk—as an infant he would break out into a cold sweat and as a toddler he would develop "goose bumps" after drinking milk.

His intake of white flour and sugar had increased over the preceding year. There was a suspicion on his mother's part that something in his diet other than food coloring was bothering him, and she wished to keep his intake as simple and "pure" as possible.

He had never had peculiar cravings or obvious sensitivities to chemicals or aversions to foods. He was thirsty and drank more than a quart of milk per day as well as several sodas.

He had been breast-fed for about 8 months, and cereals, fruits, and vegetables were introduced between 2 and 4 months. No difficulties were noted except with cow's milk, which when introduced was associated with "goose bumps" and cold sweats. As a toddler he had a strong aversion to milk but drank it at his mother's urging.

He was not taking vitamin supplements. He had been tried on Ritalin and his symptoms had worsened.

Bowels   He was toilet-trained at around 3 years of age and had no difficulty until age 6 when he became gradually unable to control the leakage of small amounts of feces in his pants. This occurred when he urinated and several times a day at home and at school. He was not constipated. He was ashamed of his difficulty, hid his soiled underpants, tried to deny the problem, but was in agony over his inability to control himself.

Urine	No problems. No bedwetting.
Activities	Poor in sports and spends most of his time alone reading, watching TV, playing games or dolls with his little sister.
Operations	None.
Illnesses	Several earaches. His attitude toward doctors was influenced by extensive psychologic testing and evaluation in which he was given a psychiatric diagnosis, and counseling had been recommended.
Injuries	None.
Allergies	As noted above, he had had insomnia related to eating foods with artificial coloring. No other allergies were noted; he had had frequent congestion in the past with earaches and he described some itching of his ear canals, the roof of his mouth, and his eyes.
Perception	Sandy's visual perception is normal. He complained at times of roaring or buzzing in his ears and had several episodes of hearing loss in association with earaches.
Taste, Smell, and Touch	His sense of taste and smell were normal, and he did not have any problems in feeling "together."
Family History	Both parents are healthy. No other family members with significant allergy, illness, or condition directly related to Sandy's. Both parents were from large families, and Sandy's uncles, aunts, and cousins all had satisfactory achievement in their careers or in school.

Physical	A single-family house, well water, gas range, oil
Environment	heat, damp basement. His room contained an average
	amount of "stuff."

Once the information about Sandy is organized in this way, three points stand out:

1. Some difficulties with development and behavior had been present from infancy.
2. The stress of his parents' separation needed to be considered.
3. His diet had become unbalanced, and there was good evidence that he had some unusual sensitivities.

Counseling by a psychiatrist had already been suggested as a way of helping Sandy communicate his difficulties and cope with the stress in the family. Remembering the cautions noted on page 286, the obvious stress of the parents' separation should not blind us to the possible role of nutritional factors. Any illness can create difficulties of communication in a family. A skilled counselor may be helpful in that process as well as in helping any individual, such as Sandy, cope with his problem. Nutritional factors were tackled promptly. Fortunately most brief trials of nutritional therapy can be completed in a matter of weeks.

It was recommended that Sandy's diet be changed to eliminate all sugar and white flour because of the general observation that many people are bothered by refined carbohydrates. Milk was discontinued because of evidence in the history that milk may have bothered him in the past and because milk disagrees with many people. A daily intake of three tablespoons of coarse, unprocessed bran, mixed with other foods was recommended. Except for people who are allergic to wheat, this source of dietary fiber is the easiest to obtain and most effective.

Within three days after he discontinued sugar, white flour, and milk, Sandy had experienced a dramatic change in the way his body worked. His bowels were completely controllable, his headaches disappeared, his thinking cleared, and his speech became more free-flowing and clear. His restless gestures ceased, and he stopped being afraid to attend school, where his performance improved dramatically and where he became better at making friends. Now, years later, he is a shy, intelligent young man, doing well in school. He is still a little hesitant in speech, but he is happy and free from difficulty in any aspect of self-control. He can tolerate small amounts of milk and "junk"* without difficulty.

Sandy's story illustrates several points:

1. A careful history outlining at least the points noted on pages 287–90 is the most important "test" needed to begin to figure out a behavior problem.

2. Nutritional stress should never be ignored even when other obvious stress factors are present.

3. In approaching any problem, it is wise to begin by trying the things that are relatively easy to do (brief change of diet) before contemplating complicated methods of diagnosis and treatment (prolonged psychotherapy).

4. It is also wise to correct things that are out of balance even if their direct connection to the problem is uncertain. This may be a very controversial point among those specialists who limit their practice to psychotherapy directed toward understanding interpersonal reactions. Many therapists feel that it is too confusing to a patient to have to think about factors (such as nutrition) that distract from understanding the "basic psychodynamics" or symbolic aspects of behavior.

5. Nutrition influences behavior. Many experts in the field of child behavior believe that the way children are nurtured is so much more important than any other aspect of a child's life after birth that psychological treatment aimed only at such issues is the only appropriate treatment. There are others who feel that drugs

---

*"Junk" refers to foods that are refined, sweetened, or adulterated in ways that decrease fiber content, freshness, and nutritional value and increase shelf life and commercial appeal.

are an important adjunct. Relatively few authorities believe as we do that the brain and other parts of the body are susceptible to the influence of nutritional factors such as are illustrated in Sandy's case. The climate of opinion is beginning to shift, but you will still find that professionals interested in child behavior are mostly oriented to psychological factors. When pressed, they will point to the lack of evidence provided by statistically validated controlled studies. It is worth remembering that in biology a single well-authenticated example is proof enough. In medicine, especially when dealing with a complex problem of learning, behavior, or health, it is not wise to dismiss a relatively simple explanation (intolerance to a food, vitamin or mineral imbalance) because it isn't proven to be "the cause of" whatever symptom.

Labels and Lists

In medical or graduate school, many of us learned that our job as physician or psychologist was to take the patients's symptoms and the results of various kinds of observations, examinations, and tests and come up with a name, or label, or diagnosis.

We also learned an idea called the *principle of parsimony*. This means that we should seek the fewest possible explanations for a person's problem and dispense with any that are not essential to the explanation. There are indeed a number of problems in health and behavior that for all practical purposes have a single cause. There are many other problems which can be understood only in terms of a web of interacting causes, and it is important not to allow the labeling process to limit the continued consideration of all the factors that can give rise to a certain kind of behavior.

Some labels such as "autism" are helpful in allowing parents and professionals a concise means for communicating a general idea of the way the problem expresses itself. Others, such as "minimal brain dysfunction" are confusing both to children and to the adults who care for them, and serve no purpose in really explaining what is going on. Even labels that help explain causes such as Down's syndrome (Mongolism, Trisomy 21, an inborn genetic error related to the presence of an extra chromosone) may be damaging if parents or professionals are led to conclude that nothing can be done in the area of nurturing or nutrition to improve the child's health or behavior.

If labeling or making a diagnosis is not to be the main emphasis in figuring out a problem in health, behavior, or development, then how can we look at our child's problems in a way that will help us get at the root of them? *It depends on understanding of health and behavior by list instead of by label.* Listing all possible contributing factors should be done as an ongoing process so long as any problem continues. A behavior problem often involves most or all of the factors included on the diagnostic list described in Chapter 18. Your map for finding a way through the problem should include at least the checking of all items on this list.

18 The Diagnostic List

QUESTION #1. NURTURE: *To what extent is this child's problem related to interactions with his or her human environment: family, teachers, friends?*

Learning the self-confidence that is needed to love and to be loved begins in the first days of life. Its importance has been stressed in most of the writings about child behavior in the last two generations.

The diagnostic list for problems in child behavior must always include an understanding of the child's experience with family and other care-givers starting from the earliest moments of life. Our own emphasis on nutritional and other ecological factors in behavior reflects our concern that the general awareness of interpersonal relationships has tended to limit recognition of factors that have to do with perceptual and nutritional abnormalities and to overemphasize the interpersonal.

Two-month-old Chris had been fretful and hardly smiled for a week after an operation for pyloric stenosis which had cured the cause of projectile vomiting that started when he was 7 weeks old. Tests done in the hospital had raised—but not answered— questions as to whether "something else" might be wrong with him. The doctors in the hospital were honest about their worries. Home from the hospital, he fed well and gained weight rapidly but his behavior was abnormally irritable and his parents were doing everything they could imagine to console him: nursing, singing, rocking, walking, bouncing, stroking, hugging, and swaddling. Nothing was working and Chris looked worried—

that's right—he was a worried-looking 9-week-old baby.

One look at his father's face revealed a possible source of worry —the father's own worry. Research in infant behavior in the past decade has changed older notions that Chris was "too young to notice" that his father's face betrayed an overwhelming and contagious concern that things were not okay with Chris. Other indications from answers to further questions on our list and from Chris's physical examination and blood tests led us to reassure his parents that things *were* okay and that they should allow their son to cry himself to sleep—which they hadn't been able to do because of their feeling that they were responsible for keeping him happy —that is, not crying. The first few times they put him down (already fed, burped, changed, cuddled, sung to, and swaddled), he cried for forty-five minutes, and his mother and father cried in the next room. But after less than two days, Chris was smiling and his parents were smiling back. No more worried looks, no more behavior problem, and a baby who had learned to console himself. No infant is too young to respond to the worry of his parents expressed in their faces or in the way they handle him!

QUESTION #2. NUTRITION—GENERAL: *To what extent is this child's problem affected by nutritional factors?*

Over the last generation the climate of opinion in institutions training most professionals dealing with child behavior has been "anti-nutrition." That is, we've been taught more or less along the lines suggested by a professor of pediatrics who said that all a modern parent needs to know about nutrition is how to use a can opener. The lessons we in our own practice have learned about severe problems of behavior and health can help guide us in milder disorders, and those lessons have increased our attention to nutrition and our respect for individuality.

It is important not to take too narrow a definition of nutrition. Taken broadly, nutrition should include not only food but the absorption of light and other forms of radiation as well as elements from the air, water, and earth through the various portals and surfaces of the body. The term *ecological* is more apt than *nutritional* because it means interaction with the whole physical environment. That interaction depends on *taking in* the right amount of things that are good for us and *avoiding* allergens and poisons.

Nutrition has a complex technical and cultural base, but what is known can be summarized by pointing to some old sayings that science had found to be either true or false. Everything we consider in a thorough approach to nutritional problems has a firm scientific basis but can still be summarized in the following statements:

TRUE

1. Everybody has to eat.
2. Some people need more than others.
3. Variety is the spice of life.
4. One person's meat is another person's poison.
5. You are what you eat.
6. Love feeds the soul.

FALSE

1. A little bit can't hurt you.
2. If it's good, it's good for you.
3. If a little is good for you, more is better.
4. You can never get too much of a good thing.
5. One more won't hurt you.
6. Moderation in all (as opposed to most) things.*

Generalizations about nutrition in clinical practice can be a source of vehement disagreement among professionals. But if agreement can be reached on these few true and false statements, then there should be no misunderstanding about the application of nutritional strategies as part of the detective work in any particular child's problem.

We usually break nutrition down into its two sides: selec-

---

*For example, it is hard to find a moderate way to roll in a patch of poison ivy.

tion (getting the right amounts of essential nutrients: vitamins, minerals, amino acids, etc.) and avoidance (staying away from poisons and allergens), but sometimes all that is needed is a general "cleanup" of a child's diet. The following example illustrates such a cleanup and points out that while breast milk is best, its effect on the infant depends on the quality of maternal nutrition.

When we met them, Susan and Sylvie were 17. Susan was 17 years of age, and Sylvie was her 17-day-old baby who wouldn't stop screaming. An inconsolable baby can put any parent to the test, but for Susan, alone, on welfare, with scarce help, it was a nightmare of self-doubt and desperation. She needed badly to be able to take care of her baby, but despite an adequate supply of milk from her mother's skinny body, Sylvie was not content. Of the many factors to consider, Susan's diet raised the most questions. Coffee, donuts, and other pastries, cola drinks, hamburgers, and french fries were her main intake. Within *hours* of a change to fresh vegetables, fruits, whole wheat, meat, and eggs, her daughter, Sylvie, settled down and has been an easy baby ever since. Susan has proven herself to be a very competent mother—steady, consistent, and able in ways that surpass those of many older, married, and better-educated women.

Sylvie's temperament improved after her mother managed a general cleanup of her diet—basically avoiding junk foods. That should always be the first step in tracking down a nutritionally based problem, and it may not always be clear whether it was sugar, various additives, or caffeine that was the main problem.

The stories of Chris and Sylvie illustrate that the same symptom—irritability—can result from two quite different stresses. The lessons we learn from newborns, who have a relatively limited "vocabulary" for expressing reactions to stress, are valuable in understanding the same phenomena in older children. Naming a behavioral illness after its symptoms in childhood can be misleading if we forget how similar the expression of different stresses can be in children.

QUESTION #3. NUTRITION—SPECIFIC AVOIDANCE, ALLERGY: *Could the child's behavior be affected by a specific intolerance or allergy to a food, or to dust, pollen, mold, or other inhalant?*

A broad definition of an allergy is "an acquired sensitivity to small amounts of a substance on an individual basis." The notion of allergy does not include any limitation as to the way it is expressed in the body, but itching, hives, congestion, wheezing, sneezing, vomiting, and diarrhea are the most common and the most obvious reactions. Fatigue, irritability, hyperactivity, perceptual distortions, and a variety of other symptoms that come out in abnormal behavior have been reliably observed as allergic reactions. Any thorough evaluation of a behavior problem should not ignore the possibility that an allergic reaction is at the root of the disturbance.

Johnny was a 2-year-old who had had twelve ear infections and was constantly stuffy. He suffered frequent bouts of diarrhea that made toilet-training difficult, and he was a cranky, irritable, worried-looking boy. His troubles had begun when he was weaned from the breast at 10 months. Tests revealed sensitivity to cow's milk, oranges, yeasts, and molds. Elimination of orange juice, milk products, and foods containing yeasts or molds resulted in the disappearance of his congestion, an end to the earaches, and a change in his personality and behavior. His obvious allergic symptoms made it easy to approach his difficulties in this fashion. Fatigue, irritability, hyperactivity, etc., can yield to the same approach even when obvious allergic symptoms are lacking.

QUESTION #4. NUTRITION—SPECIFIC AVOIDANCE, POISON: *Could the child's behavior be influenced by exposure to a poison?*

A broad definition of a poison is "a substance that is universally harmful even in small amounts." Sensitivity to poisons may vary so that it is difficult to draw a clear distinction between poisons and allergens. Lead is the most abundant poison in the environment and should always be considered when a child has a behavior problem even if exposure to this substance is not likely.

QUESTION #5. NUTRITION—DEFICIENCY: *Could this child's behavior be influenced by a deficiency of a mineral or vitamin?*
Iron deficiency is the most prevalent deficiency in the United States. No evaluation of a child's behavior should ignore this factor which can be reliably measured by a serum iron test. (A blood count for anemia is not an adequate screening test for serum iron.)

Deficiencies of other minerals and vitamins are prevalent enough so that any child whose difficulties warrant investigation should be checked from this standpoint. We have seen many children with problems in learning, behavior, and development who had vitamin or mineral deficiencies *not* related to low intake in their diet. Some children have a problem absorbing vitamins or minerals and may need large doses of supplements to overcome it (see page 327).

QUESTION #6. NUTRITION—DEPENDENCY: *Could this child's problem be related to a special need for large amounts of minerals or vitamins?*
It is not possible to make a sharp distinction among all cases of children requiring larger than average doses of certain nutrients. Some appear to have no difficulty absorbing nutrients but need to have very high levels in their body in order to overcome a biochemical error in their systems. Such an error has been described in detail in a few children, but present technology does not permit discovery of the biochemical problem in all children who will improve when given a large supplement of a vitamin.

Randy was seen when he complained to his parents that "things look small." He had been a behavior problem all his life, and he and his family had had counseling for some of the difficulties related to his behavior: irritability, hyperactivity, insomnia, difficulty getting started in the morning, soiling his pants, wetting his bed, and being unresponsive to discipline at home and at school. When he complained about his vision it was clear to us that he was having a distortion of what he saw rather than a difficulty with the sharpness of his vision. Referred to as an Alice in Wonderland effect, it is a complaint that suggests difficulty with perception related to biochemical rather than optical defect.

Because some children with major distortions of perception and communication (autism) respond to very large doses of vitamin B-6 and magnesium, Randy was given a trial of therapy with such a regimen. Neither he nor his family expected that it would alter other aspects of his behavior. However, within a few days he was a "different" boy. Patterns of sleep, urination, bowel function, activity, and learning improved dramatically.

His teacher, unaware that anything had been done, wrote a note home asking what had happened to suddenly turn him into a "new boy." Subsequent trials on and off his vitamin-mineral supplement confirmed Randy's dependency on relatively large doses of vitamin B-6 and magnesium. No test presently available other than a trial of therapy with supplements would have revealed his excessive needs. (Fortunately such a trial has never been reported to produce a serious adverse effect.)

QUESTION #7. PERCEPTION: *Could this child's behavior result from his perception of the world being damaged or disturbed?*

Perception is the way we take in the world to form our individual sense of reality and our place in it. Nutrition is the way we take in the world to provide energy and substance to our bodies. *Together perception and nutrition are the two main bridges between our internal and external worlds.* Nutrition must always be considered in all problems of health, development, and behavior because it is fundamental to the well-being of the person. Perception must always be considered in problems of health, development, and behavior for the same reason *and* because we cannot judge the meaning of behavior unless we can understand how a person experiences the world.

In the infant and young child we are limited to looking for a failure of vision or hearing. In children of all ages we may guess (and older children may tell us) that they have disturbances of their senses of vision, hearing, taste, touch, and smell, as well as of space or time that make their reality not only different from that of others but often painfully unpredictable. Information about perception is less likely than nutritional testing to reveal a specific remedy for a problem. But understanding children's perceptions of the world may increase our ability to see why they act as they do, and sometimes points the way to a remedy, as in Randy's case. Children with perceptual difficulties have special needs for help with communication that should involve their whole family. Some of those needs are met when other family members understand that certain patterns of behavior are based on an altered perception of what's going on.

Adela was a 9-year-old girl with Down's syndrome (Mongolism). She had had very slow development, and when we first saw her it was not possible to estimate whether or not she had fulfilled her potential. Routine physical examination revealed that both eardrums were congested by an accumulation of fluid in the middle ear, and a hearing test showed marked deafness. Efforts to alleviate congestion by other means failed, and she was given P.E. tubes —a surgical means of venting the middle-ear space to get rid of the fluid accumulation. Her hearing improved dramatically, and with it she experienced a sharp increase in her ability to communicate. This resulted not only in a great improvement in her I.Q. but a sudden lifting of withdrawn and cranky behavior. Her mother remarked that her doctor in the town where they lived previously had passed off Adela's ear congestion as "just one of those things that bother these children." Children whose problem has an already identified cause are particularly likely to have other aspects overlooked.

QUESTION #8. MEMORY: *What memories from the past give rise to expectations, fears or associations that influence his behavior?*

Factors of nurture and nutrition determine how a child feels and aspects of perception determine how a child realizes what is going on around him or her. In addition, memory—conscious and unconscious—will help determine behavior at any given moment. A careful reconstruction of the past will help to answer this final question on our diagnostic list.

"Memory" includes a lot: all of a child's past experience, which is often the grist for the mill of psychotherapy. Examination of this facet of a child's experience should focus particularly on loss.

The diagnostic list is short but we feel that it embraces the main factors that influence behavior. The ordering of the list does not imply priority.

Ecologic

1. Avoiding minimum amounts of allergens and poisons.
2. Getting optimum balance of vitamins, minerals, and other essential nutrients, such as amino acids and essential fatty acids, as well as light and air.

Perceptual

1. Impairment of a sense (especially hearing or vision).
2. Distortion of senses (vision, hearing, taste, smell, touch, space, and time).

Memory—knowledge

1. Conscious.
2. Unconscious (leading to expectations, fears, or associations—including present day-to-day events that may be stressful).

The examples we have given for items on our diagnostic list illustrate the way that thorough application of this list may turn up a *major* cause of a child's problem. But problems are not evenly distributed among us, and a person with one identified problem is more likely to have another. This is the most compelling argument for diagnosis by list instead of by label. It should always be remembered that problems are not evenly distributed in the population and the discovery of problem must not prevent us from searching through the entire list.

19 Tests

"All the tests are normal, so nothing is wrong" is a statement few professionals actually make, but it is one that many people "hear" when various tests fail to reveal the cause of some complaint about a child's behavior or development. The most important check is a thoughtful consideration of the history as revealed in the answers to the questions noted on pages 287–90. Beyond that, a number of questions may help define the problem or unearth the causes.

Psychological, Developmental, Vision, Hearing, and Speech

Tests that augment information taken from the history tell us about the child's performance compared to that of other children. No test is completely free of influence from the skills or biases of the person conducting or interpreting it. Care should be taken to consider the quality of the personal interaction between the child and the professional conducting any test.

Children able to do so should be asked to say how they themselves feel about their problem. This may be done through direct interviewing or by observing their drawings or their play in the office or at home. A visit to school or careful discussion with the teacher of a school-aged child should precede any testing.

Developmental testing (see page 174) reveals the child's place in life's spiral of changes. Psychometric or psychological testing reveals skill levels in various areas as well as some aspects of perception.

308

Visual perception can be evaluated in various ways. A generous part of the brain is devoted to vision, which depends on more than the clarity of the image produced by the shape, optical properties, and coordination of the two eyeballs. Six eye muscles for each eye direct constant micromovements (too fine to observe directly) of the eyes on which vision also depends. There is wide disagreement among eye surgeons (ophthalmologists), vision specialists (optometrists), and vision-and-muscle coordination specialists (developmental optometrists) concerning the extent to which careful examination of visual function in children reveals valuable aspects of visual behavior. The official position of pediatricians and eye surgeons is that detailed visual testing and training has not been proven to be helpful. We ourselves have seen hundreds of children in whom such methods have been associated with logically expected and dramatic improvement in the child's sense of his or her visual world. The impact on learning and behavior is frequently dramatic.

Analysis of the child's speech and hearing should have high priority in any child whose behavior is not completely reassuring in the area of communication.

Physical Examination

Establishment of a child's place on a growth curve of height, weight, and head circumference, as well as other physical measurements of pulse, blood pressure, and respiratory rate are part of any evaluation of behavior. A thorough physical examination includes examination of all the surfaces and every orifice of a child's body.

Evaluating a child's nutritional status by physical examination is a tricky business. Allergy often reveals itself in "shiners," or circles under the eyes, and in an itchy rash, patchy smoothness of the tongue, pitted nails, or a tendency of the skin to form welts after a mild scratch. We have seen children whose allergy is certainly a major part of their problem but who show no sign of it on physical examination.

Vitamin deficiency tends to affect the parts of the body that are "busiest" in terms of energy consumption, wear and tear: the brain, intestinal tract, and skin. Even in parts of the world where diet, economics, and politics make for a higher incidence of nutritional deficiency than in the United States, the assessment of deficiencies by physical examination is very inexact.

Bumpy "chicken skin," with raised openings for the little hairs on the skin, should raise the question of vitamin A deficiency. A child who is very bothered by bright sunlight may also be deficient in vitamin A—usually eyes or skin are affected but not both at the same time.

Chalk-white flecks in the nails, the kind that are said to come from telling little white lies, are a fairly reliable sign of zinc deficiency. Severe iron deficiency is associated with pallor from anemia (not enough redness to the blood), but iron deficiency often affects health before the blood count begins to fall.

One does see significant vitamin deficiency as measured by blood tests (see page 326) when no physical signs are present to provide clues that the deficiency exists.

Physical examination of children with behavioral problems should stress the neurologic exam, which considers developmental progress and brain function as expressed in coordination, strength, reflexes, sensation, and organization of thought and expression.

Electroencephalogram (EEG, Brain Wave)

An EEG may define the problem in terms of a specific pattern of irritability of the brain's electrical activities. Problems that are paroxysmal, or come in bursts, can be seen in terms of their similarity to seizure disorders (convulsions). Brain wave may indicate a pattern that reveals a particular type of irritability. It does not tell what a child perceives, thinks, or knows, and it is often abnormal in nonspecific ways. Abnormalities of brain-wave tracings should not be automatically taken as evidence of "brain damage" in a way that leads to the conclusion that other tests won't reveal a remedy.

Medications and the state of relaxation will influence a child's EEG, and sedation with drugs is a common practice for infants or children who may otherwise be incapable of keeping still for the 10–30-minute duration of the test. The test is carried out in a room that needs to be separated from electrical interference in the surroundings, and in some settings it may seem to a child like a cell. Wires are inserted into the skin or attached to the child's head with a paste that helps make electrical contact with the skin. Recordings of the rhythms of electrical waves associated with brain function are made on a continuous piece of paper by twelve pens during conditions of quiet rest, response to lights or sound, and sometimes sleep.

The EEG is read by a neurologist to compare the brain waves from the two sides of the brain and to see that they are normally symmetrical as well as to look for areas where there are unusual shapes of the brain waves. This test can be extremely useful in helping to understand many patterns of behavior, but in most children with behavior problems it is normal or abnormal in some very nonspecific way that does not help pinpoint the cause of trouble. Too often a mild abnormality of a brain-wave pattern is emphasized to parents who may feel that there is something horribly wrong with their child's brain.

Checking Other Body Rhythms

Other aspects of rhythmic events in children that relate to behavior cannot be measured as mechanically as the brain waves, but may be important in judging the roots of the behavior. After the first months of life outside the monotony of the womb, a baby's body responds to the regular changes of food, light, and stimulation by establishing a twenty-four-hour cycle for just about every function in the body that can be measured. Continuous monitoring of a child's body temperature (low in the morning and higher in the afternoon) is not presently used as a clinical tool, but it will probably become the first mechanical means of judging a child's obedience to the rhythmic reminders (called *zeitgebers* from the

German words meaning "time-givers") of the environment. At present we are limited to careful review of the child's daily cycles of sleeping, eating, activity, and bowel function.

An infant or older child who is all over the place in terms of body rhythms will feel better if normal rhythms are reinforced by the scheduling of meals and sleep and by emphasizing protein consumption (eggs, milk, cheese, fish, meat) in the morning and carbohydrate (vegetables) and starches in the evening. Allowing a child who is very "out of whack" in terms of sleep to suddenly stay up *very* late—even most of the night—may be a more reliable way of correcting the situation in a hurry than trying to gradually reinforce an earlier bedtime.

Babies whose rhythms haven't yet settled down will often feel and behave better if the rhythms of their surroundings are kept very regular by insistence on regular spacing of feedings and *lights-out* sleep at night. Fussy, overstimulated babies whose parents are desperately trying to console them with feeding, rocking, walking the floor, singing (and sighing), will often settle down in two or three nights if allowed to console themselves, falling asleep alone in a dark room. The first two nights may be very hard on the parents (and neighbors). Babies who have been overstimulated by their parents' constant efforts at consolation, may scream insistently for an hour or more before deciding that they will have to deal with the problem themselves.

Under these circumstances, parents should remember that their most important job is to teach their child self-confidence. Allowing a baby to learn to console himself, however painful for both parents and child, can be the most important first step in a baby's realization that however helpless he is in many ways, there are some things he can handle alone.

X-rays

X-rays are the same kind of energy as light (but more intense), and the shadows they cast can be seen in detail, thanks to a variety of photographic techniques, some of which involve computers

(ACTA or CAT scan). Limitations of X-ray studies in behavior problems are increased by the softness and complexity of the brain and its connections. An X-ray of the skull is seldom helpful in understanding a behavior problem, and it is done when doctors are looking for flecks of calcium associated with old burnt-out infections or for evidence of a tumor. If you take your child to a chiropractor, remember that a skilled chiropractor can usually judge the expression of stress in a child's body without X-rays. A behavior problem seldom warrants a child's exposure to X-ray, which should be taken only to answer *specific* questions raised by the history or other tests.

Blood Sugar

Sugar (glucose) is the first and last carrier of the sun's energy as it goes to supply the needs of our bodies (and those of most other living things). Sugar that is formed in green plants may have a long trip through many transformations in the food chain before it appears in our tissues, but when it does, it remains the fundamental "currency" of energy that our bodies use. Blood-sugar levels may lead to striking changes in mood, perception, stamina, and behavior. The most dramatic effects are associated with very low blood-sugar levels, but the matter is confusing because brain levels of sugar are not always revealed by blood levels, and blood levels do not always correspond to the expected symptoms. Children may have very low levels of blood sugar without any change in the way they feel; on the other hand, people of all ages may show typical signs of low blood sugar (hypoglycemia) when their blood-sugar level is not drastically low.

Many people now speak of "hypoglycemia" as if it were a very meaningful diagnostic label, but we feel that the term is overused since it depends on the measurement of an intermediate, not primary, cause of problems. Also, the test to discover levels of blood sugar is subject to unavoidable errors introduced by the stress of the test procedure itself. This is especially true of the glucose tolerance test. It is often reassuring for a child or his parents to know that irritability, fatigue, cold sweats, headaches, confusion, aggressive behavior, or even convulsions are associated with low blood sugar, and it may lead to better acceptance of a change in diet (no refined foods, lots of fiber foods, regular meals, and sometimes avoidance of specific allergens). But it is too bad if children get the idea that they have a "disease" called hypoglycemia. *Low blood sugar is part of the signs and symptoms which indicate that something in the body is out of kilter, but in itself it is not a disease.*

More about Diseases

Before our next section on tests—definitions and measurements that lead to action—we would like to emphasize that we are not "disease-oriented." The names or labels of behavior problems in children (autism, atypical development, hyperactivity, minimal brain dysfunction, anxiety, depression) are not well defined and often do not actually indicate causes in the same ways that measles and chicken pox are "caused" by viruses. *The language used by doctors and lay people alike implies that diseases are things (entities) that we catch and then try to get rid of.* This is a holdover from the medical imitation of the natural sciences (geology, botany, zoology, etc.) of the last century. The great discoveries of the orderliness of nature were stimulated in large measure by the classification of things (rocks, plants, animals) according to their size, structure, and distribution. *When doctors started to classify diseases along the same lines, confusion set in regarding the difference between names, notions, and things.* The discovery that germs cause disease, however crucial, tended to add to the confusion because infectious diseases are often (but not always) very consistent in the way they "behave," and this tends to make us forget that it is the germ, not the disease, which is caught. *A disease is not an entity but a complex interaction between a person and his or her environment.* The tests outlined below reveal various measurements of that interaction which may lead to corrective action (to promote balance) even when they don't lead to the labeling of a disease.

Blood Tests

For about a century the blood has been studied to reveal what's going on inside the body. Dozens of substances in the blood can now be measured quite accurately, and some tests would be appropriate in a child with almost any kind of long-standing behavior problem simply as a matter of thoroughness.

Blood Count

Counting the number of red blood cells and white blood cells used to be done by eye under a microscope; now it may be done by this means or with a counting machine. The number of red blood cells or the amount of red material (hemoglobin) and the number of white cells in a child's blood are usually checked in a test known as a blood count. Red blood cells carry oxygen from the lungs to the tissues and carbon dioxide from the tissues back to the lungs; an estimate of the blood's redness is a measure of the sufficiency of this very important function and should be included in a diagnostic workup evaluation for almost any kind of problem. The white blood cells have many functions and are particularly devoted to activities that involve allergies and infections. Counting and differentiating among the kinds of white blood cells (differential count) is usually considered part of a blood count.

Iron

Serum iron may be low even if a person is not anemic, and because low serum iron can be associated with difficulty in behavior and learning in children it is wise to include this test as a part of any evaluation of a child with a behavior problem.

Blood Chemistries

The term *blood chemistries* refers to the measurement in the blood of a wide variety of minerals, other elements, and chemical compounds that fluctuate in the blood, reflecting the function of several organs in the body, such as the kidneys, liver, muscles, and intestines. Thus, measurement often can be done in large laboratories at relatively little expense as a "package," and many doctors would choose to measure blood chemistries as a matter of routine in their evaluation of a child with a behavior problem even though the likelihood of discovering something is fairly remote.

Thyroid Test

The thyroid gland located just below the Adam's apple in the neck makes a hormone that regulates many facets of metabolism and activity. In general, when the thyroid gland makes too much of this hormone, a person becomes "hyper" in his behavior and suffers from hyperthyroidism. When a person has too little of the hormone, or the activity of the hormone is interfered with in some way, he is said to be hypothyroid and his activity is generally sluggish. Abnormalities of thyroid function are relatively rare causes of behavior disorders in children, but thyroid function should always be considered and sometimes tested when origins of any problem are puzzling.

Amino Acids

Amino-acid molecules are linked together to form protein the way boxcars form a freight train. Different proteins have different amino-acid composition, and human beings need to get some of each in order to make proteins. There are about ten amino acids which human beings cannot produce internally (like vitamins). These must be obtained from the diet. Most people can get by with an intake of the various amino acids that corresponds very roughly to average needs. Occasionally individuals have abnormal needs to obtain or to avoid certain of the amino acids which they have some difficulty in processing. PKU (phenylketonuria) is the best known disorder of amino-acid function affecting the behavior of children. Other disorders of amino-acid balance have been found in children with extremely severe disorders of development, behavior, or other body functions. As time goes by, more disorders of amino-acid metabolism will be discovered and children with milder and milder disturbances will be found to have errors of amino-acid metabolism as doctors learn to look for them. (Then such children can be treated.) A screening test on the urine or blood can be done to see if there is some striking abnormality of the amount of amino acids present. This is advisable for many children with severe problems of behavior and development. A more precise test of the actual amounts of amino acids in the blood or urine can also be carried out, but it is much more costly.

Allergy Testing

You will find that most physicians are extremely unaccepting of the idea that allergies can be related to behavioral problems. It is all too obvious that a child with diarrhea from the food he has eaten, or hives, or hay fever from exposure to some other substance may be irritable, tired, hyperactive, or depressed. But it is all too often assumed that the primary symptom is what causes the emotional or behavioral component and that behavioral or emotional reactions cannot occur as a result of intolerance to foods or inhalants. We have seen hundreds of children in whom severe disturbances of mood and behavior have been related to allergies with or without other symptoms being present. This connection has been reliably observed and reported by many physicians, and it is important to accept the fact that such reactions do occur. The frequency with which they occur may not be all that important to the family who has a child with a severe behavior disturbance. *Even if it is a long shot, it must be considered for the sake of thoroughness.*

Since we ourselves have gone from the point of utter disbelief to feeling that such reactions are common, we can sympathize with those physicians, psychologists, and teachers who still are in the utter disbelief stage; and we can sympathize even more with families who have children in whom they observe such reactions which are ignored or denied by their physicians. Fortunately a certain amount of the detective work involved in ferreting out these connections can be done by a family without the help of a professional. Several excellent books are available.* Those seeking more information on allergy testing are encouraged to read one or more of these books.

Avoidance and Challenge

If crankiness, fogginess, fatigue, or any other behavior is to be checked in terms of its possible relation to a reaction to a specific food, remove that food from the child's diet (or from your own if you are the nursing mother of a distressed baby). Observe the child's reaction when the food is reintroduced after a five-day period of abstinence. You may have to wait as long as seventy-two hours to observe a reaction, although most reactions occur within twelve hours. The reaction may mimic the child's problem (fatigue, hyperactivity, etc.) or it may be a related symptom (stuffiness, nausea, headache). If a child is bothered by many foods or inhalants, the effects of the avoidance and challenge may be submerged under the effects of the other substances to which exposure continues.

This kind of detective work is especially worthwhile under certain circumstances:

1. In babies whose diet and environment are already fairly simple and easy to manipulate.
2. In children of all ages in whom one particular food is suspected because of past reactions, such as colic in infancy due to cow's milk.
3. In instances in which other kinds of tests are unavailable or too expensive.

If one includes reactions to dust, pollen, animals, molds, chemical agents, gas odors, fabrics, food additives, and foods, attempts

---

*Crook, William G, *Tracking Down Hidden Food Allergy;* Golos, Natalie, and Goldbitz, Frances G., *Coping with Your Allergies;* Sheinkin, David; Schachter, Michael; and Hutton, Richard, *The Food Connection;* Mandell, Marshall, *Dr. Mandell's 5-Day Allergy Relief System;* Rapp, Doris, *Allergies and the Hyperactive Child;* and Feingold, Ben, *Why Your Child Is Hyperactive.*

to avoid and challenge may be prohibitively tedious, especially if your relationship with a child doesn't permit an easy acceptance of a change in diet. The effect of expectations—positive and negative—as well as a host of other variables require care in interpreting the results of an elimination and challenge, and the whole process depends on your having an accurate idea of what foods actually contain the substances you are trying to avoid. Some food substances, such as yeast, wheat, eggs, and corn, appear in disguised forms in many processed foods.

Under some circumstances this test will produce a spectacular demonstration of the cause of the problem, and it carries the especially important advantage of having the child's own body (as opposed to mother, father, or the family doctor) tell him that the food disagrees with him. If other tests discussed below point to a food that can be avoided and challenged, we would almost always advise such a challenge to confirm and demonstrate the relationship.

Keeping in mind that anything can produce almost any symptoms in someone and that a "little bit *can* hurt you," it is hard to limit the list of things to consider when seeking these kinds of ecological factors in abnormal behavior. Sugar and refined flour, food additives, cow's milk and milk products (as well as formulas made from cow's milk), foods containing yeast and molds, wheat, corn, citrus, eggs, tomatoes, and peanuts are among the most likely offenders. Suspect any food that a child seems to crave or that is known to be associated with any symptom past or present.

About Additives

We suspect that the heat generated by Benjamin Feingold's book on hyperactivity has not reflected well on the pediatric and child psychology community. Frantic arguments have been publicized as if the issue depended on deciding if behavioral reactions do or do not result from food colorings and other unnecessary food additives. Long before Feingold's book was published, it was demonstrated beyond doubt that some children and adults showed bizarre responses to small amounts of MSG (monosodium glutamate), tartrazine yellow dyes, sodium benzoate, and other additives. There are so many additives and pesticides in our foods that it is perfectly reasonable, given human individuality, for a variety of inadvertent reactions to occur in any large group of people. Questions as to the frequency of such reactions are not trivial, but it is unreasonable not to consider a reaction to food additives just because it isn't common. Thoroughness requires that all considerations be given attention. We feel that the use of drugs (admittedly and for different reasons likely "to work") is rarely justifiable before safer and more ecological measures have been tried.

When we ourselves first heard about these food additives as child behavior issues, we were somewhat dismayed—not because of a lack of statistical proof but because our training at the time left us poorly prepared to guide parents through the supermarket for a basket of sugar-and-additive-free foods to try.

We now feel that Feingold's book overestimated the frequency of food-additive reactions, was too soft on sugar, and didn't emphasize strongly enough that the same spectrum of behavior problems can come from "regular" foods. But we feel that he did a great service to children by helping to focus attention on a problem that frequently has ecological roots and is being discussed more and more as if it were a "new disease."

Blood Tests for Allergy

A RAST (also called RASP or ELISA) test measures the amount of the blood serum's allergic reactivity to various foods, chemicals, pollens, dust, molds, animals, and fibers. Only a small amount of blood is required, and the results give a good indication of a child's specific allergies. If a RAST test indicates allergy to a particular food, such as milk, the results should be considered as evidence rather than proof that milk provokes the symptoms that concern you.

Cytotoxic testing measures the tendency of the blood's white cells to "explode" in the presence of various allergy provoking substances. Like the RAST test, it is done in a test tube and requires a small amount of blood. It has roughly the same limitations and advantages as the RAST test.

We have seen instances in which each of these tests gave results that helped to clarify a difficult situation with accuracy and speed. We have also seen instances (true at times of almost all medical tests) in which the results of a RAST or cytotoxic test have been confusing and inconsistent. Used with caution and confirmed by other means, these tests can be very valuable for children because a sample of blood is all that is required.

Skin Testing for Allergic Reactions

The general average accuracy of skin testing, as well as RAST and cytotoxic testing, is about 70 percent. This figure is derived from the average accuracy as applied to large numbers of patients, and for a given patient the accuracy of a particular test can be either 100 percent or 0 percent. For a set of skin tests, or other types of tests, there may be some substances which accurately reflect the responses of the whole body to the test substance, and there may be others in which the test is either falsely positive or falsely negative. It is not possible to determine prior to testing which person is a candidate for highly accurate testing and which person will find the testing has been a waste of time and money.

Skin testing is based on one of the basic paradoxes of allergy: that a very tiny amount of a substance can sometimes evoke a dramatic reaction in the susceptible person, while the right amount of the same material may turn off a reaction (the principle behind allergy shots). We choose the skin as a site for testing because it not only provides an opportunity to introduce the substance into a person's body, giving a chance to look for general reactions (headaches, stuffiness, itching), but it also gives us a measurable bump in the skin which we can watch to determine the extent of allergy as expressed in that fashion. The type of testing we do is based on a method called serial dilution titration, or also sometimes called intradermal provocative testing. To the person undergoing the testing it seems very much like the testing done by most allergists. However, the allergy vaccines we use are made up in a different fashion, and we test the substance in a way that provides an idea of the weakest dilution of the material that gives a measurable response in the bump (wheal) in the skin. On the basis of that weakest dilution, we can determine what are referred to as the *end point* and the *neutralizing dose*. The neutralizing dose is the amount of the vaccine of a particular dilution that will turn off a patient's symptoms.

It is in the ability of this neutralizing dose to turn off symptoms promptly that this method differs from conventional allergy testing. Conventional allergy treatment depends on the notion that the dose must be gradually built up to the maximum dose tolerated by the patient in order to achieve the relief of allergy symptoms. *This sometimes takes months.* That method is more generally accepted and proven than the method that we use. With our method, if results are to be obtained, they often can be felt by the patient within a day or two after treatment starts, and we are usually able to give our vaccine from a dropper bottle under the tongue instead of by injection into the skin. When the sublingual route fails to work, it is sometimes worthwhile to try injection therapy before going on to the next step simply because the ability to turn off the symptoms in this way is sometimes much less troublesome for a patient than extensive changes in environment or diet.

It is inherently risky to give something to a person who may be allergic to it. We wait ten minutes between each test in order to take advantage of the possibility that a patient may develop some symptoms which will give us a much better notion of the accuracy of the test than the simple reading of the skin wheal. (Occasionally the test will produce a reaction in a person that is both very informative and perhaps uncomfortable for the patient—wheezing, hives, extreme fatigue, depression, or other generalized symptoms. Severe allergic reactions can be reversed rapidly by the administration of Adrenalin.)

Skin testing and allergy treatment can be carried out successfully even in young infants. The skill of the person actually doing the test (in terms of relating to infants and children) is an extremely important variable in the outcome.

Test of Poisons

Chemical poisoning through contamination of our soil, food, water, and air has now become so well recognized that it needs no special emphasis. Understanding of even the most ancient poisons, such as lead, in terms of their effects on human behavior lags far behind their proliferation in the environment. Our understanding of the effects of hundreds of thousands of synthetic and natural poisons will never catch up to their ever more widespread use. At the present time, only a handful of poisons can be checked for by readily available tests of a child's tissues.

Lead

We recommend that every child with a behavior problem be checked for lead poisoning. Tests of hair, teeth (with the help of the tooth fairy), nail clippings, blood, and of a sample from a collection of a child's twenty-four-hour urine (every drop) all provide an indication of an excess body burden of lead. Such an excess may be a part or all of the cause of a behavior problem. We prefer to screen for lead by hair analysis and confirm suspicious levels with the study of blood and urine.

Copper

While the ingestion of part of an old lead soldier could be a serious threat to a child—as can be the frequent intake of small quantities of lead from other sources such as paint—a copper penny will usually pass through the body without danger. Unless it becomes stuck somewhere, the penny will cause no harm, and similar exposures to swallowed copper objects are of no great concern. Copper is a trace nutrient needed by the body in tiny amounts that are present in many foods.

Some people have a tendency to absorb and retain more copper than others from the small amounts in drinking water that passes through copper pipes. (The first water taken after it has not run for a few hours has much more copper in it than water that has been running freely for a while.)

Relatively little is known about the behavioral effects of a large amount of copper stored in a child's body. Correlations that have been made suggest that the presence of too much copper in some individuals gives rise to irritable feelings and behavior. Hair analysis is a good way to screen for copper excess, and the results can be confirmed with studies of twenty-four-hours' worth of urine. A copper overload can be treated with a medicine that removes copper from the body—the same medicine used to treat lead poisoning—or the copper can be lowered gradually by limiting its intake and providing supplements of vitamin C, calcium, zinc, and other nutrients.

Mercury and Arsenic

These two elements are detectable by hair analysis. When found in large amounts in hair, they are sometimes the result of direct contamination of the hair and less often from poisoning of the child. These elements are often measured as part of a hair analysis profile. Elevated levels found in the hair should be confirmed with other tests before specific treatment is undertaken.

Formaldehyde

Formaldehyde is a very simple substance that is poisonous to everyone at a certain level. Some people are allergic to small amounts that may be released from new clothing (as in a fabric in a department store) or from insulation (in mobile homes or urea-formaldehyde foam that is hosed into existing wall spaces). Its presence in the body as a poison is not detectable, and tests rely on measuring the levels found in the air. Your state environmental health department may be able to advise you on how to have the necessary tests carried out.

Carbon Monoxide

If a child is exposed to carbon monoxide from the faulty exhaust system of an engine or a heater, the effect can be confirmed by a blood test done soon after the exposure. Chronic exposure to low levels of carbon monoxide should be considered in any child with a behavior problem if such an exposure is a reasonable possibility.

Other Poisons

The individual expression of the effects from chemicals known to be poisonous, such as PCB's, is so varied that it is difficult to categorize the problem as allergy or poisoning. Tests for the presence of poisons other than those mentioned above in a child's body or environment require special arrangements that can be made through consultation between your physician, the local health department, and the toxicology branches of state and federal health agencies.

Tests for Minerals

We derive energy from food no matter what kind of protein, fat, sugars, or starches we consume. We could get by on a very monotonous diet if it were only a question of getting energy. This would suit the 4-year-old noodles-and-butter addicts or the 5-year-old peanut-butter-and-jelly junkies just fine. But what about their bodies' need for various amounts of sodium, potassium, calcium, magnesium, phosphorus, chlorine, sulfur, iron, zinc, chromium, manganese, vanadium, selenium, iodine, molybdenum, cobalt, titanium, nickel, copper, and other elements of which trace amounts may be essential to the optimum health of some or all people?

The saying that variety is the spice of life is true in at least two ways: monotonous consumption of a food makes the development of allergy more likely, and it is only through consumption of a variety that we insure our bodies opportunity to absorb various elements that are needed in differing amounts by all of us.

The present state of knowledge about requirements for the minerals and trace elements is firm for a few elements in regard to behavior and health, but for others we can only depend on common sense: correcting wide departures from expected levels based on averages.

Certain minerals belong in the blood, and blood levels are an accurate representation of the body's overall useful content. Iron, zinc, manganese, cobalt (in vitamin B-12), iodine (measured in thyroid tests), can be tested for wide departures from normal. We feel that when abnormalities are found, it is reasonable to try to correct the abnormality even though its connection to a specific problem is unknown. Health is a matter of balance, and we should always try to provide nutrients in the proper amounts before resorting to more artificial forms of treatment.

Analysis of the hair is done to reflect abnormalities of the body's content of some minerals. Care must be taken by professionals not to overinterpret the results of hair analysis. Zinc deficiency, a relatively common finding in American children, is reliably screened for by hair analysis and often occurs in the presence of copper excess, for which hair analysis is also a good detection method. Interpretation of levels of trace elements in the hair requires confirmation by other means, and the prescription of a large supply of supplements solely on the basis of a hair analysis is not usually justified on the basis of present technology.

Vitamins

Because we have known about vitamins for the last twenty to forty years, you would think that a method for analyzing blood for their content would have been available for many years. As it happens, a blood test for determining the proper amounts of various vitamins in a person's blood wasn't available until the early 1970s, and even now it is used by only a few physicians. Some hospital laboratories and other large commercial laboratories are able to provide a test reflecting the blood levels of vitamin A, folic acid, and vitamin B-12. Very few laboratories are able to do more than this, but if your physician contacts Dr. Herman Baker at the New Jersey College of Medicine, 88 Ross Street, E. Orange, N.J. 07018, he or she can make arrangements to have blood vitamin levels done for all the vitamins, except vitamin D, at that laboratory. This test is highly accurate, reliable, and reproducible and the results are very "solid." That is, if the test indicates that the level of vitamin A in your blood is below par, it is very unlikely that this is "normal" for you. (It is not a foregone conclusion that correcting a vitamin deficiency will in all cases lead to an improvement or correction of all a person's problems, and it is sometimes difficult to predict which type of deficiency will present itself in which kind of problems in a given individual.)

For a set fee, a vitamin profile can be obtained which includes blood levels of the following vitamins: B-12, folic acid, B-6, thiamin, niacin, biotin, riboflavin, pantothenic acid, vitamins A, C, E, and beta-carotene. While we think it is advisable to obtain vitamin levels for all of these in a person who has any chronic illness, the vitamins which are most likely to be abnormal in a child with a behavior problem are vitamins A, B-12, folic acid, niacin, and thiamin. If a clear-cut deficiency of any of these vitamins is documented, then the first step would be its correction by giving a larger than usual amount and rechecking the blood level to assure that it has gotten into the bloodstream. Other tests are available to reveal if a vitamin present in adequate amounts may not be getting used effectively in the body.

The correction of vitamin deficiencies and abnormalities of mineral balance supersedes other forms of diagnosis or treatment. A few years ago we would have said that vitamin deficiency must be so infrequent in this country that looking for it, even in a child with a health or behavior problem, would be a waste of time and money. Our recent experience and that of many other doctors who have made use of the tests performed in Dr. Baker's laboratory indicates that a clear-cut vitamin deficiency exists in a sufficiently large proportion of children with problems of behavior and health to make such testing a very reasonable first step in the diagnostic list.

Air and Light

No tests are available to determine which children are sensitive to the so-called ion effect that is associated with air pollution and certain natural climatic conditions in some areas. Air ionizers will correct the air indoors and may be tried as a means for testing the influence of this effect on your child's behavior.*

We think of light mostly in terms of its role in vision, and many people are unaware of its role as a nutrient. The energy of various wavelengths of light (different colors of the rainbow) affects the brain in ways that modify behavior and health without involving the parts of the brain devoted to seeing.

There are no standardized tests to determine whether a person is suffering from an imbalance of light. Most artificial lighting is very different from natural sunlight in its color balance. Switching to lighting that mimics natural sunlight and eliminating tinted lenses will produce dramatic changes in the health and behavior of some children. The only way to find the children who will benefit is to try a change in lighting.†

---

*Soyka, Fred. *The Ion Effect*. New York: E. P. Dutton, 1979.
†Ott, John. *Health and Light*. Old Greenwich Conn.: Devin-Adair, 1974.

20 Applying the Diagnostic List and Where to Look for Help

Applying the Diagnostic List

Eddie was seven. His mother brought him to us because he was slow in learning, could not stick to a task long enough to absorb it, had difficulty relating to other children, would "go off into his own world," and seemed anxious and unhappy much of the time. He had had numerous ear infections all during infancy, and after age 5 he had developed recurring painful ulcerations inside his mouth. From 6 months to 2 years he seemed preoccupied with lights; he blinked and rubbed his eyes a lot. After age 2, he seemed very sensitive to sunlight, and an eye doctor said he had *photophobia* (which his mother understood to be the name of a disease. It is only a word meaning light sensitivity). He also seemed to have a very acute sense of hearing and was bothered by loud noises—often covering his ears and crying when surprised by the ringing of the phone. He was a deep sleeper and wet his bed two hours after going to sleep. He had always tended to be constipated. His nose was constantly stuffy, worse in winter; and his nose itched frequently, as did his anus. The itching of his anus decreased after his mother found it was related to chocolate consumption and eliminated chocolate from his diet. Eddie had been evaluated by an allergist and found to be sensitive to tree pollen, dust, and molds and was receiving allergy shots.

Test results showed additional allergies which were treated by elimination of some foods and by desensitization of his allergies. Other tests showed low blood levels of manganese and a very low vitamin A level (9; normal is 25–75). This was corrected by providing a supplement of manganese and 30,000 units of vitamin A, which brought his level to the range of 30–40. Eddie subsequently underwent a transformation in which all of his symptoms improved dramatically. His attention and learning abilities picked up, he appeared more comfortable, happy, and calm, and his sensitivity to light and noises disappeared.

Prevention

The message carried by most of this book is that behavior problems in children are a reflection of temporary imbalances which occur during the course of normal growth, development, and life events. Adhering to the following general principles, you will be able to prevent or manage most behavior problems yourself, or you will at least have the assurance that they are temporary and part of normal development.

1. Know what to expect from your child at each stage of development and match your expectations to his or her skills.
2. Set clear and consistent limits.
3. Set a good example.
4. Provide an environment as balanced as possible with regard to nutrition and other ecological factors.
5. Plan the (lifelong) process of separation from you carefully, and anticipate your child's potential for independence as it evolves.
6. Remember that one of the most important tasks in parenting is to teach the self-confidence that is required for self-care. Encouraging self-confidence and teaching self-care from infancy onward will maximize your child's opportunities for coping with life's stresses.

Seeking Outside Help

If your child seems to be in "real" difficulty, we assume that you will seek professional help after taking the time to observe his or her problem for a while and then discussing the matter with your family, friends, and other parents. If the problem persists, you should organize information about your child along the lines of the questions listed on pages 287–90. If you then wish to explore the diagnostic list, you will need guidance from one or more professionals.

Aware of the various tests that make up a complete diagnostic list, you will find that some of the professionals you consult specialize in helping to understand only part of the list. You should make every effort to find someone who will consider the *whole list* before accepting a specialized form of treatment that focuses on isolated findings.

Choosing help and knowing when you have chosen well will be easier if you heed the following suggestions:

1. Choose a professional who will answer your questions clearly and patiently and who is comfortable saying "I don't know, but I'll help you find out."

2. Choose a professional who will deal, at least some of the time, directly with your child. A professional person who speaks to your child indifferently, examines him roughly, or fails to treat him like a person is likely to be of little help.

3. Beware of labels. Most of the diagnostic names for behavior problems in children are simple descriptions that make it easier to talk about the problem. Very few names of childhood behavior problems identify the real cause or point to a remedy. Taking a child's symptoms and grouping them under a heading such as "hyperactivity" or "minimal brain dysfunction" or "learning disability," "dyslexia," or "attention deficit disorder" is useful only when we all keep in mind that nothing is really explained by such

labels. A diagnostic list must be explored before deciding on treatment.

4. Watch out for parsimony (see page 296). Remember that many professionals feel that it is important to narrow down the name and explanations of a problem so that a *specific* treatment can be prescribed. We feel that it is usually best not to even try to decide if a problem is "physical" or "emotional." The lessons we learn from the very young teach us that these factors are too intertwined in children to ignore either in any kind of problem. The lessons we learn from children with "strictly physical" illness such as cystic fibrosis or diabetes teach us that communication troubles in a child's family can weaken child and family as much as the disease itself.

Good professionals in all fields are able to keep an open mind about the multiple factors that lie behind most human difficulties.

5. Above all, share in controlling the diagnostic process. Do not allow the person treating your child to make all the decisions without consulting with you and discussing the options. Every problem affecting a child's behavior tends to rob him or her of some aspects of control. Every opportunity should be taken to leave children in control of those things they can manage by themselves. Your own ability to understand and share control with the professional people involved will help a lot.

21 Treatment

Treatment restores balance. It may be effective even when the exact relevance of unbalanced factors (deficiencies, allergies, family problems) is not known. Many aspects of a child's future behavior patterns are determined by genetic factors present at the time the egg and sperm join to form a new—and unique—human being. We know also that many aspects of behavior are expressions of a child's nurturing, and it has become accepted that diagnosis and treatment of problems involves detection and correction of many such factors. The remedy for psychological factors may proceed without a clear understanding of the precise role of each abnormality or stress in a child's past or present life.

The same is true of ecological and nutritional factors. Our goal is to achieve a balance that offers each child an optimum chance to fulfill his or her potential. The nonspecificity of psychological, nutritional, and ecological factors is a biological reality that many modern physicians find hard to accept because we have learned to search, sometimes successfully, for *specific causes* and *specific treatments* in human illness. If one pays careful attention to the web of causes that produces behavior, specific factors will not be missed. If one zeros in on specific factors and ignores the rest of the web, the majority of behavioral illness will be mismanaged.

Behavior Therapies

Individual Therapy

Individual therapy with a pediatrician, child psychiatrist, psychologist, social worker, or other child-oriented therapist may be appropriate at any age over approximately 12 months. The most important aspect of individual therapy is the relationship that grows between the child and the therapist. It should strengthen the child in ways that are often quite nonspecific because it provides an extra and special kind of nurturing and learning from a nonfamily adult. Children do not usually sit and talk with a therapist but engage in play and games that help communicate the children's memories and perceptions of their world. Individual therapy is not specific to any particular kinds of problems and may benefit children whose diagnostic list reveals any combination of abnormalities. A skilled therapist may be of great value to a child in just a few sessions, but individual therapy is often a long-term process.

Group Therapy

A nursery, kindergarten, or school situation that focuses on children's individual needs is an especially important treatment for some. It emphasizes opportunities to communicate with other children in the course of normal daily activities, and it gives the therapist an opportunity to observe the child in a group situation. Children whose perceptual problems make it difficult for them to cope with many sights and sounds at once may need a small group.

Family Therapy

No illness affecting a child's body and behavior can fail to affect his or her family. The desirability of family members meeting together to communicate feelings and points of view is not limited to behavior problems that stem from family problems as such. It is often difficult to tell if a family problem is the cause or the effect of a child's problem, and family therapy may be begun and concluded without complete agreement on that matter.

Drug Therapy

We wish that the general reluctance to use drugs on children applied to adults as well! Few drugs are useful in treating disorders of mood, perception, or attention in children. Every effort should be made to understand and treat nutritional imbalance before resorting to drugs. The following drugs are presently in use for treatment of behavior disorders in children.

Stimulants

Dextroamphetamine (Dexedrine), methylphenidate (Ritalin), and pemoline (Cylert) are used to treat a variety of problems associated with hyperactivity and difficulty attending to a task. None of these drugs treats the cause of the problem, and the benefit or risk to a particular child cannot be predicted. We have seen a few children in whom the positive effect of the drug was so great as to outweigh our reluctance to use such medications. The bad side effects most often reported by parents are that their child has become too much like a zombie, spacey, cool, or sometimes too restless, talkative, or sleepless at night. Children can be taken off such drugs with little difficulty. If you are having trouble deciding whether to allow your child to be treated with one of these drugs, the decision may be easier after a very brief trial to see what the effect really will be.

It was felt for some time that stimulant medications had a different effect on children than on adults. Now it is understood that the general effect—apart from individual peculiarities—is similar: They help increase alertness and ability to stay with a task. (Dexedrine gained use during World War II as an aid to radar-screen watchers, who were found to watch better on the drug.)

Since we have learned of the nutritional approaches to problems usually treated with stimulant medications, we have needed to prescribe the drugs only rarely. But we will always remember one little boy whom we had known from birth to have slow development and an odd appearance. When he began school it was found that he was able to learn to read but not to write, so he was frustrated and unhappy. After many other approaches were tried, a brief trial of methylphenidate produced a remarkable improvement in every aspect of his life. His sudden abilities to communicate and find contentment enabled us to continue the medication enthusiastically after a few trials on and off convinced us of its worth.

Sedatives

The only sedatives commonly used for children are phenobarbital—usually used to prevent seizures—and diphenhydramine (Benadryl), an antihistamine that also has a numbing effect when applied to the gums.

Phenobarbital is so well known for producing wild, aggressive, or irritable behavior in some children that it is seldom prescribed except for seizures. We know several children who were maintained on phenobarbital for seizure prevention (often done till age 5 for children who have had seizures with a sudden high fever) who underwent a total transformation when the drug was discontinued. "You have given us our child back again" said David's parents when, because of extremely irritable behavior, he was taken off phenobarbital "early" at age 3. In his case, the very small risk that he might have another seizure with a fever was well worth taking considering the restoration of behavioral health to a boy who had been extremely troubled while on the drug.

Benadryl is used to calm infants who are teething and as a general sedative for children. A young mother about to leave for a long cross-country trip with 2-year-old twins and their 3-year-old sister and a Labrador retriever implored her pediatrician to give her something to calm the twins. Their response to the first dose converted an ordeal into an emergency as they screamed and fought to find physical release for their volcanic feelings—in the confines of a heavily loaded station wagon.

Several antihistamines are sold over the counter in many combinations for congestion, and they have a good safety record. Considering that they interfere with the action of a very important body chemical (histamine), relatively few obvious adverse effects have been observed with their use. A calming effect in children is usually achieved with antihistamine, but reactions such as those described above may sometimes occur.

Major Tranquilizers

There are more than a dozen trade names and four categories of those drugs known as major tranquilizers because they tend to help organize perception and thought as a remedy for major disturbances in those areas. Many belong to a group called the phenothiazines and may involve serious long-term dangers. This group of drugs is used mostly in the management of children whose mental disorganization causes them a lot of pain. Short-term use as a means of determining the effect in a given individual is especially justifiable if it helps to establish communication with a child who is lost alone in his own mind. These drugs have been called a "chemical straight jacket" and sometimes abused as such by professionals caring for disturbed individuals. Adult patients with an opportunity to abuse this group of drugs on their own rarely do so because the effect is too much like a warm, wet blanket.

Anticonvulsants

Even when a child does not have seizures, Dilantin (diphenyl-hydantoin) may be given to see if it will alleviate a variety of behavior problems—usually aggressive, irritable, tempestuous activity, or unprovoked anger. A behavior problem associated with various kinds of seizures may also respond to Dilantin or other anticonvulsant drugs. Anticonvulsant drugs, other than phenobarbital, usually do not have very many side affects that produce behavioral difficulties unless their dosage is too high. The variability of absorption of these drugs into the bloodstream from the intestinal tract requires monitoring of blood levels.

Lithium

This drug is known for its effectiveness in helping adults with a variety of problems of mood and perception, and it is reasonable to consider that there are some children for whom its use would be appropriate. That is the case. But at present there is not widespread use of lithium with children.

Antidepressants

The only group of antidepressant drugs that has wide use with children includes the so-called tricyclic and quadricyclic antidepressants. Imipramine (Tofranil, Imipramine Pamoate, Imavate, Presamine, Janimine, SK Pramine) is one that has been used to treat bedwetting with doses that are sometimes relatively large by adult standards. The mechanism of relief from betwetting is separate from the antidepressant affect, and children who take it rarely show changes of mood except in relation to a dry bed in the morning.

Stephanie still wet her bed at age 9. She had tried no drinking after supper, being awakened, a bed buzzer, and visits to her pediatrician to explore her feelings. Her father had had the same problem as a child and his had disappeared in his tenth year. Both parents wished to avoid drugs, so they were waiting it out and neither catered to nor scolded Stephanie about her problem. A visit to her grandmother usually resulted in dryness because Stephanie tended to stay dry away from home. Her doctor prescribed a small supply of Tofranil for the visit because Stephanie had had an accident the previous year and the grandmother had not been kind about it. Stephanie made it through the week dry and no one knew for sure if it was really the little red pill that worked, but it was a big relief. Stephanie was completely dry by the age of 10.

Imipramine has been proven effective in the short run in some cases of bedwetting, and a few drugs of the same group will calm some hyperactive or frightened children. There is growing concern about the possible side effects on the heart, so more than the usual hesitation to use this group of drugs should be applied for now.

Pain Medications

All the most effective pain medications originate from the poppy plant or are partly synthetic imitations of its derivative (opium). Demerol, codeine, morphine, and other opiate narcotics provide welcome relief from the pain of severe injuries or operations. Their potential for producing behavior changes is often more recognizable at night when vivid dreams—often very frightening—may be so troublesome that the pain relief is not justified.

Aspirin is also sometimes associated with hallucinations, but the association may be only through the fever being treated. Yolanda had been sick in bed all day with a fever that seemed to have no particular focus of illness in her body except that she ached all over and was a little sick to her stomach. At 11 P.M. her mother and father were watching TV after sponging her down with tepid water, tucking her in bed, and giving her one and a half "adult" aspirins. Terrified, they ran to her room in answer to her desperate cries for help. Sitting bolt upright in bed, she waved her arms in the air and screamed so loudly that their neighbors' lights went on. Nothing in her seven years of watching Saturday morning TV matched the horrors that surrounded the child as she battled with birds and lizards that her brain invented so convincingly. Her hallucinations lasted for twenty minutes, with periods of wakefulness and sleep mixed in. Her temperature had shot up to 105 degrees F (40.7 C), and she quieted down only after a trip back to the bathtub where the birds and lizards finally dissolved.

All drugs have the ability to affect the behavior of children. The drug itself or some coloring, flavoring, or other ingredient of the preparation may sometimes produce behavioral changes that seem unrelated to the supposed action of the drug. Ten-month-old

Eric had his first earache. He was fretful, not interested in nursing, pulled at his left ear. His pediatrician treated him with a red, fruit-flavored suspension of ampicillin, and a half hour later Eric became wide-eyed. He flailed, kicked, and screamed his way through the next six hours. Given the same medicine in the morning, he "climbed the walls" again. The pediatric medication was switched to the contents of an adult capsule (no red dye, sugar, or flavoring) suspended in water and squirted into his throat with a vitamin dropper. He made a face but slept beautifully after that. The remainder of the treatment was uneventful, but when the same medication was prescribed for him during a subsequent trip away from home, the story was repeated.

Nutritional Therapy

Vitamin Deficiencies

Nutritional balance is a concept that we all accept. If your child is found to be out of balance, it is reasonable to correct it even without knowing exactly how the imbalance is related to whatever problem you have observed. The standards by which normal values for the body's content of nutrients have been set are very broad. (For example, the normal range of vitamin B-12 level in the blood includes values of 115 to 800 pg/ml.) Correction of a vitamin deficiency may fail to be a specific remedy for your child's behavior problem, so you may need to look further in the diagnostic list.

Before we made use of a reliable test for blood vitamin levels, we believed that vitamin deficiency would be rare. Even so, we felt it was a factor to consider for the sake of thoroughness just as we consider a variety of rare possibilities whenever we study a child's problem carefully. Now we find nutritional imbalance to be a factor in *many* children with problems and we urge that this possibility be explored carefully if your child has a problem.

The Megavitamins

Correction of a deficiency often requires doses of vitamins far in excess of the average requirements for children. If the dose exceeds ten times the average, it is referred to as *megavitamin* therapy. Many people would make a distinction between large-dose treatment to provide normal blood levels and large-dose treatment that appears to meet needs for much-higher-than-normal levels in the body.

The controversy about the use of large doses of vitamins does not hinge on the question of whether such excessive needs exist in some children. Very well-documented examples prove that they do indeed exist, but there are various opinions as to how frequently this is the case. We do not think that the question of frequency will be answered very soon, and our experience indicates that looking for such children is well worthwhile. The efficacy of large doses of vitamin B-6 and moderate doses of magnesium in children with severe disorders of mood and perception (autism) has been proven in a carefully designed scientific study. There has been no reported case of a serious complication from this form of treatment, so the decision to try it on a child with certain disorders is reasonable.

We would never withhold a brief trial of treatment with large doses of vitamins (other than vitamin A or D *which can be hazardous*) in a child who has a complex problem that has not yielded to other remedies. With the exception of the vitamins A and D, trials of large doses of these nutrients can be undertaken with great safety. Adverse reactions do occur and are not infrequently due to a preservative or some other material that accompanies the vitamin in the pill or liquid. We resort to a trial of large doses of vitamins only after the question of vitamin deficiency has been resolved, and we recommend that any megavitamin treatment be carried out under the supervision of a knowledgeable professional.

We encourage the use of "natural" vitamins only in the sense that they are usually free of sugar or additives. Except for vitamin E, which has different forms, "natural" and synthetic vitamins have identical chemical structure and effect.

Allergy Treatment

If a child is found to be hypersensitive to a food or any other substance, it should be avoided. If it cannot be avoided, as is the case with pollens, dust, and molds, there are means for altering a child's sensitivity by deliberate administration of small amounts of extracts of the offending substance. This allergy vaccine can be introduced into a child's body by injection through the skin or by placing it under the tongue where it enters the bloodstream without going through the digestive tract.

We prefer to try sublingual treatment (under the tongue) at first and go on to injections only if this doesn't work. Most of our own allergy patients use sublingual drops.

22 Application

The Web

So far we have discussed diagnostic strategy and treatment without mentioning *specific diagnoses*. There are dozens of behavioral symptoms in children, and there are more than fifty labeled childhood psychiatric disorders in the *Diagnostic and Statistical Manual* of the American Psychiatric Association (DSM III). For only five of the labels listed in this reference work—all varying degrees of mental retardation—is *cause* mentioned in the definition of the problem. A cause when known is essential to the definition of a disorder. We know of no behavior symptoms in children that point automatically to a specific cause, and we feel for many reasons already referred to that a variety of stresses should be considered when attempting to understand a child's difficulty.

We see these causes as a web of interacting factors. Children with problems should have all the strands of their web strengthened until the problem is defined in terms of a specific narrow cause. Stress of all kinds tends to be disorganizing, and sometimes we have to repair the effects of disorganization even when we cannot fix the main trouble.

David was 2½ when his mother became concerned about his constant stuffiness and frequent earaches. He looked more and more pale and his behavior was irritable and cranky much of the time. Both his parents were busy with his father's new business, which was thriving thanks to a lot of work and worry. When David's father gave up a safe job with a corporation and went out on his own, it seemed certain to be a good thing for the family in the long run, and there were no major ways that the process affected the family in the meantime—no fights, no big changes in schedule, no changes in activities—just the normal worries of a new business. When David was taken off milk and milk products, his stuffiness, frequent infections, and irritable behavior improved dramatically. Two years later David was able to be free of congestion and to stay in good health even without milk avoidance. Looking back, we and his parents agreed that finding the milk allergy was the key to helping David feel better at the time, but certainly the effect of general stress on the family was an important factor in making David vulnerable.

Major Labels

This section focuses on symptoms and lists and sees problems in terms of a web of interacting factors that are not revealed by a single label. Labels are helpful for comparison and communication so long as we don't take them too seriously and don't confuse names, ideas, and things. Five major divisions of labels for childhood behavior problems have been described in DSM III.

1. Intellectual
2. Behavioral
3. Emotional
4. Physical
5. Developmental

Subgroupings of these categories are defined in terms of the kinds of behavior that a child needs to display in order to fit into any given label. For example, a common category—"Attention Deficit Disorder with Hyperactivity" is defined as follows:*

A. Inattention (three of the following)

    1) Fails to finish tasks

---

*DSM III, American Psychiatric Association, p. 43.

2) Often seems not to listen
3) Easily distracted
4) Difficulty concentrating
5) Difficulty sticking to play activity

B. Impulsivity (three of the following)

1) Often acts before thinking
2) Shifts excessively from one activity to another
3) Difficulty organizing work
4) Needs lots of supervision
5) Frequently calls out in class
6) Difficulty waiting for turns

C. Hyperactivity (two of the following)

1) Runs about or climbs on things excessively
2) Has difficulty sitting still or fidgets excessively
3) Has difficulty staying seated
4) Moves about excessively during sleep
5) Is always "on the go" or acts driven by a motor

D. Onset before age seven
E. Duration of at least six months
F. Not due to Schizophrenia, Affective Disorder, or Severe or Profound Mental Retardation

If your child is labeled with this diagnosis, you don't actually have any information that you didn't already know—his symptoms. The label permits shorthand communication to describe the difficulty, but it has nothing to do with causes.

Dwayne is a 7-year-old first-grader who has an "Attention Deficit Disorder with Hyperactivity." His symptoms are present more at school than elsewhere. A videotape taken of his classroom by an unseen camera reveals his constant motion and total inability to attend to a task. Unknown to Dwayne, an experiment is carried out that involves changing the fluorescent lighting to full spectrum lighting that has the same balance of colors as natural sunlight. With full spectrum lighting Dwayne's behavior becomes calm and attentive, but it reverts to hyperactive when the lights are changed back.

Many factors may have contributed to Dwayne's hyperactivity, but his sensitivity to an imbalance of light was the key to the remedy. We do not know how many children are sensitive to this effect of light, but we do know that the effect occurs and we feel it should be considered as part of the diagnostic list for any hyperactive child.

Wishing and Willing

Many aspects of a child's difficult behavior may be studied and described without revealing the cause. One important test must accompany all other efforts detailed in this chapter: *look carefully at the effect of the behavior.* As the path of an arrow reveals its source, the results of a child's behavior often suggest the causes that lie in the child's will. A child's wellness depends on his early discovery that he can affect the behavior of the people who care for him. A child's wishing and willing things to happen are more confused than are those of most adults, so that many unrealistic plans are launched on the basis of inappropriate and sometimes reasonable wishes.

If the effect of a child's behavior keeps Mother from going to work—or gains more of Father's attention, it pays to wonder if that effect has to do with a cause in his will or perhaps in that of another family member who puts him or her up to it in various ways—spoken and unspoken.

Prevention

This section states our understanding of the causes of a child's behavior—normal and abnormal—in terms of a web of interacting forces: a child's inborn potential, perceptual world, interaction with other human beings and the physical environment, and memory—conscious and unconscious—of his or her life experience. This is an ecological view and differs from the usual medical and psychiatric models in that it is not concerned with a descriptive diagnosis. We do not reject the idea of specific therapy, but our experience leads us to believe specific therapy is an illusion in most of the behavioral illness we see.

What we have presented is above all a practitioner's view, and as such it responds to our need to understand the problems and potentials of single individuals as opposed to groups of individuals or averages. We have known many normal children, but we have never seen the "average" child. We have studied many children with similar behavior problems, but we have never seen the same mosaic behind any two. We believe that prevention of problems depends on parents understanding their child as an individual rather than applying rules based on average needs.

We feel that parenting is one of the most demanding and creative tasks of today's culture, one in which we all need as much help as we can get. It is helpful to keep in mind that love heads the list of essential nutrients. The most important thing we ever teach our children is to love and to be loved by others.

References

Alexander, Martha. *When the New Baby Comes, I'm Moving Out.* New York: Dial, 1979.

Ames, Louise Bates. *Is Your Child in the Wrong Grade?* Lumberville, Pa.: Modern Learning Press, 1978.

Ames, Louise Bates, and Chase, Joan Ames. *Don't Push Your Preschooler,* rev. ed. New York: Harper & Row, 1981.

Ames, Louise Bates; Gillespie, Clyde; Haines, Jacqueline; and Ilg, Frances L. *The Gesell Institute's Child from One to Six.* New York: Harper & Row, 1979.

Ames, Louise Bates, and Ilg, Frances L. *Your Two Year Old: Terrible or Tender?* New York: Delacorte, 1976.

——. *Your Three Year Old: Friend or Enemy?* New York: Delacorte, 1976.

——. *Your Four Year Old: Wild and Wonderful.* New York: Delacorte, 1976.

——. *Your Five Year Old: Sunny and Serene.* New York: Delacorte, 1979.

——. *Your Six Year Old: Loving and Defiant.* New York: Delacorte, 1979.

Ames, Louise Bates, and Learned, Janet. "Imaginary Companions and Related Phenomena." *Journal of Genetic Psychology* 69 (1946): 147–167.

Beekman, Daniel. *The Mechanical Baby: A Popular History of the Theory and Practice of Child Raising.* New York: Lawrence Hill & Co., 1977.

Berman, Claire. *Making It as a Stepparent: New Roles, New Rules.* New York: Doubleday, 1980.

Brazleton, T. Berry. *Infants and Mothers.* New York: Delacorte, 1969.

——. *Toddlers and Parents.* New York: Delacorte, 1974.

Bunin, Catherine, and Bunin, Sherry. *Is That Your Sister?* New York: Pantheon, 1976.

Calladine, Andrew, and Calladine, Carole. *Raising Siblings.* New York: Delacorte, 1979.

Chase, Joan Ames, "A Study of the Impact of Grade Retention on Primary School Children. *Journal of Psychology* 70 (1968): 169–177.

Crook, William G. *Tracking Down Hidden Food Allergy.* Jackson, Tenn.: Professional Books, P.O. Box 3494, 1978.

Delacato, Carl. *The Ultimate Stranger.* New York: Doubleday, 1974.

Dodson, Fitzhugh. *How to Parent.* Los Angeles: Nash, 1970.

————. *How to Discipline with Love.* New York: Rawson, 1977.

————. *How to Grandparent.* New York: Harper & Row, 1981.

Ernst, Kathryn. *Danny and His Thumb.* Englewood Cliffs, N. J.: Prentice Hall, 1972.

Feingold, Ben. *Why Your Child Is Hyperactive.* New York: Random House, 1975.

Fisher, Florence. *The Search for Anna Fisher.* New York: Arthur Fields, 1973.

Gardner, Richard A. *Understanding Children.* New York: Aaronson, 1974.

————. *The Parents' Book About Divorce.* New York: Doubleday, 1977.

————. *The Family Book About Minimal Brain Dysfunction.* New York: Aaronson, 1973.

Gesell, Arnold; Ilg, Frances L.; and Ames, Louise Bates. *The Child from Five to Ten,* rev. ed. New York: Harper & Row, 1977.

Gold, Phyllis. *Please Don't Say Hello.* New York: Human Sciences Press, 1975.

Goldfarb, William; Myers, Donald; Florsheim, Judy; and Goldfarb, Nathan. *Psychotic Children Grow Up: Prospective Follow-up Study in Adolescence and Adulthood.* New York: Human Sciences Press, 1980.

Golos, Natalie, and Goldbitz, Frances Golos. *Coping with Your Allergies.* New York: Simon & Schuster, 1979.

Grollman, Earl A. *Talking About Death: A Dialogue Between Parent and Child.* Boston: Beacon Press, 1976.

Hartley, Ruth E. *Children Vis-à-Vis Television and Filmed Material.* Archives Division of the Library of the University of Wisconsin. Green Bay, Wisc.: Joint Committee of Research on Television and Children, 1968.

Ilg, Frances L.; Ames, Louise Bates; Haines, Jacqueline; and Gillespie, Clyde. *School Readiness,* rev. ed. New York: Harper & Row, 1978.

————. *The Years from Ten to Sixteen.* New York: Harper & Row, 1982.

Levine, Milton M., and Seligmann, Jean. *The Wonder of Life.* New York: Simon & Schuster, 1940.

Maddox, Brenda. *The Half-Parent.* New York: Evans, 1975.

Mandell, Marshall, and Scanlon, Lynne Waller. *Dr. Mandell's 5-Day Allergy Relief System.* New York: Pocket Books, 1979.

Mayle, Peter. *Where Did I Come From?* New York: Lyle Stuart, 1973.

Meredith, Judith C. *And Now We Are a Family.* Boston: Beacon Press, 1971.

Nilsson, Lennart. *How Was I Born?* New York: Delacorte, 1975.

Ott, John. *Health and Light.* Old Greenwich, Conn.: Devin-Adair, 1974.

Paton, Jean. *The Adopted Break Silence.* Philadelphia: Life History Center, 1954.

Rapp, Doris. *Allergies and the Hyperactive Child,* 2nd ed. New York: Cornerstone Library, 1980.

Redlich, Fritz, and Bingham, June. *The Inside Story—Psychiatry and Everyday Life.* New York: Knopf, 1953.

Rimland, Bernard. *Infantile Autism.* New York: Appleton Century Crofts, 1964.

Rogers, Florence. *Parenting the Difficult Child.* New York: Chilton, 1979.

Scheinkin, David; Schachter, Michael; and Hutton, Richard. *The Food Connection: How the Things You Eat Affect the Way You Feel and What You Can Do About It.* New York: Bobbs, Merrill, 1979.

Scott, Betty, and Ames, Louise Bates. "Improved Academic, Personal and Social Adjustment in Selected Second-grade Repeaters." *Elementary School Journal* 69 (1969): 431–439.

Sheldon, William S. *Varieties of Temperament.* New York: Harper & Row, 1942.

Smith, Lendon. *Improving Your Child's Behavior Chemistry.* Englewood Cliffs, N.J.: Prentice Hall, 1976.

———. *Feed Your Kids Right.* New York: McGraw Hill, 1979.

Soyka, Fred. *The Ion Effect.* New York: E.P. Dutton, 1979.

Spock, Benjamin. *Baby and Child Care.* New York: Hawthorn, 1976.

Stein, Sara Bonnett. *Making Babies: An Open Family Book for Parents and Children Together.* New York: Walker, 1974.

———. *That New Baby.* New York: Walker & Co., 1974.

Stevens, Laura, and Stoner, Rosemary B. *How to Improve Your Child's Behavior through Diet.* New York: Doubleday, 1979.

Straus, Murray A. "A Sociological Perspective on the Causes of Family Violence," in Maurice R. Greer, ed., *Violence and the American Family.* Washington, D.C.: American Association for the Advancement of Science, 1980.

Straus, Murray A.; Gelles, Richard J.; and Steinmetz, Suzanne K. *Behind Closed Doors: Violence in the American Family.* New York: Anchor/Doubleday, 1980.

Thevenin, Tina. *The Family Bed: An Age-Old Concept in Child Rearing.* Minneapolis, Minn.: P.O. Box 16004 (privately printed), 1979.

Ward, Scott; Wackman, Daniel B.; and Wartella, Ellen. *How Children Learn to Buy.* Beverly Hills, Calif.: Sage Publications, 1977.

Wolde, Gunilla. *Betsy's Baby Brother.* New York: Random House, 1975.

Wunderlich, Ray C. *Allergy, Brains and Children Coping.* St. Petersburg, Fla.: Johnny Reads Press, 1973.

Yahraes, Herbert. "Learning Disabilities: Problems and Progress," *Public Affairs Pamphlet No.* 578. New York: Public Affairs Committee, Inc., 1979.

Index